THE FUTURE OF HOUSING FINANCE

THE FUTURE OF HOUSING FINANCE

Restructuring the U.S. Residential Mortgage Market

MARTIN NEIL BAILY

editor

BROOKINGS INSTITUTION PRESS
Washington, D.C.

Copyright © 2011
THE BROOKINGS INSTITUTION
1775 Massachusetts Avenue, N.W., Washington, DC 20036
www.brookings.edu

Library of Congress Cataloging-in-Publication data

The future of housing finance : restructuring the U.S. residential mortgage market /
Martin Neil Baily, editor.
    p.   cm.
    Includes bibliographical references and index.
    Summary: "Evaluates the options open to policymakers as they reassess the federal
government's role in the U.S. residential mortgage market and consider a new system
that reduces risk in mortgage lending, maintains a limited government role, and
gradually removes the government-sponsored enterprises (Fannie Mae and Freddie Mac)
from the mortgage market"—Provided by publisher.
    ISBN 978-0-8157-2208-3 (pbk. : alk. paper)
    1. Mortgage loans—Government policy—United States. 2. Housing—United
States—Finance. I. Baily, Martin Neil. II. Title.
    HG2040.5.U5F88 2011
    332.7'220973—dc23   2011033694

9 8 7 6 5 4 3 2 1

Printed on acid-free paper

Typeset in Adobe Garamond

Composition by Cynthia Stock
Silver Spring, Maryland

Printed by R. R. Donnelley
Harrisonburg, Virginia

Contents

Preface

The financial crisis that started in the summer of 2007 and subsequently triggered a deep and persistent recession was centered in the U.S. housing market. The price of homes dropped by 30 percent as the crisis unfolded, and this was a prime factor in the rash of defaults and mortgage foreclosures as millions of homeowners began to go "underwater"—owing more on their mortgages than the value of their homes.

Policies to encourage homeownership have been supported by both political parties for many decades, making the real estate market a prime candidate for a bubble. The housing bubble that preceded the post-2007 financial crisis was financed in large part through the use of securities, consisting of bundled mortgages that were sold either to the government-sponsored enterprises (GSEs, especially Fannie Mae and Freddie Mac) or to the private market. Once the underlying mortgages began to default, the market prices of the securities collapsed, bringing down large banks such as Lehman Brothers, which started a panic on Wall Street, as well as many small banks. Fannie Mae and Freddie Mac were the largest holders of mortgage-backed assets, and they were in the middle of the storm. Holding a paper-thin layer of capital to protect themselves against losses, they were forced into a Treasury conservatorship in September 2008. In order to avoid losses on the mortgage-backed securities that had been issued by these institutions, the U.S. Treasury has had to put up hundreds of billions of dollars of taxpayer funds.

Rather than close down the operations of Fannie and Freddie, the government made the decision to have them continue to buy mortgages because the housing market and the overall economy were both so weak, and closing their doors would have been catastrophic given the value of their holdings ($3.8 trillion in 2008) and the tightening of credit throughout the economy. Private sector financial institutions were not able to provide sufficient new mortgage finance or to refinance old mortgages at lower interest rates, so Fannie and Freddie (and the Home Loan Banks) became almost the only game in town supporting the ailing mortgage market. In 2010 more than 8 in 10 new mortgages carried a federal guarantee.

In the spring of 2010, the Business Initiative at Brookings commissioned a set of papers to look at the future of Fannie and Freddie and to present the findings at a conference in February 2011. The purpose of the papers and conference, and this resulting volume, was to set out alternative views of what should be the right role, if any, of government in the housing and mortgage market going forward and how Fannie and Freddie might or might not fit into that role. Almost everyone agreed that the structure of Fannie and Freddie was not one that should be sustained into the future. The sternest critics of the GSEs argued that they had caused the financial crisis by buying securities backed by subprime or Alt-A mortgage loans, riskier loans that did not meet the standard for prime loans. They relied on the implicit government guaranty they enjoyed to borrow at lower rates of interest and used the proceeds to hold mortgages on their books, making large profits for shareholders for a number of years before the bubble burst. Others did not see Fannie and Freddie as the cause of the crisis, but agreed that their structure was flawed, with government sponsorship and private ownership epitomizing the problem of the public assumption of risk while rewards accrue to the private sector.

The chapters, together with a summary chapter by Douglas Elliott of Brookings, reflect the alternative views presented at the conference, from those who believe the GSEs should be phased out as soon as possible to those who continue to see a role for government in the mortgage market in the future. An important purpose of the conference was to provide a guide to Congress and the Obama administration as they weigh alternative proposals for the future of the GSEs. No one proposed keeping Fannie and Freddie in anything close to their current form. We had asked representatives of these GSEs to participate in the conference, but they did not accept. We were, however, fortunate to have Treasury Secretary Timothy Geithner roll out the administration's proposals for the GSEs to the audience to open the conference and to have former Federal Reserve Chairman Alan Greenspan as the keynote speaker. Greenspan had expressed deep concerns about the safety of Fannie and Freddie before the crisis and his address is included in this volume. We did not include the Treasury proposals because they were laid out in a White Paper released on the same day as the conference.[1] However, it is worthwhile briefly to review what Geithner proposed.

Geithner argued first the importance of winding down Fannie and Freddie and substantially reducing the government's footprint in the housing market. This must happen gradually, because they are now the dominant source of housing finance. Second, for the private market to take on a greater share of the burden of providing housing finance, a new set of rules of the game has to be in place for all the pieces of the mortgage market, covering capital requirements, underwriting standards, consumer protection, oversight of mortgage servicers, better incentives for securitization, and clarification of risk retention rules. The third piece, he argued, is to define a substantial but more targeted role for the government in supporting affordability—both for people who want to own a home and those who wish to rent. The Treasury White Paper lays out a series of basic elements of a reformed role for the government—concentrating on the FHA—in helping support those basic objectives. There are three specific reform options laid out, and the first is an approach that would be limited to the role the FHA now provides, while the second would complement that role with an emergency back-stop mechanism to be deployed only in crisis. The third option is an FHA, alongside a redesigned and much more limited but standing guarantee or insurance mechanism that would be available for a broader class of homeowners. Geithner said that it would be fundamentally untenable for the country to adopt a model where the government plays no role. And he also thinks it would not make sense for the government to be in the position, on an ongoing basis, of guaranteeing 80 or 90 percent of the mortgage market.

Elliott's summary of the papers in this volume points out there were a number of points of agreement among the authors that emerged, including a general concern that the stability of the mortgage market was vital to the overall stability of the economy. Any disagreement was about the extent to which there should be a continuing government role in the market and what form that should take.

We are very grateful to many people who worked hard to make the conference and this published volume happen. Brookings received generous support in this endeavor from a private nonprofit foundation that sponsors nonpartisan independent research. The financial support was, of course, essential and the authors and discussants worked very hard and constructively. Douglas Elliott

1. U.S. Department of the Treasury and U.S. Department of Housing and Urban Development, *Reforming America's Housing Finance Market: A Report to Congress,* February 2011, available on the departments' websites.

worked with me on the design of the conference, and Lindsey Wilson, DJ Nordquist, and Elaine Yang contributed enormously to the running of the event and to preparing the papers for publication. Robert Faherty, the director of the Brookings Institution Press, was willing to stretch our meager finances to make sure the book would be published. It was a privilege for me to work with such a great set of authors and support staff, and I hope and believe this volume will contribute to the important policy debate on the GSEs.

1

The Federal Role in Housing Finance: Principal Issues and Policy Proposals

DOUGLAS J. ELLIOTT

Fannie Mae and Freddie Mac dominate the American housing market, backing more than 62 percent of recent new mortgages and holding more than $5 trillion in accumulated mortgage risk. Unfortunately, their traditional structure as government-sponsored enterprises (GSEs for short) is clearly broken. The GSEs are a kind of public-private partnership in which private capital, motivated by the pursuit of profits, is channeled toward the accomplishment of government objectives for housing. For a while, the GSEs generated very high earnings while meeting increasingly challenging public goals with no cost registering on the federal budget. However, the structures came crashing down in 2008, requiring a rescue that has effectively given the federal government ownership of the two GSEs in exchange for a projected $224 billion in capital injections and the promise of more, if needed.[1]

Fannie Mae and Freddie Mac are coming to a crossroads where the government will have to make key choices about their structure and, indeed, their very existence. This volume is an outgrowth of a conference held by Brookings to better inform these decisions. To begin, this chapter provides some background on the GSEs and the federal role in supporting the U.S. housing market and then summarizes and compares key proposals offered by the remaining chapters. The good news is that these chapters reflect what appears to be a growing

1. Projection from the president's proposed budget for 2012 for the maximum cumulative capital injections.

consensus on several public policy issues critical to the design of a restructured housing finance system. This is particularly good news since the authors were chosen to represent a fairly wide range of views and analytical perspectives.

At the same time, important areas of disagreement remain. In addition, it is not clear that the emerging public policy consensus will be that of the politicians who will ultimately determine the fate of the GSEs and the housing market.

The key elements of consensus among the researchers, and with a Treasury white paper outlined at the conference, appear to be the following:

—The federal government has an appropriate role in stabilizing housing finance markets and assisting low- and middle-income home buyers.

—However, the government has been doing too much in this area and doing it too expensively. It should step back and let the private markets do more.

—Mixing credit guarantee and affordability efforts so intimately in the GSEs was a mistake. Going forward, the housing affordability mission should lie with the Federal Housing Administration (FHA), the Department of Housing and Urban Development (HUD), and similar entities.

—Any government credit guarantees, apart from the affordability mission, should be priced explicitly at "actuarially fair" rates and not be provided implicitly at zero cost, as before, or even explicitly but at a low cost.

—Any private credit guarantors with government backing should be severely limited in their ability to own substantial portfolios of mortgages or related securities. This becomes even more important to the extent that such entities have a structural ability to earn arbitrage profits by borrowing at rates close to Treasury rates.

—Any government housing subsidies should be calculated accurately and recorded in the federal budget.

—A multiyear period is needed to transition from the current housing finance regime to any of the proposed ones. Housing finance is too troubled and the GSEs are too important to move immediately, although that does not need to hold back the decisionmaking, just full implementation.

Despite these areas of agreement, the authors disagree about the right structure for the housing finance system, including differences of opinion about the extent of the federal role. Before addressing these areas of disagreement, this chapter offers some background on housing finance in the United States.

Overview of the Federal Role in Housing Finance

The federal government has played an important role in the U.S. housing market since the early 1930s, when a number of programs were set up in response to the Great Depression. The recent housing and financial crisis caused the government role to expand still further, to the point where it clearly dominates the mortgage market, at least temporarily. As Dynan and Gayer note in chapter 4 of this volume, 88 percent of new mortgages were backed in some manner by the federal government in the first three quarters of 2010, roughly double the average share from 2000 through 2007.

Tax subsidies may be the single strongest, and most expensive, support that the federal government provides. Individuals and couples who itemize their deductions for federal income tax purposes are allowed to deduct the cost of mortgage interest, within fairly wide constraints. The federal government forgoes approximately $100 billion a year in tax revenue as a result, and many states subsidize homeownership in the same way.[2]

The federal government also provides mortgage guarantees to a wide swath of Americans through the FHA, the Veterans Administration (VA), the Rural Housing Service of the Department of Agriculture, and other bodies. In addition, the Government National Mortgage Association (Ginnie Mae) guarantees mortgage-backed securities containing mortgages with federal guarantees. These entities were set up to assist either groups who are viewed as particularly worthy of government aid, such as veterans, or low- and middle-income borrowers who are believed to have the financial ability to carry a mortgage, but need help in buying a first home or trading up to a larger home. Critics argue that the latter role has been stretched considerably to include aid for many Americans who could afford homes without the help. In addition, the government sponsored the two GSEs that are described next.

Background on Fannie Mae and Freddie Mac

For decades the government used an unusual form of public-private partnership with the two huge GSEs to achieve key goals in the housing market. Originally, Fannie Mae and Freddie Mac were both wholly owned government corporations. However, the government's stakes were sold to the public over time, starting under President Lyndon Johnson, apparently primarily for budgetary

2. The conceptual analysis of the subsidy is more complex than normally presented. Ideally, an income tax system matches income with the expenses related to its production, taxing the net difference between the two. Rent payments are taxable to the landlord, net of expenses related to the rental property. Homeowners, however, are not taxed on the value of the "implicit rent" they receive from owning a home, but they *are* allowed to deduct many expenses related to the production of that implicit rent, including the mortgage interest deduction. Thus the tax subsidy could be eliminated either by taxing the implicit rent or by eliminating the interest and other deductions associated with homeownership. The author is grateful to Bill Gale for his careful explanation of the issue.

reasons.[3] In addition, there were policy arguments that the hybrid form could bring the benefits of a private sector, profit-focused approach while still achieving the broader housing goals. These arguments are similar to those advanced in regard to federal credit programs, such as student loans or FHA mortgages, for guaranteeing private sector lending rather than making direct federal loans.

Each GSE was given a special federal charter, created by an act of Congress, which was intended to provide an element of continuing government control, such as through presidential appointment of a certain number of members of the board of directors, and special privileges that would allow the GSEs to function more effectively and profitably than purely private competitors. Both the government control and the special privileges in the charters were enhanced by additional regulatory actions. These charter provisions and regulations evolved over time. By 2001 the key elements in the balance of government control and special privileges were as follows:

—The board of directors was now completely chosen by the shareholders, with no presidential appointees.[4]

—The Office of Federal Housing Enterprise Oversight, later restructured as the Federal Housing Finance Agency (FHFA), acted as the primary regulator. The agency set capital standards, within congressional rules that locked in fairly light requirements, enforced safety and soundness regulation, and determined whether the GSEs could introduce new products. The FHFA worked in concert with HUD on new product introductions and some other issues.

—Each GSE was given "affordable housing" goals intended to ensure that a stated percentage of the mortgages that it owned or guaranteed were for low- and moderate-income, central city, or rural households. These goals generally rose over time.

—The GSEs were only allowed to purchase mortgage-related assets where the underlying mortgages were for principal amounts below specific limits set by law. In addition, the GSEs imposed additional requirements regarding the form of the mortgage and the underwriting process. Those mortgages that met the legal and other requirements were referred to as "conforming" mortgages.

—GSE debt was treated in a privileged manner that gave the firms a strong advantage in raising funds in large volume at low costs. Most important, banks and some other regulated entities were allowed to treat GSE debt as if it were

3. The sale produced some cash that counted immediately against the growing deficits. More important, credit programs were still budgeted on a cash basis at that point in time, which meant that each dollar of new loan added to the deficit just as much as the purchase of military equipment, for example. Repayments worked in the opposite direction, but the growth of the GSEs would have continued to increase the deficit for years to come.

4. The George W. Bush administration chose not to appoint anyone to the board and proposed eliminating presidential appointments from the charters of the firms.

Figure 1-1. *GSE Obligations Outstanding, 1998–2010*

Dollars (billions)

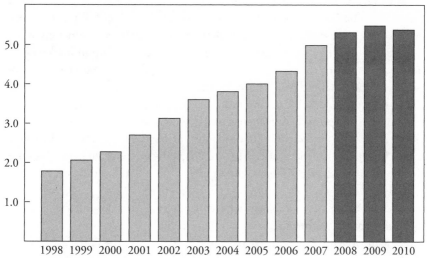

Source: Author's calculations.

U.S. government debt for the purposes of calculating risk-based capital require-ments. This meant that banks generally needed to hold little or no capital against these instruments, a preference that could be worth 30 basis points annually to a bank.[5] Further, GSE debt was not subject to credit concentration limits at these regulated entities, which could otherwise have constrained their GSE exposure. GSE debt was also settled through the same systems as U.S. Treasury securities.

—The specific debt privileges, combined with the GSEs' important public policy roles, their special charters, and their origins as government agencies, left investors with the strong impression of an implicit government guarantee of the debt. This, of course, proved to be true in practice. That implicit guarantee fur-ther reduced the GSEs' funding costs.

—GSE capital requirements were calculated differently than the require-ments for banks, their closest competitors. Congress clearly sent the message to the regulators, both explicitly and implicitly, that they should calculate the

5. A bank that was aiming to hold capital equal to 8 percent of risk-based assets, and would otherwise own assets with a risk weighting 25 percentage points higher than that for GSE-backed securities, would avoid allocating capital of 2 percent of the principal amount to this investment. Internal capital charges were generally set at 15 percent or higher, creating an advantage of 30 basis points in this example.

capital needs in ways that gave the GSEs a significant market advantage by letting them put up less capital for each dollar of principal.

The GSEs grew strongly in recent years, until the housing crash, as shown in figure 1-1. The GSEs' mortgage exposure grew an average of 9.8 percent annually during this period. Part of this growth reflected what was happening in the mortgage market as a whole, and part of it was due to a pickup in market share. The biggest part of that gain in market share arose from the purchase of pools of mortgages that were held as investments, rather than securitized. The GSEs found their capital levels growing nicely as they profited each year from a combination of their powerful advantages and a benign mortgage market. They, and their investors, came to realize that the most effective way to employ the capital was to hold on to the mortgages. This employed the excess capital while still producing significantly higher returns on equity than investors could expect to earn elsewhere, due to the GSEs' funding and capital cost advantages. Securitization was also profitable per unit of capital, but it put little capital to use.

Both the Bush administration and the Federal Reserve under Chairman Greenspan were quite concerned about the potential risk the GSEs posed to the taxpayers and the financial system if they ran into trouble. Their high growth rates, particularly in their investment portfolios, were viewed as a dangerous response to distortions produced by their excessively favorable structural benefits.

The administration therefore pushed for a stronger regulator, higher capital requirements, and limits on the size of the GSEs' investment portfolios. Congress, however, blocked most of the serious reforms in these areas, although some steps were taken.

Ironically, the major fear of critics was that the mismanagement of interest rate risk would bring these giants down, when in fact the basic business of taking credit risk on mortgages was the proximate cause of their failure. The fear about interest rate risk management was considerably heightened when it became clear that there were significant accounting failures at both of the GSEs with regard to how they calculated their exposure to losses on their massive books of interest rate derivatives. In 2003 Freddie Mac had to acknowledge that investors should not rely on their financial statements, and Fannie Mae followed in 2004. It took approximately three years to create acceptable accounting systems that allowed newly issued financial statements to be certified as accurate. Thus critics may well have been correct about the dangers on the interest rate side, but they largely missed what turned out to be the bigger issue.

The bursting of the housing bubble and the ensuing severe financial crisis put the GSEs in an untenable position. Impending large credit losses started to raise some doubt in investors' minds as to the seemingly risk-free nature of their debt, forcing the GSEs to pay higher and higher spreads and raising the prospect that a day might come when they would not be able to roll over their debt at a reasonable interest rate. This had become particularly critical since the GSEs borrowed most of their funds on a relatively short-term basis, certainly much shorter than the long-term mortgage assets they held as investments. In the end, the federal government, primarily through the Treasury Department, had to step in to recapitalize the two mortgage giants, effectively making the implicit debt guarantee explicit going forward.

Current Status of the GSEs

The financial state of the GSEs, and the associated concerns in the financial markets about their solvency, reached a critical point in September 2008 that forced the federal government to intervene directly. A law had been passed in July 2008 establishing a mechanism that would allow the FHFA to take over a GSE under a "conservatorship." The conservatorship would allow the GSE to continue operating, but under close government control. It would also give the FHFA the ability to determine which classes of investors would suffer financial losses, if any, much as the Federal Deposit Insurance Corporation is empowered to do for banks.

The FHFA used this authority on September 7, 2008, to put both GSEs into conservatorships. The Treasury stepped in the next day with an initial purchase of $1 billion of senior preferred stock in the two firms and a pledge to invest as much as $100 billion more, per firm, if needed to maintain positive net worth. (This cap was removed at the end of 2009 for capital needs through 2012.) This aid came with a high cost to the shareholders, since the Treasury received the right to buy 79.9 percent of the common shares of each of the firms for a few dollars.

The FHFA's conservatorship effectively gave it the powers normally belonging to shareholders and the board of directors, in addition to its standard regulatory authority. The agency used those powers to remove some of the key managers and board members who were in charge when the GSEs failed.

Today, the federal government effectively owns the GSEs and exerts strategic control. In conjunction with this, the GSEs are being used more explicitly than ever as an arm of federal housing policy, although they are still theoretically nongovernmental entities. For example, the GSEs are required to participate in two sets of foreclosure mitigation programs established under the Making Homes Affordable Program. Of one of these programs, Fannie Mae's Form 10Q filing for the third quarter of 2009 stated that the program would "likely have a material adverse impact on our business, results of operations, and financial conditions, including our net worth."[6] The GSEs presumably would not have chosen to participate if they had been privately owned and operated entities.

6. I am indebted to Dwight Jaffee for pointing out this statement in the regulatory filings.

The federal government's conservatorship and overall regulatory powers, combined with its effective ownership of 80 percent of the common and all of the senior preferred stock, give it the ability to direct the actions of the firms now and to determine their future shape and course. In practice, the government is allowing existing management[7] to operate the firms as private sector companies, except where regulators or the Treasury deem there to be significant public policy considerations or concerns about the effects on the safety and soundness of the GSEs. For example, the GSEs have been required to participate in fairly generous mortgage foreclosure mitigation efforts.

In addition to their importance to the economy, the GSEs also represent a considerable threat to the federal budget. The Obama administration has projected cumulative total capital injections from the Treasury Department of $224 billion, at its peak. (The net loss to taxpayers would be somewhat lower, since the government would benefit from dividends minus government funding costs, plus any repayment of the capital injections that might occur.) Moreover, external analysts have projected that the loss could rise to as high as $400 billion, although most estimates run significantly lower. Whatever the figure turns out to be, it is almost certain to be substantial and to represent the government's biggest loss on its emergency responses to the financial crisis.

The current legal situation is unstable. Conservatorships are not intended to be long-term arrangements, but rather to allow a continuation of normal operations while a stable solution is developed. Nor does it make policy sense for the government to own the GSEs on behalf of the taxpayers, but to treat them in certain measures as private entities, with minority shareholders.

Chapter Summaries with an Emphasis on Policy Recommendations

This section provides summaries of the five chapters, with particular emphasis on their policy recommendations.

In chapter 3, Pozen provides an overview of the issues relating to home mortgages, beginning with an analysis of the public policy goal of promoting homeownership, in order to assess whether and to what extent the federal government should favor this policy. He concludes that homeownership has various advantages for society as a whole, such as the much-cited research papers showing that people behave better (from society's point of view) in multiple ways when they own a home. However, he also emphasizes the considerable damage to society that can result from booms that divert excessive resources to housing and

7. The regulators did require certain changes in management and the board, so current management is not entirely the same as the group that led the firms into trouble.

busts that destroy the finances and lives of many marginal owners of homes. He stresses that we need to be careful in designing government subsidies for home-ownership. In addition, he states, most of the U.S. subsidies for homeownership are not very effective, and some of these subsidies increase the default rate on home mortgages—a key negative externality.

For example, the mortgage interest deduction is not well designed to promote homeownership and costs roughly $100 billion a year in lost tax revenues. To reduce the costs of the deduction and strengthen its link to homeownership, Congress should (a) eliminate the mortgage interest deduction for second homes and home equity loans and (b) provide a tax credit for mortgage interest on a primary residence or reduce the ceiling on the mortgage interest deduction from $1 million to $500,000 per couple. The second part of Pozen's recommendation is intended to eliminate or mitigate the problem that the current tax treatment of mortgage interest heavily favors the better-off because they itemize their deductions, which is a requirement for receiving the benefit. They are also in higher tax brackets, increasing the value of each dollar of deductions; and they have larger mortgages on which to deduct the interest.

Pozen also cites the problems he believes are created by the "nonrecourse" nature of mortgages in many states. (Homeowners in those states can effectively eliminate their mortgage debt by handing the house keys back to the lender.) In almost all other countries, and the rest of the states in our country, lenders have the legal ability to pursue the borrowers for any loss taken on the sale of a fore-closed home. He believes that nonrecourse mortgages encourage homeowners to make excessively low down payments and to walk away from their mortgages if their house values drop too far. He suggests that Congress should (a) supersede state laws prohibiting personal recourse on mortgages and (b) allow individual hardship cases to be adjudicated by bankruptcy judges.

He believes that the FHA and VA perform valuable functions, but that they allow borrowers to make down payments that are too low—creating moral hazard and generally raising the risks in the system too far. In addition, Pozen believes that the benefits of these subsidized loans are not targeted sufficiently well toward low- and middle-income borrowers. Therefore, Congress should (a) gradually raise the down payment requirement for these programs to a rea-sonable percentage of the purchase price and (b) establish an income limit for these programs, such as the median income level for the metropolitan area.

Pozen proposes that Fannie Mae and Freddie Mac should be phased out gradually. Where there is an appropriate role for government support, it should be performed where possible by direct on-budget subsidies for housing or by an increased role for Ginnie Mae, FHA, and VA activities. The rest of housing finance should be performed through the private sector, including securitiza-tion of conventional mortgages. However, the Federal Reserve should provide liquidity to the mortgage securities market, if and when necessary, in order to mitigate the ill effects of housing busts.

He recognizes the need to revive the private market for mortgage-backed securities in order for his proposal to succeed and therefore proposes that federal regulators should (a) adjust capital requirements of bank sponsors of mortgage-backed securities to reflect the actual allocation of risk in these deals; (b) require more disclosure on the individual loans in the pools supporting mortgage-backed securities; (c) encourage simpler structures for such deals; and (d) minimize ratings shopping by allowing an independent party to choose the ratings agency for large structured finance deals.

Finally, Pozen addresses the question of how best to define qualified residential mortgages (QRMs), which he sees as "a middle tier of mortgage-backed securities, between the private tier and the government-subsidized tier." (Dodd-Frank mandated that regulators define such a category of mortgages.) As he notes, since mortgage-backed securities based solely on QRMs would be exempt from risk retention requirements and certain other protections, regulators should mandate high down payments and strict underwriting standards for them. In addition, the criteria for QRMs should be designed to (a) phase out Fannie Mae and Freddie Mac by limiting the QRM status of their mortgages to a specific number of years; (b) promote long-term, fixed-rate mortgages by allowing prepayment penalties for the initial five years of high-quality mortgages; and (c) increase the standardization of home mortgages in the United States, including flexibility for mortgage servicers to modify loans in appropriate circumstances.

In chapter 4, Dynan and Gayer emphasize the importance of transitional arrangements in any housing finance overhaul, given that 88 percent of recent mortgages are backed by the government in some manner. However, they also emphasize the importance of making the *decisions* soon, even though there will be delays before all the changes are fully phased in. They fear that uncertainty about the future shape of housing finance could hold back the recovery of the housing market and the overall economy. Roughly the first half of their chapter is dedicated to explaining the current state of the housing market and reviewing the past and present role of the GSEs in housing finance.

The authors begin their policy recommendations with a strong critique of the fundamental structure of the GSEs. They state that the "conflation of the GSEs' private and public goals is financially and fundamentally unsound. The implicit government backstop incentivized the GSEs to take on excessive risk. Because their debt was perceived as backed by the federal government, they were able to engage in a massive amount of arbitrage by borrowing at low rates and purchasing mortgage products with higher yields for their portfolios." In addition, it is clear that "the future structure of mortgage finance should prevent the conflation of public goals and private goals within any one entity. Any public goals for mortgage finance should be explicitly provided by the federal government."

They go on to describe a second concern: "Another problem with the pre-crisis GSE model arose from how the two primary public goals of the agencies interacted with each other. The GSEs were to provide liquidity in mortgage markets by purchasing and securitizing mortgages and then selling them with a credit guarantee attached. And they were to promote affordable housing by subsidizing mortgages for low- and moderate-income families. As it turned out, the pairing of these two goals was a key factor behind the GSEs' substantial credit losses." In essence, the issue is that liquidity provision could be achieved at the lowest cost, and the least disturbance to the private market, by pricing the guarantees at an actuarially fair level. However, the promotion of affordable housing leads to pressures to subsidize the guarantees by charging premiums that are less than actuarially fair. And, indeed, this conflict appears to have contributed to the GSEs' slide into insolvency. Further, the authors question the extent of the benefits of assigning an affordable housing mission to the GSEs: "The available evidence suggests that the GSEs—despite their affordable housing goals—have had only limited effects on the supply of affordable housing."

These points lead the authors to make the following policy suggestions:

—*Separate out the affordable housing mission.* The entity offering the credit guarantee should not have an affordable housing mission and should charge actuarially fair prices. HUD could carry the affordable housing mission, "whether by expanding FHA programs or by providing direct, explicitly funded assistance to targeted borrowers."

—*Restrict portfolio holdings of the credit guarantor.* To the extent that the GSE or credit guarantor has access to funds at better than a market rate, it should be restricted from holding large investment portfolios, since there would be too much temptation to arbitrage the difference between the government-supported borrowing rate and the market rate.

—*Provide government-backed guarantees at actuarially fair, or higher, prices.* The authors acknowledge that there are risks of "government failure" analogous to the risks of "market failure" that a government role would be designed to fix and that the former risks might even be larger than the latter. However, the market undoubtedly assumes a future and ongoing implicit guarantee. With this inevitable moral hazard in place, it is better to make the guarantee explicit, to contain it, and to attempt to price it accurately, rather than to leave an expansive and implicit guarantee that is more likely to be mispriced.

They go on to say that the market failure warrants a government role in insuring mortgage credit risk, but one that is sensitive to the risk of the sort of government failure described above. This can be achieved by limiting the government guarantee to easily priced, plain-vanilla, high-quality mortgages.

The authors acknowledge that offsetting increases may be needed in other affordable housing programs to make up for the decreased access created by raising the standards for mortgages eligible for government credit support. They also note that the market share of government-backed entities should decline, but view this as an upside, not a downside, of their proposal.

—*Allow many securitizers, not just two GSE-like entities.* The authors believe that the careful restrictions on the quality of mortgages eligible for government backing should make it possible to have a considerably more competitive securitization sector; therefore, they oppose the idea of having a small number of GSEs operating on a "public utility" model, whereby they are each carefully constrained, but essentially also privileged.

In chapter 5, Wallison argues, "Fannie and Freddie should be eliminated and not replaced because the U.S. housing finance system would function well without them, or any other government financial support, and the removal of any government role in housing finance would free the U.S. taxpayers from the costs of yet another massive bailout in the future. However, because of the central role of the GSEs in the current housing finance system, removing them from that system without a replacement is complicated and depends on factors that do not exist today."

He then briefly surveys the role of government support to housing from the Great Depression through 2008, concluding that "two facts stand out" from his survey. "The government role in housing finance has been successful in standardizing mortgage terms and creating a national market for mortgages, largely through the sale and distribution of mortgage-backed securities. This has drawn financial resources from institutional investors in the United States and around the world, supplementing the funds previously supplied primarily by banks and by savings and loans. But these benefits have come at a huge cost to U.S. taxpayers, who have supplied in the past and will have to supply in the future hundreds of billions of dollars to bail out the losses incurred by government in its financial support for housing. In addition, once the government gets involved in assisting housing finance, its role will expand over time."

He continues, "The massive government losses described above occurred because government agencies do not have either the incentives or the means to price accurately for the risks they are taking. Even if that were not true and the government could price for risk like an insurance company, political pressures would not allow a government agency to accumulate the reserves (as insurance companies do) during the good times that would be necessary to meet its obligations during the inevitable bad times."

Wallison does not believe that providing the guarantees as backstops for securitizations would work any better than direct lending or guarantees of mortgages: "It is an illusion to believe that the government would be taking fewer risks and suffering fewer losses if the government is only guaranteeing mortgage-backed securities." Major moral hazard issues would arise because a government guarantee "will eliminate investor concern about both the quality of the underlying loans and the financial capacity of the issuer." In fact, he believes, "Any continuing government support for housing finance is highly likely to result in massive taxpayer losses and thus, as a matter of policy, should be rejected as a valid policy path."

Further, Wallison argues that better targeting of the benefits to those in greatest need is impossible in the long run, since "experience in the housing field shows that the benefits associated with government financial support cannot be effectively limited." Political pressure will always cause a widening of the eligibility requirements. "Thus, once a government subsidy program is established, it will expand to cover larger and larger portions of the population and will drive out all competing private sector activity."

He goes on to reject four arguments that he encounters in favor of continuing government involvement. First, he dismisses the argument that thirty-year, fixed-rate mortgages cannot exist without government support. He points out that even today a Google search turns up a large number of offers for thirty-year, fixed-rate jumbo mortgages, which are, by definition, not supported by Fannie and Freddie or another government body. Second, he does not see a valid reason why the housing industry, in preference to other industries, must be guaranteed a steady source of funds. In fact, he muses that government support for the steady availability of funds for housing finance may well have fueled housing bubbles in the past by eliminating some concerns about risk.

Wallison also rejects what he views as "probably the key reason for the support this idea enjoys in Washington," which is that institutional investors might buy U.S. mortgages, or securities backed by those mortgages, only if they are supported by a government guarantee. He believes that high-quality mortgages will be attractive to institutional investors. "The key to a successful mortgage market is not providing a government guarantee—which will inevitably cause serious losses to the taxpayers—but ensuring that the mortgages made in the market are of prime quality."

Finally, he believes that government backing is necessary to provide the concessionary rates or other benefits that will enable low-income families to become homeowners. He notes, however, that this objective can be achieved if government assistance is targeted to low-income home buyers and is not available to those who can participate in the prime market.

Wallison continues by asserting that the massive federal support for housing has not brought results remotely commensurate with the cost. He quotes a table developed by Dwight Jaffee to show that the U.S. housing system performs poorly when compared with other countries that provide much less government support.

He briefly reviews the housing market fluctuations of the last several decades and discusses why he believes that the recent housing bubble was so much worse than the others. He attributes this to a government-sponsored move to increase homeownership among low-income borrowers by reducing underwriting standards.

If the history of housing bubbles suggests that human nature fosters repeated and reinforcing market failures, what can be done? Wallison argues that regulation is necessary to assure that the bulk of mortgages in the system are of truly prime quality.

Steps to achieve this include requiring that all securitized mortgages meet certain underwriting standards, barring the use of nonprime loans as collateral for private mortgage-backed securities, covered bonds, and Federal Home Loan Bank advances. Rules for loans held in the portfolios of banks and other financial institutions could be looser, but full disclosure about the quality of loans in the portfolio is key. The last point, bringing more information to bear on the housing market, is relevant not only for the investor but also for the consumer. Something as simple as a one-page mortgage information form, signed early on when the home price is negotiated, would give the buyer a fuller understanding of potential costs under different scenarios.

Finally, countercyclical measures have a role to play in diluting the presence of weak mortgages. Mandating an increase in the down payment when home prices have risen by a certain amount could tamp down bubbles. And requiring countercyclical loan loss reserves during boom times could soften the impact of a crash, especially since banks are currently obligated to account only for expected losses.

Finally, Wallison concedes that it will take time to phase out the GSEs. First, a robust private securitization market needs to be restored, which he thinks will take perhaps two more years. He does not see delay as a practical issue, since Congress and the administration are unlikely to reach agreement on GSE reforms faster than that anyway. Second, he lays out a series of steps to provide a smooth phasing out of the GSEs over five years.

In chapter 6, Hancock and Passmore survey a history of failure in mortgage securitization and pose three questions:

1. Why is mortgage securitization fragile?

2. Would government provision of catastrophic insurance for mortgage credit likely improve financial stability?

3. Is there a potential role for Fannie Mae and Freddie Mac to provide government-backed insurance for mortgage-backed instruments?

To answer the first question, the authors analyze mortgage market equilibriums. They note that the liquidity that comes from securitization, irrespective of its effect on primary mortgage rates, creates the potential for a run. Investors who are sensitive to the presence of a guarantee will flee to safety if they doubt the quality of mortgage-backed bonds and the associated guarantee, leaving only the highest-quality mortgages as a source of credit in times of stress. The results are tighter credit, greater declines in home prices, and weaker economic growth.

In answer to the second question, the authors argue that only the federal government, with its massive size and its power to tax, can credibly provide wide guarantees on a market as large as mortgage-backed securitizations. Private efforts to achieve the same result, including even the recent experience of the GSEs with their implicit government guarantee, are doomed to eventual failure. Private entities cannot credibly guarantee these obligations when confronted with the most severe crises of housing finance. Therefore, there will come a tipping point when the many investors who essentially relied on the guarantees, rather than on the quality of the underlying assets, will flee in a panic analogous to a bank run. This panic fuels itself and creates substantial disruptions in housing finance.

The authors propose that the federal government provide insurance for mortgage-backed securities, potentially including covered bonds, but only at a level of protection sufficient for catastrophes and not for more ordinary swings in housing markets. They fear that protecting against more ordinary events would create major moral hazard problems and lose many of the efficiency benefits of a solid private sector role in housing finance. They further propose that the government charge appropriate risk-based premiums for the protection.

To the third question, the authors also note that Fannie and Freddie could be used to provide the insurance, if they were appropriately structured, severely constrained, and given an explicit federal backstop. Such an approach involves relatively straightforward changes to the existing organizations, making it a feasible way to reestablish a robust private market for housing finance.

In chapter 7, Scharfstein and Sunderam begin with an economic analysis of the two main types of housing finance reform proposals: (a) maintaining government guarantees of mortgage-backed securities with adjustments to the past forms of guarantees and (b) privatizing mortgage markets by eliminating government guarantees altogether. Each type of proposal has strengths and weaknesses. On the one hand, guarantees are valuable during periods of great financial stress. On the other hand, they have limited benefits in normal periods; they may instead encourage moral hazard without substantially lowering mortgage rates. While private markets are capable of providing adequately priced mortgage credit in normal times, a wholly privatized market is prone to instability.

Their analysis of these two policy approaches leads the authors to believe that the purpose of housing finance policy should be fundamentally reoriented. Rather than trying to lower mortgage interest rates—especially when the tax code already incentivizes investment in housing—the main goals of housing finance policy should be to reduce volatility in the supply of housing credit and to prevent shocks to the housing sector.

With that new framework in mind, the authors propose a hybrid plan that draws from both approaches. First, Fannie Mae and Freddie Mac should be phased out to achieve a greater privatization of the market. Indeed, they argue that the main source of housing finance should be from the private market with no direct government guarantees. However, given the role of the private market in providing unstable and imprudent forms of housing finance—even at the peak of GSE involvement in subprime and Alt-A lending, the private market provided 70 percent of these types of loans—they argue that this market should be stringently regulated. Given the importance of securitization, they point to a variety of new approaches to ensuring some degree of safety in privately issued mortgage-backed securities, such as limits on the inclusion of risky mortgages and rules for the capital structures of securitization trusts. They go on to argue that no system of private finance can be foolproof and that a government-owned corporation could play a useful role as a guarantor of last resort during times of crisis. In their proposal, the government-owned corporation would "ensure the supply of high-quality, well-underwritten mortgages during a period of significant market stress" by guaranteeing newly issued mortgage-backed securities in such periods. The government corporation would not guarantee securities previously issued by private entities, but might need to have a small market presence as a guarantor during normal times to be able to ramp up its role quickly during a crisis.

In sum, their proposal seeks a well-regulated privatized mortgage finance market combined with a government agency that could serve as a backstop for new mortgage credit in times of crisis.

Key Policy Points

There is a surprising degree of consensus across the five chapters and between the authors and the Treasury white paper, despite the intense political and ideological struggles that have surrounded the GSEs in recent years. In particular, there is essentially no appetite to have the GSEs operate in something close to the manner in which they did in recent decades. For example, most of the proposals discussed here would abolish them or have their role taken over by the government; the rest would give them a much more circumscribed role, if they did survive. There also appears to be a complete consensus among this group that the affordable housing mission needs to be detached from the credit guarantee mission and moved to the FHA. The remainder of this section compares the views of the various chapters on key policy points.

Overall Role of the Federal Government in Supporting Housing

All of the chapters advocate a continuing federal role to support housing finance. Pozen is the most explicit in discussing the pros and cons, referencing the various studies showing that homeownership encourages socially desirable behaviors. He views these benefits as worthy of federal support, but argues strongly for targeting subsidies to those households where the aid would make an appreciable difference in their ability to own a home rather than remain as renters. He suggests several changes to the current system of support, which he believes provides much more support to the relatively affluent than to those who would be able to support mortgage payments with some aid, but would otherwise be unable to afford a home.

Scharfstein and Sunderam include some modest discussion of broader housing policy goals, but focus very strongly on financial stability, arguing that the key objective should be to "reduce excessive volatility in the supply of housing credit and protect the financial system from adverse shocks to the housing market." They do not find convincing the arguments for providing a widely spread pricing subsidy, such as by undercharging for a government guarantee. They share Pozen's concerns that such a subsidy encourages overinvestment in housing and essentially subsidizes existing homeowners, with little benefit for new home buyers, who face an offsetting increase in the price of the home they must purchase.

They also acknowledge the "significant benefits of meeting" the policy objective of encouraging housing affordability for low- and moderate-income households, while focusing on enhancing the safety of the housing finance system.

Dynan and Gayer implicitly take as given two existing policy goals: assuring the stability of housing finance and enhancing the affordability of housing for marginal home buyers. They address GSE reform as a better way to achieve these goals, without discussing whether these goals are justified. Presumably they would have addressed the desirability of these goals if they had disagreed with the consensus supporting those objectives.

Hancock and Passmore focus more narrowly on the stability of the housing finance system, but clearly believe that a federal role as a guarantor is necessary to assure that stability.

Wallison does not believe that federal support is necessary for housing finance as a general matter, either to encourage housing broadly or to assure stability beyond the normal role of regulating financial institutions. He leaves open, and seems implicitly to endorse, a federal role to assist low- and middle-income home buyers through a reformed FHA. However, he does not go so far in this chapter as to state explicitly that there should be such a federal mission.

In sum, there is a broad consensus among the authors that the federal government's role in supporting housing finance was too broad and deep even before the housing crisis caused the government's market share to skyrocket. They are all searching for a way to retain whatever government role is necessary to maintain the stability and smooth working of the housing finance market, while pulling back in those areas where the private sector can take over.

Role of the FHA

There is virtual unanimity among the authors that a housing affordability mission is appropriate and should be handled primarily through the FHA and not mingled with a credit guarantee mission, such as was the case with the GSEs. Pozen, Dynan and Gayer, and Wallison are all specific that there should be no mixing of those missions, a view also supported by the Treasury white paper. Scharfstein and Sunderam are less specific about the housing affordability mission, but seem to support both the existence of that mission and its clear separation from the credit guarantee role. Hancock and Passmore focus on a narrower question and do not seriously address this question.

Those authors who address the point are unanimous in calling for any federal subsidies to be accurately calculated and fully shown on the federal budget, in order to encourage the best decisions.

Importance of the Transition

There is also virtual unanimity that GSE reform must take several years, given the difficulties of the current housing market and the high proportion of new mortgages now guaranteed by the government, mostly through the GSEs. Wallison, along with Dynan and Gayer, puts the most emphasis on the transitional arrangements, but Pozen as well as Scharfstein and Sunderam also discuss the issue. Hancock and Passmore once again have a narrower, and somewhat more theoretical, focus that does not explicitly address this issue. The Treasury white paper also affirms the belief that a transition will take time and must be carefully designed.

Undesirability of Large Portfolio Holdings at a Government-Backed Credit Guarantor

Most of the chapters oppose the past practice of the GSEs (or some equivalent future private sector credit guarantor with government backing) of holding large portfolios of mortgages or mortgage-backed securities. Wallison underlines the dangers in this practice, Pozen calls for very significant limitations on it, and Dynan and Gayer agree that it should be limited, unless structural reforms create a competitive dynamic that sharply mitigates the risk to the public. Scharfstein and Sunderam, along with Hancock and Passmore, essentially avoid the issue by minimizing the extent to which government-backed private entities would be in the guarantee business. The Treasury white paper also calls for sharp cutbacks in the portfolio holdings of GSEs or their future equivalents.

Use of Actuarially Fair Pricing of Government-Backed Credit Guarantees

There appears to be unanimity that any direct or indirect federal guarantee of mortgages should be at actuarially fair, or higher, prices with the exception of the affordable housing mission, which would generally be carried out separately by the FHA and similar entities. The partial exception to this statement is that Wallison does not want the government to do this at all, since he believes that it would be technically and politically difficult to achieve actuarially fair pricing, although he would favor such rates if the government had to be involved and could manage to charge at those levels.

The term "actuarially fair" leaves open the question about the extent to which taxpayers should receive compensation for taking risk, over and above covering the expected losses. Since guarantee fees would be charged in advance of the losses they would be expected to cover, it is necessary to bring the future losses back to a value in today's dollars, using an interest rate known as a discount rate that represents the time value of money. If the discount rate for the actuarial calculation is a risk-free rate, then taxpayers would be paid nothing to compensate them for taking the risk that results are worse than expected. Scharfstein and Sunderam explicitly call for use of a risk-adjusted rate, whereas most of the other papers are silent on this important issue. (Fortunately, this issue is less critical for high-quality mortgage lending than for many other areas of finance, since the market assessment of the risk on these loans is not terribly far above U.S. Treasury rates. Nonetheless, the large dollar amounts involved do call for clarity on the ultimate decisions about how to price such guarantees.)

Existence of a Federal Credit Guarantor

The consensus breaks down on the question of whether the federal government should provide a credit guarantee for mortgage-backed securities, other than perhaps in support of a tightly focused housing affordability mission. Wallison clearly rejects this approach altogether. Pozen has a somewhat more nuanced approach, but essentially supports the elimination of government guarantees of securitization on private mortgage loans. Scharfstein and Sunderam strongly prefer a private market solution in normal times, but they want the government to be able to spring into a support role in crisis times and therefore see the need for a modest government role in normal times in order to maintain the capacity to ramp up in a crisis.

Dynan and Gayer support offering explicit federal guarantees of mortgage-backed securities, but at actuarially fair, or higher, prices. They believe that this would give the private market room to provide cheaper guarantees or learn to invest without credit guarantees, while maintaining the stability of the housing finance markets through a government backstop. However, this government backing would only be available for quite safe, standardized types of mortgages.

Hancock and Passmore take a similar approach to that of Dynan and Gayer, in that they recommend a government guarantee at actuarially fair prices, but only for super-safe mortgages. Essentially, the government would be there for "catastrophic" credit risk, but would leave the normal run of credit losses for the private sector to bear. The underwriting criteria they suggest would therefore be considerably more strict even than those suggested by Dynan and Gayer.

The Treasury white paper leaves a range of potential options, making it difficult to compare the "Treasury view" directly with that of the authors.

At the risk of repetition, it is significant that none of the proposals offered in these papers would involve GSEs, or equivalents, nearly as large or as active as Fannie Mae and Freddie Mac were prior to the collapse of the housing bubble. The authors differ on the role of a federal guarantee, but all see the appropriate scale of that activity as much more restricted than how the GSEs operated.

2

The Cycle in Home Building

ALAN GREENSPAN

While the rest of this volume is devoted to the structure of mortgage finance, it might be useful to discuss what mortgage finance is ultimately all about: home building.

The last twenty years have exhibited the longest uninterrupted rise in single-family housing starts, and by far the sharpest collapse, in the postwar years. Starts in recent months have languished at an annual rate of a little more than 400,000, less than a fourth of where they stood at the top of the boom in early 2006. Nothing resembling this collapse had occurred in the six decades following the war. To find such data, we have to go back to the 1930s, when single-family housing starts fell almost 90 percent between 1925 and 1933. Housing starts did not regain their 1925 levels over the next eight years prior to the war. Starts, in fact, did not recover to their 1925 levels until 1947. I do not expect a similar hiatus this time, but the trudge uphill is not going to be easy.

During the recent boom years, the demand for single-family units, and their financing, was predominantly demand for owner occupancy. The level of additions to ownership was driven significantly by the rate at which households chose to own rather than rent and could afford to do so. The ownership rate, in turn, was fostered by rising home prices and the implementation of affordable housing goals.

This chapter is based on a presentation made on February 11, 2011.

After a protracted period of stability, the ownership rate, at 64 percent in 1994, began its historic rise to more than 69 percent a decade later, producing from 2001 to 2004 an annual average increase in new single-family owner-occupied dwelling units of approximately 1.2 million, absorbing all, and more, of the gain in household formation. In addition to the demand for owner occupancy was the significant demand for single-family residences by investors. According to Home Mortgage Disclosure Act data, the share of total investment and second home purchases rose from 9 percent of home originations in 2001 to 14 percent in 2004. That combination, coupled with an annual rate of 200,000 demolitions and some loss of single-family units to multiunit conversions, supported, over those years, an average annual level of single-family unit completions and mobile home placements amounting to 1.5 million.

The demand for homeownership peaked at the end of 2004, as the limited backlog and higher prices began to take their toll. Ownership rates turned downward in the fourth quarter of 2006 (falling below 67 percent, seasonally adjusted, by September 2010). Single-family housing starts peaked in early 2006. But it took another seven months for starts to turn to completions, and not before adding an unstoppable (once started, aborting construction is expensive and rare) and unprecedented 430,000 units to the inventory of single-family homes for sale over the four quarters of 2006. This was on top of 170,000 added during 2005.

By the end of 2006, the level of vacant single-family homes for sale had reached 1.8 million, a staggering historic overhang of more than 700,000, the equivalent of six months of sales. For years prior to the surge, completed homes, available for sale, had been relatively stable, at a little more than 1 million units. Following the topping out of demand late in 2006, home prices proceeded to fall for three years in a largely futile endeavor to uncover enough demand to absorb the excess inventory. But homeownership, by then, no longer held the seemingly irresistible profit-making attraction of earlier years.

Home builders and other owners of newly constructed, but vacant, houses have been able through price discounting to liquidate their full share of the overall excess inventory—about 200,000 of the more than 700,000 excess units for sale. The remaining vacant homes offered for sale by investors—the bulk of the vacant market—were still hovering around the (seasonally adjusted) 1.5 million level, less than 6 percent below their all-time peak, reached at the end of 2007. The level of home completions declined more than two-thirds, but demand fell almost as much, placing new supply only modestly below demand.

Even at current depressed levels of new single-family construction, the inventory overhang cannot be credibly absorbed quickly. A stabilization of the home-ownership rate would help in the sense that a *falling* ownership rate severely undercuts the demand for single-family units. The ownership rate moving from negative to zero is in that sense a positive. Nonetheless, market pressure could keep completions below demand for much of this year or longer, as excess inventories are gradually brought under control.

New demand must come from either an increase in the rate of household formation or an increase in the share going toward owner occupancy. Temporary tax credits rarely do either. It is thus no surprise that the recent first-time home buyer tax credit produced little, if any, permanently higher demand.

Certainly, the more than 2 million single-family units currently in foreclosure have not helped. Recent history suggests that approximately two-fifths of the surge in foreclosed properties, on completion of the foreclosure process, will be sold, possibly into a still troubled market. That would amount to an additional several hundred thousand overhang, bringing the total excess to more than 1 million units.

After falling almost 30 percent from their peak in late 2006, home prices stabilized by most measures between early 2009 and the spring of 2010. By summer of last year, however, they began to soften again, largely as a consequence of the pickup in distressed (foreclosure) sales, especially in December. There was, however, some evidence of price stabilization at the end of 2010. Seasonally adjusted CoreLogic prices, excluding stressed sales, rose, as did the median price of newly built homes.

Stabilization is important not only to the housing market, but also to economic recovery as a whole, since approximately 8 million homes were financed with conventional (conforming) mortgages during 2005 and 2006. Most of their 20 percent and more original down payment plus recent amortization of that debt has been eaten into by the 25 percent price decline since origination. Another 5 to 10 percent decline in home prices, which many are forecasting, would place a significant part of the 8 million homes underwater.

To be sure, the propensity to default on underwater conventional (conforming) mortgage debt has been much lower than on the more vulnerable subprime and Alt-A mortgage-financed homes. Nonetheless, a price weakening itself could set in motion the contagion for a further decline. However, with the rest of the economy recovering rather impressively, I am hopeful that such an outcome can be avoided. But it would be unwise to rule it out fully.

As a consequence of the near 30 percent decline in home prices, equity in homes by the end of the third quarter of last year had retraced all of the $7 trillion rise between 2000 and 2006, but its composition had changed. Currently, it is highly concentrated. Subprime and Alt-A mortgage-financed homes are, net, underwater. There is some net equity in prime jumbos and, which is surprising, in the niche market of homes financed only with home equity loans. Nationwide, well over half of home equity is currently in homes free and clear of debt. Conventional (conforming) mortgage-financed homes are running a distant second. Prior to the crash, in 2006, they had similar shares of net equity, but that was a time when virtually all homeowners had positive net equity.

With home prices flattening out over the past year, the number of homes underwater has stopped rising. The number of homes in foreclosure has also stabilized at approximately 2.3 million, seasonally adjusted, at least for now, but they presumably would move higher should home prices slide again.

The rapidity of the housing recovery, when it gets under way, is going to depend, in large part, as it has in the past, on trends in what we used to label equity extraction—the raising of cash by borrowing against the market value of equity in homes. Equity extraction has faded as a key determinant in economic activity, but it remains important to the housing and mortgage markets, and it will surely reemerge as a factor driving the household saving rate and personal consumption expenditures. Today, equity extraction is negative, as debt write-offs and new owners add equity to, rather than extract it from, the nation's owned homes. Despite flat home prices, equity has risen by half a trillion dollars since March 2009.

The overall stock of home mortgage debt is in a constant state of turnover and revaluation, owing largely to changes in home prices and the degree of refinancing of the debt. But to understand the equity extraction process better, we can usefully separate quarterly changes in debt into two components: (1) the part of the increase (or decrease) that is solely the difference between mortgage origination on newly built homes and the scheduled amortization of debt that exists at the beginning of each quarter—in short, the amount of debt accumulation that occurs solely from the financing of newly built homes—and (2) the part that owes wholly to actions that in total we measure as equity extraction. Equity extraction is capable of being fully accounted for in three buckets:

—Debt changes owing to the sale (that is, turnover) of existing homes. The buyer of an existing home will almost always add more debt on that home than the seller will repay as part of the transaction.

—"Cash out" refinancing: the difference between the balance on a refinanced mortgage less the mortgage balance being refinanced.

—Unscheduled repayment of debt unrelated to a property transfer or a refinancing, including especially delinquent scheduled amortization, that may or may not more than offset burgeoning write-downs.

In years past, Jim Kennedy of the Federal Reserve Board and I went through a set of detailed calculations to estimate each of these three components separately.[1] But equity extraction, *in total,* can be approximated more expeditiously from

1. For a detailed explanation of these series, see Alan Greenspan and James Kennedy. 2005. "Estimates of Home Mortgage Originations, Repayments, and Debt on One- to Four-Family Residences." FEDS Working Paper 2005-41. Washington: Federal Reserve Board.

a simple regression in which equity extraction per capita is regressed against the refinanced share of total home mortgage originations and a cumulative, moving, four-year change in home prices. The results over the past fifteen years are statistically highly significant.[2] Moreover, the regression accurately traced equity extraction in the boom years as well as its small negative during the past year. What the price variable suggests is that it takes four years of cumulative capital gains on homes, on average, before homeowners endeavor to extract equity, mainly through sale of the home or cash-out refinancing.

The regression coefficients can be employed, along with the calculated amortization rate (given average maturities and interest rates) and the value of home originations estimated as the product of the number of one- to four-family completions and the average price of sales of newly constructed homes. These inputs estimate the change, and hence the level, of one- to four-family regular mortgages. This simple model suggests that home prices will have to rise 10 percent or more before signs of a full-fledged recovery in housing, and the mortgage finance that goes with it, becomes unambiguous.

---

2. R^2 = 0.88 for refinance share, t = 6.1, and, for the four-year price average, t = 22.0. Durbin-Watson = 1.85.

3

Toward a Three-Tier Market for U.S. Home Mortgages

ROBERT C. POZEN

Home mortgages constituted the single largest type of credit in the United States at $10.6 trillion as of September 2010. Almost half of this amount took the form of mortgage-backed securities (MBS) that were formally or informally guaranteed by the U.S. government—$2.55 trillion by Fannie Mae, $1.7 trillion by Freddie Mac, and $1 trillion by Ginnie Mae. As of September 2010, the other half of outstanding home mortgage credit was composed of $1.557 trillion in MBS not backed by the U.S. government and $3.837 trillion in whole mortgage loans (Bank of America–Merrill Lynch 2010, p. 3).

Since the financial crisis started in 2007–08, however, the annual flow of new home mortgages has shifted even more from the private to the public sector. In 2006 only 5 percent of the home purchase mortgages originated were insured by the Federal Housing Administration (FHA), and less than another 5 percent were insured through programs at the Veterans Administration (VA) and the U.S. Department of Agriculture (USDA). By contrast, these three agencies together insured close to half of all home purchase mortgages originated in 2009—38.4 percent for the FHA, 6.9 percent for the VA, and 4.4 percent for the USDA (HUD 2010, p. 6).

Similarly, the government's role in issuing MBS soared from 2006 to 2009. Many of the federally insured mortgages mentioned above are securitized by Ginnie Mae, part of the Department of Housing and Urban Development (HUD). Ginnie Mae's share of new MBS originations rose from 4 percent in 2006 to 25 percent in 2009. Private lenders may sell their conventional mortgages (not government insured) up to a specified size to either of two government-chartered corporations, Fannie Mae and Freddie Mac, which were put into conservatorship by the U.S. government in September 2009. The portion of MBS issued by these two corporations was 72 percent in 2009, up from 40 percent in 2006. Ginnie Mae, Fannie Mae, and Freddie Mac together accounted for 97 percent of all MBS issued in 2009 (FHFA 2010, p. 5).

During the same period, the securitization of U.S. home mortgages by the private sector plunged. In 2006 the private sector securitized $723 billion in home mortgages, including $154 billion in subprime mortgages. In 2009 the private sector securitized only $48 billion, with only one small deal for subprime mortgages (Federal Reserve 2010b, p. 29).

In short, by 2009, the U.S. home mortgage market was totally dependent on government insurance programs and purchases of mortgages. In 2010, 95 percent of all the home mortgages originated in the United States were either insured by a federal program or purchased by Fannie Mae or Freddie Mac (Haviv 2010).

Nevertheless, none of the 2,400 pages of the Dodd-Frank Act, passed in the summer of 2010, attempted to reform these two corporations; the act "kicked the can down the road" by directing the administration to publish proposals on this subject by the end of January 2011. Instead, the statute contained a 5 percent requirement for risk retention—subject to regulatory exemptions—by certain originators and securitizers of mortgages. It also established tougher rules for credit rating agencies and stricter standards for private mortgage products.

Given the enormous problems in the U.S. market for home mortgages and the modest legislative response to date, this chapter addresses the key policy issues related to government support of home mortgages in four main sections. It begins by tackling the fundamental question of whether government subsidies are necessary to promote the social benefits of homeownership. It reviews the evidence in the United States and other similar countries—such as Australia, Canada, and England—that have higher homeownership rates than the United States, with much lower levels of government subsidies. The second section critiques the current approach of the federal mortgage insurance programs—based primarily on the size of the home mortgage with minimal requirements for down payments. Instead, it proposes new criteria, based primarily on homeowner income, for allocating government subsidies for home mortgages. Recognizing that the revival of the private market for home mortgages is necessary to reduce the degree of government mortgage support, the third section recommends the adoption of specific measures to revive this private market. These measures relate to capital requirements, disclosure rules, deal structure, and credit ratings. The fourth section explains how exempting qualified residential mortgages from the risk retention requirements of the Dodd-Frank Act will create a middle tier of

MBS between the private tier and the government-subsidized tier. It addresses how this exemption should be designed to reduce the chances of another credit crisis. A final section delineates the conclusions for each of the three tiers of the home mortgage market.

I. Societal Justifications for Promoting Homeownership

Why does the U.S. government supply so many subsidies to promote home-ownership? For this purpose, subsidies include any benefit or protection beyond that provided by the private market. Such subsidies include direct government appropriations as well as lower-than-market interest rates, minimal down payments on government-insured mortgages, tax deductions for mortgage interest and property taxes, capital gains exemptions on home sales, government institutions to buy or securitize home mortgages, and personal immunity against deficiencies in home mortgage foreclosures.

Externalities of Homeownership

Government subsidies for homeownership are typically justified by their benefits to the rest of society. For example, homeownership is strongly connected to better maintenance of the house and garden as well as higher levels of participation in civic and political groups (Glaeser and Shapiro 2003). Other people are willing to pay more to live near homeowners because of their beneficial effects on the local neighborhood (Coulson, Hwang, and Imai 2001). In other words, government support of homeownership for certain families is positively correlated with social benefits for the larger community.

However, certain aspects of homeownership are closely associated with negative externalities, although these have been much less studied. For instance, Paul Krugman has suggested that high levels of homeownership impose social costs because homeowners are less mobile than renters (Krugman 2008). This reluctance to move to a different location reduces to some degree the efficient functioning of labor markets.

More important for the financial crisis, researchers have shown that mortgage defaults and home foreclosures have a significant adverse impact on other homes in the neighborhood. For instance, researchers have estimated that a single foreclosure decreases values of nearby houses by as much as 1 percent (Campbell, Giglio, and Pathak forthcoming). This occurs because the foreclosed home is quickly sold at a very low price or the foreclosed house remains a vacant eyesore.

Thus if government subsidies that are intended to promote homeownership in practice increase the level of mortgage foreclosures, these subsidies will have negative social externalities. The main culprit has been a well-intentioned drop in the down payment requirement for certain types of mortgages, together with lax underwriting standards. In 2005 and 2006, for example, 40 percent of all first-time buyers took out mortgages with no down payment (ElBoghdady 2007). Yet having no equity in a home is the single best predictor of mortgage defaults (Pozen 2010, p. 256). When housing prices turn down or other problems arise, it is too easy for homeowners with negative equity simply to walk away from their mortgages.

Home buyers are more likely to have no equity in their homes, and therefore more likely to default, in states that limit the ability of lenders to attach the personal assets of borrowers to satisfy deficiencies after mortgage foreclosures. In states like California and Arizona, the borrower is not personally liable for any shortfall if the lender forecloses on a home and sells it for less than the outstanding mortgage amount. In states like Florida and Nevada, "homestead" exemptions generally prevent creditors from reaching owner-occupied homes to satisfy mortgage deficiencies of homeowners. Although correlations are not necessarily causations, the percentage of "underwater" mortgages—with outstanding amounts above the current value of their homes—far exceed the national average in all four states (Pozen 2010, pp. 22–23). More systematically, recent empirical research shows that the existence of personal recourse in a state decreases the probability of mortgage default when there is a substantial likelihood that a borrower has negative home equity (Ghent and Kudiyak 2010).

In summary, we should carefully design any subsidies to promote the positive, and not the negative, externalities associated with homeownership. Although low down payments encourage homeownership, they increase the adverse neighborhood effects of mortgage defaults and foreclosures. Given the strong connection between mortgage defaults and negative home equity, we should move away from government-supported mortgages with minimal down payment requirements. Instead, we should gradually increase down payment requirements for such mortgages and adopt realistic income standards for such mortgage holders to avoid defaults—even if housing prices fall in the future.

Similarly, Congress should override broad protections in certain states against personal recourse on home mortgages—legal immunity for homeowners who default on their mortgages and whose homes are sold in foreclosure for less than the outstanding mortgage amount. Nonrecourse mortgages increase the number of defaults and their negative externalities. Nonrecourse mortgages also encourage people to walk away from mortgages that they could afford to pay.

Nevertheless, there may be individual cases where a homeowner does not have sufficient personal resources to pay a deficiency after a mortgage foreclosure. These situations should be addressed by bankruptcy courts, which are in the best position to evaluate the overall financial situation of the borrower. In specific, states should recognize a home mortgage as a senior lien on the property and an unsecured claim to the extent that the proceeds from the sale of the property are less than the outstanding mortgage. Thus the lender could enforce this unsecured claim for such a deficiency against a former homeowner, who could in turn choose to file for bankruptcy. Then the judge could decide to eliminate, reduce, or reschedule this unsecured claim in light of the total creditor claims against the borrower and his or her financial resources.

Tax Deductions for Mortgage Interest

One of the largest subsidies for homeownership in the United States is the income tax deduction for interest paid on home mortgages. Each year the U.S. government loses approximately $100 billion in tax revenues due to this deduction (Joint Tax Committee 2010). Furthermore, some states allow income tax deductions for interest paid on home mortgages.

The parameters of this federal tax deduction are quite broad: it is allowed for interest paid on all home mortgages, including vacation cottages and other second homes, with principal totaling up to $1 million per couple. In addition, a couple may deduct interest on a home equity loan up to $100,000. A home equity loan is typically a second mortgage on a home that already has a first mortgage, even if the loan proceeds are not used to buy or improve the home. These deductions for mortgage interest, including interest on home equity loans, are available to all homeowners who itemize their tax deductions, instead of taking the standard deduction.

Nevertheless, as explained below, despite its magnitude and breadth, the mortgage interest deduction does not promote homeownership in many locations. And in those locations where the tax deduction does promote homeownership, it does so mainly for high-income families.

The actual impact of the mortgage interest deduction depends heavily on the nature of the local market for home mortgages. In "tightly regulated" markets with limited vacant land and strict land use controls, such as Boston, Massachusetts, the mortgage interest deduction tends to raise the price of homes rather than the quantity of homeownership. In other words, when the supply of prime residential lots is relatively inelastic, an increase in demand through tax deductions will have price rather than quantity effects. For this reason, researchers have found that eliminating the income tax deductions for mortgage interest and property taxes would reduce home prices by 2 to 13 percent, depending on the metropolitan area (Capozza, Green, and Hendershott 1996).

By contrast, we would expect the mortgage interest deduction to increase the quantity of homeowners in "loosely regulated" markets (for example, Houston, Texas), where there is an ample supply of residential lots and the land use controls are relatively light. In loosely regulated markets, however, it is unclear in theory what the distributional effects of the mortgage interest deduction would be. On the one hand, this deduction benefits only the one-third of taxpayers who itemize, mainly from the top half of all filers, who buy relatively pricey homes (Poterba and Sinai 2008, pp. 84–89). On the other hand, it seems logical that the decision to purchase a home is much less influenced by home prices for high-income families than for low-income families.

In a recent paper, Hilber and Turner (2010) resolve these theoretical arguments through an extensive empirical analysis of metropolitan areas in the United States. In tightly regulated markets, they conclude that mortgage tax subsidies have a significant adverse impact on homeownership: "They reduce the likelihood of homeownership, with the effect being slightly more negative for moderate-income households (–3.7 percentage points) than high-income households (–3.4 percentage points)" (Hilber and Turner 2010, p. 22). In loosely regulated markets, they conclude that the mortgage interest deduction "has a positive effect on homeownership attainment, but only for higher-income groups, increasing their likelihood of homeownership by about 3.6 to 5 percentage points depending on income status, with the effect being stronger for higher-income than moderate households" (Hilber and Turner 2010, pp. 21–22). Finally, they conclude that the mortgage interest deduction has no material impact on low-income families in either tightly or loosely regulated housing markets.

These conclusions suggest the need for fundamental rethinking about whether the mortgage interest deduction is justified as promoting homeownership. A positive effect on homeownership is achieved only in loosely regulated housing markets; in tightly regulated housing markets, this deduction significantly decreases the level of homeownership. Moreover, the positive effects of this deduction are highly skewed in favor of homeownership for high-income families: it has little impact on homeownership for low-income households since they do not itemize their deductions.

To promote homeownership for low-income and moderate-income families, we could transform the interest deduction into a tax credit. A tax credit—for example, equal to 20 percent of the interest payments on a home mortgage—would be much more effective than a tax deduction in moving families at these income levels from renters to homeowners. According to one study, transforming the mortgage interest deduction into a tax credit on a revenue-neutral basis would increase the national homeownership rate by 3 percent (Green and Vandell 1999). But this transformation may not be politically feasible.

Alternatively, Congress could adopt either or both of the following measures, which would help to reduce the budget deficit without reducing homeownership for low-income and middle-income families. First, Congress could limit the interest deduction to the mortgage on a couple's primary residence—in other words, no interest deductions for vacation or second homes. Second, Congress could limit the interest deduction to home mortgages up to $500,000—down from the current maximum of $1 million. Both of these measures were contained in the proposals by the co-chairs of President Obama's deficit reduction commission.[1]

In addition, the co-chairs proposed eliminating the current interest deduction for home equity loans up to $100,000. This aspect of the interest deduction has a weak relationship to promoting homeownership, since the proceeds of home equity loans are rarely used to improve homes. These proceeds are often used to purchase goods, pay tuition, or reduce credit card debt. However, these uses of home equity loans are inconsistent with the congressional decision several years ago to eliminate tax deductions for interest on consumer loans.

Of course, all of these proposals should be implemented gradually over many years to prevent a major blow-up in the U.S. market for homes. For the twelve years before 2000, the United Kingdom gradually eliminated its tax deduction for mortgage interest without a material impact on its homeownership rate (Kalita and Timiraos 2010). Over the next decade, it is estimated that these three proposals together would increase federal tax revenue by roughly $150 billion.[2]

International Perspective on Homeownership

The tax deduction for mortgage interest is just one of many U.S. subsidies to promote homeownership. In this chapter, we have already mentioned three others: government insurance of FHA, VA, and USDA home loans; government-backed purchase and securitization of home mortgages; and state laws limiting personal recourse for deficiencies on home mortgage foreclosures.

Table 3-1 compares these four types of homeownership subsidies for the United States and five other advanced industrial countries, together with their homeownership rates expressed as a percentage of families owning a home. Three of these comparison countries—Australia, Canada, and the United Kingdom—were chosen because they, like the United States, have an Anglo-Saxon legal system. The two remaining comparison countries—France and Germany—were chosen because they are the largest European countries and have legal systems based on civil law.

A review of the data in table 3-1 reveals several important differences among these countries:

—None of these five comparison countries allows tax deductions for mortgage interest, and none offers nonrecourse mortgages to home buyers.

—Only Canada and the United States have established government programs for mortgage insurance and mortgage securitization.

1. Proposals by the co-chairs of the President's Deficit Commission (2010).
2. Estimates from the Tax Policy Center at Brookings Institution based on data from the Congressional Budget Office.

Table 3-1. *Government Support of Home Mortgages in Select Industrial Countries*

Country	Percent of households owning homes	Tax deduction for mortgage interest	Availability of nonrecourse mortgages	Government insurance for mortgage defaults	Government-backed mortgage securitization
Australia	70	No	No	No	No
Canada	68	No	No	Limited	Limited
England	68	No	No	No	No
France	57	No	No	No	No
Germany	46	No	No	No	No
United States	67	Yes	Yes	Extensive	Extensive

Source: Pollock and Lea (2010).

—The homeownership rate of all three Anglo-Saxon countries is slightly higher than that of the United States, while the homeownership rate of France and Germany is much lower than the U.S. rate.

These factual differences strongly suggest that the broad array of U.S. subsidies for homeownership is not essential to promoting high rates of homeownership. This is the key lesson from the comparison between the United States and the three Anglo-Saxon countries. But the differences in homeownership rates between these three Anglo-Saxon countries and the two civil law countries show that other types of factors are at work. For instance, neither the United Kingdom nor Germany provides significant monetary subsidies for homeownership, so the 22 percent difference in homeownership rates between these two European countries must be attributable to factors such as cultural preferences, historical patterns, and legal traditions.

Since international comparisons like the one above are inherently superficial, it is helpful to look more closely at the differences between the United States and Canada—the country whose housing system is most similar to that of the United States (a detailed description of the Canadian mortgage market is contained in Lascelles 2010). Of course, there are many differences between Canada and the United States with respect to tax rates and income distribution. Nevertheless, it is surprising that Canada has achieved a slightly higher rate of homeownership than the United States without most of the subsidies in table 3-1. This comparison suggests that many of the U.S. subsidies for homeownership may raise the price of American homes rather than increase the rate of homeownership.

In the private market, Canadian lenders have traditionally required down payments of 20 percent or more of a home's purchase price. Canadian lenders also have recourse against personal assets in the event of a mortgage foreclosure deficiency. Although American lenders once insisted on a similar down payment level, they substantially dropped their down payment standards in the years leading up to the financial crisis. The combination of low down payments and no personal recourse on foreclosure deficiencies led to high levels of mortgage defaults in the United States when housing prices plummeted (Pozen 2010, pp. 20–23, 256–57). This comparison suggests that no-down-payment and no-recourse mortgages may decrease, rather than increase, homeownership in the long term.

In the public sector, Canada has relatively small programs for government insurance and securitization of home mortgages, although these programs have grown rapidly over the last few years. Moreover, these government programs now require down payments of at least 5 percent of a home's purchase price, together with private mortgage insurance for another 15 percent. As a result, the default rate for mortgages in these Canadian programs has been much lower than the default rate in their American counterparts. Thus the Canadian example demonstrates that large public programs, which allow home purchasers to obtain mortgages with little private equity, are not necessary to achieve high rates of homeownership.

II. The Who and How of Federal Mortgage Subsidies

Since homeownership has both negative and positive externalities, we should carefully design any government subsidies for homeownership. The interest deduction for home mortgages in the United States, for example, has an adverse impact on homeownership in many metropolitan regions and does not promote homeownership for low-income families in any region. The homeownership rate is lower in the United States than in Australia, Canada, and the United Kingdom, despite much lower government subsidies for home mortgages in all three countries.

Nevertheless, given the political support for homeownership in the United States, Congress will almost certainly maintain certain types of subsidies for homeownership. In the previous section, we recommend narrowing the scope of the mortgage interest deduction and reducing state support for no-recourse home mortgages. Here, we suggest stricter limits on the FHA, VA, and USDA programs for insuring home mortgages and a narrower role for the federal government in securitizing home mortgages.

Federal Insurance Programs for Home Mortgages

The federal government insures mortgages issued by private lenders against losses on default through three main programs—FHA, VA, and USDA. Eligibility for all three programs is limited by the dollar amount of the mortgage, with minimal down payment requirements. We suggest eligibility criteria more geared to home-owner income, with a gradual phase-in of higher down payment requirements.

Critical Review of Existing Programs

The FHA is the largest federal program for home insurance, insuring almost 40 percent of the U.S. home purchase mortgages in 2009. The reserves for this program have dropped below the statutory requirement of 2 percent of out-standing loans insured. While FHA officials believe that its home insurance pro-gram has enough of a cushion to stay solvent, even some of them admit that the program could need a federal bailout if housing prices remain depressed.[3] To remain solvent, the FHA is raising its fees to home borrowers. In April 2010 FHA increased the up-front fee from 1.75 to 2.25 percent of the insured mort-gage, since FHA could not change the annual premium without legislation. In October 2010 Congress increased the annual premium from between 0.50 and 0.55 percent to between 0.85 and 0.90 percent of the insured mortgage, so the FHA reduced the up-front fee to 1 percent.

Yet the minimum down payment for an FHA mortgage is only 3.5 percent of the purchase price of the home, and most closing costs can be included in the mortgage amount. Moreover, the FHA website touts several federal programs for down payment assistance: Nehemiah grants up to 3 percent toward the down payment, the Housing Action Resource Trust grants up to $15,000 toward down payment and closing costs, and Neighborhood Gold Grants allow "homebuyers to purchase a home with no down payment and no closing costs by providing the money necessary to purchase without repayment."[4] In addition, the FHA website lists various state and city programs for down payment assistance, such as Access 2000, a no-money-down program for California.

Besides this minimal requirement for down payments, the FHA insurance program is limited by the dollar amount of the mortgage. The standard FHA mortgage limit is $417,000 for one-unit dwellings, with a floor of $271,050 based on local prices in lower-cost areas. However, the effective ceiling for such mortgages is $625,500 in most high-cost areas (temporarily raised to $729,750 from 2008 thru 2011) and $938,250 in a few extremely high-cost areas such as Alaska and Hawaii.

The FHA imposes no income limit on home buyers who want to participate in a mortgage insurance program. While it does review whether the home buyer has the financial capacity to meet his or her mortgage payments, it does allow

3. "The FHA Rethinks Its Mortgage Lending," *Smart Money*, August 9, 2010. Quote from Bob Ryan, chief risk officer of the FHA.
4. See the FHA website, Neighborhood Gold Down Payment Assistance (FHA-Home-Loans.com).

more flexibility in calculating household income and payment ratios than entities offering conventional mortgages.[5]

The VA mortgage insurance program is even more favorable to home buyers than the one run by the FHA.[6] The VA allows an eligible buyer to finance 100 percent of the purchase price of the home through a mortgage issued by a private lender. In other words, it does not require a down payment. The borrower pays the VA an up-front insurance fee of 2.15 percent of the mortgage amount, but no annual insurance fee. The up-front insurance fee may be financed as part of the VA-insured mortgage. In addition, the VA allows the seller of the home to contribute 3 to 6 percent of the purchase price to offset the buyer's closing costs.

In 2010 the maximum guarantee amount for a VA mortgage was 25 percent of the local VA limit. The highest local limit was $625,000. Therefore, the maximum mortgage amount for a VA-insured mortgage was $625,000, of which the VA would insure $156,250 against losses on default.

Under the VA's rules, no more than 41 percent of a home buyer's income can be devoted to mortgage payments and other housing costs such as property taxes and fire insurance. But the VA has no upper limit on the homeowner's overall income. Instead, it focuses on whether the homeowner can demonstrate enough qualifying service in the U.S. armed forces.[7]

Like VA-insured home mortgages, mortgages insured by the USDA do not require any down payments and allow sellers to help pay the buyer's closing costs. Similarly, the USDA charges an up-front insurance fee, which can be financed as part of the mortgage, but no annual insurance fee.[8]

In contrast to the VA program, the USDA program has an upper income limit for eligibility—115 percent of the median income for the area. But the USDA program has no maximum for either the purchase price of the home or the size of the mortgage.

The USDA program is intended mainly to encourage homeownership in rural areas. Nevertheless, the Government Accountability Office found 1,300 instances of so-called rural areas that were closely integrated with urban areas. For example, in 2005 the USDA considered Belpre, Ohio, to be rural. That same year, the U.S. Census Bureau reported that Belpre was "densely settled," with 1,000 residents per square mile, and that it was contiguous to the urban community of Parkersburg, West Virginia, with a population of 33,000 (GAO 2005, p. 7).

5. See the HUD website (www.hud.gov/offices/hsg/fhahistory.cfm).

6. See the Department of Veterans Affairs website, Pre-Loan Frequently Asked Questions (www.benefits.va.gov/homeloans/faqpreln.asp).

7. See the HSH Library website, VA Home Loans: A Quick Eligibility Guide to Homebuyers (http://library.hsh.com).

8. See USDA website, Rural Development Housing and Community Facilities Programs (www.rurdev.usda.gov/rhs).

A Different Approach to Government Mortgage Insurance

The price of mortgage insurance is substantially lower in the public sector than in the private sector. The private sector also charges up-front and annual premiums for mortgage insurance, while the VA and USDA programs do not charge annual premiums. Moreover, private mortgage insurance imposes stricter underwriting standards than its government counterparts. In short, government insurance of home mortgages constitutes a significant public subsidy to promote homeownership.

Should U.S. taxpayers subsidize a $617,600 mortgage on a $640,000 home for a family with a joint income of $300,000 a year? Even worse, should U.S. taxpayers subsidize a $617,600 mortgage for a $640,000 home for a couple with a joint income of $500,000 a year? These examples can occur because both the FHA and the VA have no maximum limits on homeowner income, just maximum limits on the size of the insured mortgage. Only the USDA program has limits on homeowner income, but not on the size of insured mortgage.

In my view, the key criterion for all government-insured mortgages should be homeowner income below a specified level—for example, below the median family income for the metropolitan region. If we want to promote homeownership, we should focus our limited public resources on those least likely to buy homes without government assistance.

If Congress would adopt a relatively modest income limit for government insurance of home mortgages, it might not be necessary to have a size limit on insured mortgages. Nevertheless, to avoid unforeseen consequences, Congress should set a size limit—for example, the median price of a home in a metropolitan region should not exceed $350,000 (indexed to inflation in the future). In light of the looming federal budget deficits, it is hard to justify federal subsidies (that is, below market rates) for home mortgages over $500,000 even in relatively expensive cities.

Most important, Congress should gradually raise the down payment requirements for all federal mortgage insurance and eliminate the various methods (for example, grants or seller contributions) of avoiding these requirements. As discussed, the best predictor of mortgage defaults is negative equity. When home purchasers begin with minimal down payments, they will quickly have negative equity in their homes if local prices fall. A mortgage default not only causes tremendous personal problems for the homeowner, but also imposes substantial social costs on the neighborhood.

Of course, we need to proceed cautiously when raising down payment requirements, given the fragility of the current housing market. Therefore, we should announce a schedule for incremental increases over the next decade. For example, the down payment requirement for home mortgages in all federal insurance programs could increase by 0.5 percent a year until it reaches 8.5 percent of a home's purchase price.

The Government's Role in Mortgage Securitization

Besides insuring mortgages through the FHA, the VA, and the USDA, the federal government has supported home mortgages by chartering two shareholder-owned corporations, giving them special privileges and directing them to purchase a specified percentage of low- and moderate-income mortgages. This percentage was increased gradually from 42 percent in 1996 to 56 percent by 2008, and this category was explicitly defined to include subprime mortgages (Pozen 2010, pp. 30–31).

To facilitate their purchases of low- and moderate-income mortgages, Congress exempted from state and local income tax the interest payments on the debt securities issued by Fannie Mae and Freddie Mac. Congress also granted them a $2.25 billion line of credit from the U.S. Treasury. In addition, both of these corporations did not have to register with the Securities and Exchange Commission (SEC) their public offerings of securities, which could be acquired without limit by banks insured by the Federal Deposit Insurance Corporation (FDIC). See Pozen (2010, pp. 29–30).

Because of these privileges normally associated with a federal agency, investors widely perceived the bonds of Fannie Mae and Freddie Mac as constituting a moral—though not a legal—obligation of the United States. Due to this perceived implicit guarantee, interest rates on the bonds of both corporations were significantly lower than those of other top-rated financial institutions. However, Fannie Mae and Freddie Mac bonds were not subject to the statutory ceiling on federal debt. In 2007 the debt of these two corporations was $5 trillion, roughly equal to the total U.S. Treasury debt held by investors that year (Pozen 2010, p. 33).

Fannie Mae and Freddie Mac issued so much debt in part to build up their own portfolios through huge purchases of MBS from the secondary market. In effect, these corporations used their implicit federal guarantee to borrow cheaply, buy MBS for their own portfolios, and profit from the spread. The portfolios of Fannie Mae and Freddie Mac peaked in 2004 at $1.6 trillion and have stayed below that level in response to public criticism (OFHEO 2008, pp. 83, 100). Since 2008, a strong consensus has developed that Fannie Mae and Freddie Mac should not issue bonds to finance the purchase of MBS for their own portfolios.

The debate is now centered on whether Fannie Mae and Freddie Mac should continue in their role as mortgage securitizers—purchasing mortgages from the private sector, turning these mortgages into MBS, and selling these MBS with guarantees to the investing public. Let us consider the four main arguments for allowing Fannie Mae and Freddie Mac to continue playing this role.

Subsidizing Home Mortgages for Needy Families

The FHA, the VA, and the USDA already subsidize home mortgages through below-market insurance in certain circumstances. As suggested above, these programs should be limited to needy families with incomes below specified levels (as well as meeting other relevant standards). Without Fannie Mae or Freddie Mac, we can focus these mortgage insurance programs on helping needy families, as Congress decides to define them.

In addition, the federal government offers needy families other types of assistance in purchasing homes. These include HUD's interest subsidies for loans and direct loans from financial agencies to first-time homeowners. These other programs can target needy families better, and provide assistance to them more efficiently, than Fannie Mae or Freddie Mac.

Guaranteeing MBS Sold to Public Investors

Ginnie Mae currently securitizes only mortgages insured by the FHA and other federal agencies. To the extent that Congress decides to subsidize other types of home mortgages for needy families, it should do so directly through on-budget appropriations. These other home mortgages can also be securitized by Ginnie Mae if desired by Congress. As a federal agency under HUD, Ginnie Mae is an appropriate and competent securitizer of home mortgages subsidized by the federal government. Ginnie Mae's guarantee of mortgage securities should be aimed at covering its costs, and its finances should be included in the federal budget.

Mortgage bankers have suggested that a federal agency like Ginnie Mae should purchase and securitize conventional mortgages not insured by any federal program. As part of this process, they want this federal agency to provide private lenders with a guarantee against default of home mortgages meeting the criteria now used by Fannie Mae and Freddie Mac (Kopecki 2009). In other words, since Fannie Mae and Freddie Mac went bankrupt with their implicit federal guarantee of conventional home mortgages, they believe the United States should move to an explicit federal guarantee of such mortgages.

However, why should the federal government directly or indirectly guarantee MBS for homeowners with incomes above whatever criteria are chosen to define needy families? In my view, the securitization of these home mortgages for middle- and higher-income families should be left to the private sector through a gradual phaseout of Fannie Mae and Freddie Mac. Of course, private sector securitization will mean less favorable rates and terms for these home mortgages than those eligible for securitization by Ginnie Mae. But most of the holders of these higher-end private mortgages already receive government support through the interest deduction on their mortgages (Joint Tax Committee 2010, table 3).

A practical argument against my view is that mortgage securitization in the private sector has virtually stopped since the financial crisis. In part, this has happened because Fannie Mae and Freddie Mac have been so active in buying home mortgages from private lenders—up to $729,000 in amount. No private party can compete with these two corporations now that the federal government explicitly backs their guarantees. In part, this has happened because investors have lost confidence in private sector securitization after the huge spike in defaults during the financial crisis. The third section of this chapter delineates the reforms needed to revive private securitization of home mortgages.

ATTRACTING MORE CAPITAL TO THE MORTGAGE MARKETS

Some commentators would leave the allocation of mortgage capital to the normal functioning of the financial markets. In their view, capital would be attracted to home mortgages to the extent that home mortgages would be more profitable than competing uses of capital. If excess capital is drawn into home building as a result of government subsidies, they would argue, then such capital is being taken away from more productive uses for the American economy.

Other commentators would counter with the argument that mortgages are special due to the societal goal of promoting homeownership. In their view, the market left alone might not allocate enough capital to support that goal. This latter view underlies the case for Fannie Mae and Freddie Mac as shareholder-owned corporations with special privileges tied to serving the U.S. mortgage market. By selling debt securities to the public and buying mortgages, these two quasi-public corporations bring more capital into the mortgage market.

However, even if we decide to attract more capital to building homes, the structure of these two corporations does not meet the cost-benefit test. The implicit federal subsidy to Fannie Mae and Freddie Mac has been estimated to be as high as $143 billion in 2003. Roughly half of this subsidy went to the shareholders and executives of these two corporations, yet this subsidy reduced home mortgage rates in the United States by only seven basis points (7/100 of 1 percent; Passmore 2003, pp. 2–3, 27).

To reduce these benefits to their shareholders and executives, some have proposed that Fannie Mae and Freddie Mac be turned into public utilities with rates of return set by a regulator. The history of rate regulation in industries like airlines and electric power, however, is not encouraging. Regulators found it very difficult to calculate reasonable rates of return, and utilities managed to engage in risky activities outside the regulated envelope. Due to these drawbacks, the public utility format is usually reserved for industries characterized as natural monopolies. The mortgage market, with its many players and diverse products, does not appear to be a natural monopoly.

Stabilizing the Mortgage Market in Tumultuous Times

The last argument for continuing Fannie Mae and Freddie Mac is that they stabilize the trading market for mortgages in times of financial turmoil. When the secondary market becomes illiquid, these two institutions continue to purchase mortgages or MBS for their own portfolios.

However, these purchases entail much more risk than securitizing and selling mortgages. If these two corporations buy mortgages and MBS during a period of falling home prices, they are likely to incur large losses from credit defaults, as they did in 2008 and 2009. If they issue fixed-rate bonds to finance purchases of mortgages or MBS and then rates decline significantly, they will suffer substantial losses as homeowners refinance at lower rates. If the top officers of Fannie Mae and Freddie Mac manage these risks well, their shareholders will reap large profits. However, if they do not manage these risks effectively, the two institutions can easily become insolvent, as they did in 2008. Their insolvency imposes large costs not only on their own shareholders but also on all U.S. taxpayers who are forced to pay for the bailout of these institutions.

A better approach would be to ask the Federal Reserve to perform the function of stabilizing the secondary market for MBS—in those extraordinary circumstances where such stabilization is necessary. The Fed is in the best position to evaluate the need for government intervention in any or all of the trading markets for debt securities. To promote stability in those markets, the Fed in 2009 made large purchases of MBS and other asset-backed securities. The Fed also created temporary liquidity facilities to swap high-quality, asset-backed securities for U.S. Treasuries. All taxpayers bear the risk of losses from those purchases by the Federal Reserve, but they also reap the profits if those purchases turn out well.

Alternatively, David Scharfstein, in chapter 7 of this volume, proposes creating a backup federal agency that would buy mortgages in the event of a liquidity crisis. To ensure that the agency would be prepared for such a crisis, he suggests that it operate on a regular basis by buying less than 10 percent of U.S. mortgages. While a thoughtful proposal, it seems to require a significant expenditure of government resources each year to deal with a potential liquidity crisis in the mortgage market. Such annual expenditures seem hard to justify because these liquidity crises happen so rarely—perhaps once every twenty years. Moreover, it would be politically difficult to limit the agency's purchases of home mortgages when there is no liquidity crisis.

Nevertheless, given the importance of Fannie Mae and Freddie Mac to the U.S. housing market, Congress should not abruptly stop these institutions from buying home mortgages and securitizing them. Instead, Congress should gradually lower the maximum for their mortgage purchases from $729,000 to

$650,000—and $50,000 a year thereafter—until the maximum size (for example, $350,000 or $400,000) is reached for mortgages eligible for the federal insurance programs and securitization by Ginnie Mae.

At that time, federal insurance programs and Ginnie Mae should replace Fannie Mae and Freddie Mac as the primary vehicle for supporting all types of subsidized home mortgages. By that time, the conventional market for home mortgages should have revived through the reforms suggested in the next section of this chapter. In specific, Fannie Mae and Freddie Mac should go into "wind down" mode—servicing existing mortgages and MBS, while reducing their staff and other resources as well as limiting the large compensation packages paid to their senior executives. At some point, it may make sense to make these two corporations a part of HUD or the FHA.

Unfortunately, in passing the continuing budget resolution for fiscal 2010–11, Congress prevented the maximum mortgage purchased by Fannie Mae and Freddie Mac from dropping to $650,000 from $729,000, as the maximum was scheduled to do in 2011.[9] These two corporations have already cost the U.S. taxpayers $145 billion, which could easily rise to $500 billion or even $1 trillion, according to various analysts (Woellert and Gittelsohn 2010). We need to start weaning the mortgage market off its addiction to mortgage securitization by these two corporations, as we adopt reforms to revive the private market for securitization. In October 2011, the maximum mortgage eligible for purchase by Fannie Mae and Freddie Mac will fall to $625,000 unless Congress intervenes. It is hoped that Congress will allow this statutory downsizing to proceed as originally planned.

III. Reviving Private Mortgage Securitization

If we want to reduce the amount of government support for homeownership, we need to revive the private market for mortgage originators. The total amount of U.S. bank loans of all types was $7.4 trillion in 2010,[10] only two-thirds of total U.S. housing credit outstanding at that time. The volume of new mortgages originated depends primarily on the pace of mortgage securitization. For example, a bank can originate a mortgage for $500,000, sell it to investors as part of the securitization process, and then use the proceeds to make another $500,000 mortgage. If this cycle happens once a month, a bank can originate many times the volume of home mortgages it could without securitization.

Moreover, mortgage securitization provides the benefits of diversification to both lenders and investors. Without securitization, lenders hold local mortgages

9. Section 145 of continuing budget resolution for fiscal 2011 (passed on September 30, 2010).
10. See FDIC website (www.fdic.gov).

for years and thereby are exposed to a potential economic downturn in that region. By selling local mortgages for cash, or swapping them for MBS, lenders can build a diversified portfolio of mortgages from around the country. Similarly, investors can attain a more geographically diversified portfolio by buying MBS than by buying whole mortgages from local banks. In addition, investors can easily buy and sell MBS, as opposed to home mortgages that do not have well-developed trading markets.

However, the private market for mortgage securitization has contracted sharply—from a peak of $60 billion a month in 2006 to a trickle today. Without securitization, the mortgage volume of banks is limited to the maximum amount supportable by their regulatory capital. And there are many competing demands on the regulatory capital of banks. Without securitization, many nonbank lenders, such as independent mortgage banks and real estate brokers, do not have enough capital to make home mortgages and hold them for ten to fifteen years. Such nonbank lenders normally originate a substantial portion of all home mortgages in the United States.

The private market for mortgage securitization has virtually disappeared in the United States because it was subject to so many abuses in 2004 to 2008.[11] As a result, investors no longer have confidence in MBS, unless guaranteed by the federal government. Thus to revive the private market for mortgage securitization, reforms are needed to prevent these abuses from occurring again.

This section reviews the major types of prior abuses in the private market for mortgage securitization and proposes specific reforms for each type of abuse. It begins with the private sponsors of MBS, proceeds to the special-purpose entities issuing MBS, and ends with the credit rating agencies.

Private Sponsors of Mortgage Securitization

While there are many forms of private mortgage securitization, they all involve a sponsor—typically some type of bank—creating a special-purpose entity (SPE) to purchase a pool of mortgages from multiple originators. The sponsor establishes the SPE as a legal entity, arranges temporary financing for it to acquire the pool of mortgages, designs the various tranches of securities issued by the pool, selects a credit rating agency to rate the various tranches, and helps to sell these securities to public investors. In addition, the sponsor may enhance the attractiveness of these securities by providing credit support to the pool if a specified amount of its mortgages default or by agreeing to buy back these securities from holders if the trading market for these criteria becomes sufficiently illiquid.

Until quite recently, the sponsors of SPEs were able to keep them off their balance sheet by exploiting certain loopholes in the accounting rules. As a result,

---

11. These abuses are well documented. See, for example, McLean and Nocera (2010); Shiller (2008).

the sponsor of an SPE was usually able to avoid allocating capital under banking rules to support the SPE and minimize disclosures about the sponsor's obligations to the pool. Under the new accounting rules, as explained below, SPEs will almost always remain on the balance sheet of their sponsoring bank. Furthermore, this bank sponsor will be required to allocate capital to support mortgages in the pool, even if investors in its securities have assumed significant risks of loss from those mortgages.

In other words, the accounting and capital treatment of SPEs has gone from one extreme to another. In the following subsections I outline the abuses of the prior off-balance-sheet arrangement and then suggest a more functional, intermediary approach to the current on-balance-sheet system.

ACCOUNTING ISSUES

An SPE is a legitimate method for any company to finance the purchase of assets (this section is based on Pozen 2010, pp. 51–54). The SPE should not be put on the balance sheet of the company if most of the risks related to the assets and liabilities in the SPE are assumed by other investors in the SPE. However, this device can easily be abused, so the Financial Accounting Standards Board (FASB) has established rules for when an SPE may be kept off the balance sheet of the sponsoring bank or other type of company. In the late 1990s, the FASB allowed an SPE to be kept off the balance sheet of the sponsor only if at least 3 percent of the voting equity of the SPE was held by a party not affiliated with its sponsor. When Enron set up SPEs in the late 1990s, it violated that FASB requirement.

After the failure of Enron, the FASB in 2003 adopted new rules on when most types of SPEs could be kept off the balance sheet of their sponsor. Unfortunately, it took Wall Street only a few months to figure out how to avoid the constraints in the FASB's new rules. As a result, the assets and liabilities of most SPEs did not appear on the balance sheets of most banks sponsoring these SPEs, and there were few public disclosures about the potential obligations of these banks to these SPEs.

In response to the circumvention of its 2003 rules, the FASB adopted new rules in 2009 that effectively forced all SPEs financing mortgages onto the balance sheet of their sponsoring bank. As a result, bank sponsors have to make public disclosures about the mortgages held by the SPEs. For example, banks have to disclose their potential obligations to support an SPE experiencing a specified level of mortgage defaults.

In particular, the SEC has recently adopted rules requiring any sponsor of SPEs to disclose fulfilled and unfilled repurchase requests in all relevant deals over the last three years (SEC 2011). These disclosure requirements apply both in the original offering document and in annual reports. They are designed to inform investors about the actual experience of SPE sponsors in supplying ongoing liquidity for short-term securities issued by their SPEs.

Capital Requirements

While putting SPEs on balance sheet significantly improves disclosures by bank sponsors, it also increases the capital requirements for these banks. Subject to a six-month delay, the federal banking agencies at the end of 2009 adopted rules confirming that assets in bank-sponsored SPEs are fully subject to regulatory capital requirements and eliminated the prior exclusion from these requirements for asset-backed commercial paper programs that were consolidated on the bank's balance sheet (FDIC 2009).

However, these capital requirements for bank sponsors of SPEs are inconsistent with the actual allocation of risks between the bank and investors in the SPE's securities. Three main types of risks are involved with private mortgage securitization deals: interest rate, credit default, and liquidity risks. In general, the investors in securities issued by SPEs fully assume the risk of fluctuating interest rates.

The allocation of credit default risk is more complex: the sponsor usually retains a significant portion, but not all, of the SPE's credit risk. In some deals, the sponsor agrees to substitute good mortgages for all nonperforming mortgages above a specified threshold. In other deals, the sponsor creates a cushion against credit defaults by initially capitalizing the SPE with mortgages worth more than 100 percent of the total value of its securities or by holding subordinated tranches of the deal to absorb the first losses on these mortgages.

Similarly, the allocation of liquidity risk varies a lot from deal to deal. When selling short-term securities in some SPEs, the sponsor represents that it will buy back all such securities if an auction for such securities fails. In other MBS deals, the sponsor does not provide the buyers of the SPE's securities with any assurances about repurchases in illiquid markets, although the sponsor can be sued by the buyers if there are material breaches of representations and warranties in connection with these deals.

In sum, the actual retention of risks by a bank sponsor can range from roughly 20 percent to 80 percent of all the risks involved in the SPE's underlying mortgages. If the regulators nevertheless force all banks sponsoring an SPE to support its assets with enough capital to cover 100 percent of the risks involved, most banks will stop sponsoring SPEs. A bank cannot afford to over-allocate capital and lower its returns on mortgage securitizations.

Instead, federal regulators should encourage bank sponsors to disclose in detail their potential obligations to any SPE or its investors, along the lines of the SEC proposals mentioned above. Then they should impose a partial capital charge on the bank for these obligations, based on an actual allocation of risks, which should be updated periodically in light of the experience of the SPEs sponsored by the bank.

Disclosure and Design of SPEs

Moving SPEs onto the balance sheet of bank sponsors will improve the disclosure of the bank's potential obligations to these SPEs. In addition, the SEC is moving to enhance the information available about the mortgages held by the SPEs. This additional step will be important to renewing investor confidence in mortgage securities. A broad survey of MBS investors concluded that the highest reform priority should be enhanced disclosures about individual loans in the underlying pool, rather than its aggregate characteristics, presented in a standardized format to the maximum extent feasible (American Securitization Forum 2008, pp. 39–40).

In response, the SEC has proposed detailed disclosure requirements for each loan or other asset in the pool.[12] Such data would have to be provided in a machine-readable, standardized format so that they would be useful to investors. Furthermore, the SEC proposals would require every SPE to provide investors with a computer program that gives effect to the cash flow provisions of the "waterfall" structure in most deals.

In the past, an SEC rule allowed an SPE to stop filing quarterly and annual reports within a year after the initial public offering. This rule was used by SPE sponsors to limit the ongoing flow of information about the status of mortgages or other assets in the pool. Under the SEC's recent proposals, the SPE would be required to file quarterly and annual reports as long as nonaffiliated investors hold any securities sold initially by the SPE in an SEC-registered offering. The SEC also proposes to narrow the exemptions from registration available to SPEs selling securities backed by asset pools.

At the same time, participants in the private market have begun to simplify the structure of asset-backed issuances of securities. Before the financial crisis, the structure of SPEs was inordinately complex. SPEs often issued many tranches of MBS based on the same pool of mortgages. Moreover, some SPEs issued securities based on pools of MBS, rather than a pool of mortgages, in arrangements known as collateralized debt obligations (CDOs); other SPEs issued securities based on pools of CDOs.

Ultimately, the value of such multilayered products depended on the actual payment record of the mortgage pools at the bottom of the pyramid. In such multilayered products, a small mistake in estimating the default probability of the bottom pool of mortgages has a huge impact on the risk profile of the top

---

12. SEC Release nos. 33-9117, 34-6185 (April 7, 2010). See also SEC Release no. 33-9165 (December 16, 2010).

tier. For example, an increase from 5 percent to 7 percent in the default rate on the mortgage pool at the bottom of a CDO deal could increase the default rate in the top tier more than 100 times (Pozen 2010, app. to ch. 4).

By contrast, underwriters have recently started to develop simpler deals with high-quality "jumbo" mortgages—mortgages too big to be eligible for government-backed programs. In April 2010, for instance, Redwood Trust issued $238 million in MBS with senior tranches priced to yield 4 percent, supported by junior securities paying 6.5 percent. BlackRock has been trying to revamp the U.S. mortgage market with a new fund that buys loans with high down payments and borrowers with good track records of repayment. To reduce potential conflicts of interest, BlackRock hired a loan servicer independent of the lenders participating in the program (Currie 2010).

This example represents the future of mortgage securitization—a small number of tranches of securities, based directly on a pool of high-quality mortgages, serviced by a truly independent party. This new model for private MBS deals will be reinforced by two recently adopted SEC rules. In any asset-backed securities deal, the issuer will be required to perform a review of the assets as well as to disclose the findings and conclusions of such a review.[13] Second, the credit rating agency will be required to describe the representations and warranties made by the sponsors of the deal or originators of the assets in the pool, as well as the enforcement mechanisms available to investors in the pool.[14]

Credit Rating Agencies

Within the context of this new model for private MBS deals, what will be the role (if any) for credit rating agencies? A few MBS deals have been sold without credit ratings in private offerings to institutional investors. But many investors will still be looking to rely on an outside expert to assess the quality of the various tranches in private MBS deals. Thus it will be difficult to revive the private market for MBS unless and until credit ratings again have credibility with investors.

Investors no longer have confidence in credit ratings because so many AAA tranches of MBS and other asset-backed deals went into default during the financial crisis. The dismal record of credit ratings was due to several factors: the complexity of the deals, the short historical record for certain types of mortgages, and, most important, the conflicts of interest built into the issuer-pays model. Since the issuer selects and pays the credit rating agency, the issuer has an incentive to shop for the agency most likely to give the highest rating to the most tranches of an MBS deal. In response, regulators and commentators have offered four main types of regulatory proposals to reform credit rating agencies.

13. SEC Release nos. 33-9176, 34-63742 (January 20, 2011).
14. SEC Release nos. 33-9175, 34-63741 (January 20, 2011).

As discussed below, most of these proposals would be ineffective or unworkable.

The first set of proposals is based on the premise that the core problem is the oligopolistic structure of the ratings industry—its domination by three large firms. To promote competition in the ratings industry, Congress in 2006 directed the SEC to increase the number of rating agencies whose ratings were approved for use in SEC filings (Pozen 2010, pp. 60–61). As a result, the number of approved agencies quickly rose to nine. However, since the issuer-pays model is still prevalent, this increase merely expanded the chances for issuers to shop for ratings. If one rating agency would not give a AAA rating to most tranches in an MBS deal, the issuer could then shop around for higher ratings with eight other agencies instead of two.

Other efforts to promote more competition among rating agencies have reduced the information available to the agency hired by the issuer. The SEC now requires any issuer to disseminate to other credit agencies all of the information provided by the issuer to the agency hired by the issuer.[15] This dissemination requirement was supposed to encourage other agencies to promulgate ratings on deals for which they have not been hired. In fact, the potential for dissemination reduces the willingness of the issuer to provide detailed information to the hired agency. Without a clear source of payment, however, other agencies have little incentive to do the work necessary to promulgate a rating.

Similarly, to promote competition, the Dodd-Frank Act directed the SEC to remove the existing exemption for credit ratings from Regulation FD.[16] To prevent selective disclosure, that regulation generally forces issuers to publish a press release with any material information it provides to any one party. In the past, Regulation FD contained an exemption to encourage issuers to supply confidential data to credit rating agencies in order to improve the quality of their ratings. By removing this exemption, Congress did not persuade most issuers to share more information with the investing public; instead, issuers generally reduced the information they gave to the credit rating agency they selected.

The Dodd-Frank Act includes a second approach to credit rating reform. It directs the SEC and other federal authorities to remove requirements in their rules based on a high rating by an agency approved by such authorities.[17] While some references to ratings have been removed by the federal authorities, their removal has encountered considerable opposition in other areas. For instance, the investment management industry has vigorously opposed the SEC's proposed

15. SEC Release no. 34-61050, November 2009. Amendments to Rule 17g-2 under the Securities Exchange Act.

16. Section 939B of the Dodd-Frank Act, SEC Release nos. 33-9146, 34-63003 (September 29, 2010).

17. Section 939A of the Dodd-Frank Act.

deletion of the high ratings requirement for commercial paper held by money market funds.[18] In their view, these funds should be legally limited to highly rated commercial paper and their managers should also be required themselves to conclude that the paper is high quality. Similarly, the banking industry has opposed the proposed deletion of references to credit ratings from the bank capital requirements (Federal Reserve 2010a). In their view, these ratings represent a useful starting point for risk analysis, though not necessarily the ultimate determinant.

In any event, the laws of most states allow local pension plans and insurance companies to buy only bonds with investment-grade ratings. These state laws would be difficult to change since they provide useful guidance to small pension plans and insurance companies without the resources to evaluate a broad range of bonds. Similarly, for all their shortcomings, credit ratings provide individual investors with useful guidance on choosing bonds, especially state or municipal tax-exempt bonds.

Since it is not feasible to do away with all required credit ratings, commentators have suggested a third approach: moving to an investor-pays model, currently used by Egan Jones. Under this model, investors would choose the rating agency for major MBS offerings and pay for the agency's services. As a result, so the argument goes, the agency would seek the most accurate rather than the highest rating.

However, this proposal does not appear to be workable. The largest investors in bonds are mutual funds, hedge funds, and corporate pension plans. Since many of them do their own in-depth analysis of bonds, they object to paying for credit ratings. Yet it would be politically unacceptable for ratings to be paid for only by small, and not by large, investors. Even if institutional investors were willing to select and pay for credit ratings, this would not be a good idea for other investors. Institutional investors have a perverse interest in inaccurate ratings. When the rating of a bond is too high or low, then institutional investors can profit by selling or buying the bond.

A final group of proposals involves the selection of a credit rating agency by a government process designed to represent all investors. One suggestion is to establish a credit rating agency as a public utility, with rates and methods approved by a government body. This proposal would, of course, eliminate any potential benefits from competition, such as lower prices or more expertise on certain types of deals. Moreover, a public utility structure would subject the credit rating agency to political pressures on ratings for government bonds.

Another suggestion, advocated by Senator Al Franken (D-Minn.), is to allocate credit ratings randomly among a pool of credit rating agencies, subject to a standardized fee schedule. The pool would include any agency meeting standards

18. SEC Release no. IC-28327 (July 1, 2008); see also SEC Release no. IC-29592 (March 3, 2011).

set by the SEC, which would run the allocation process. Franken's proposal is now under study by the SEC.[19] However, a random allocation process would undermine the incentive of any rating agency to develop expertise in evaluating specific types of complex offerings. For investors in complex offerings, the rating by a randomly selected and little known agency might not be credible.

A better approach would be for FINRA—the Financial Industry Regulatory Authority, the self-regulatory organization for the securities industry—to establish a group of independent consultants, such as retired executives, who would select the rating agency for each major bond offering. This group would be similar to the cadre of independent arbitrators maintained by FINRA to deal with customer-broker disputes. FINRA would pay the independent consultant a modest fee for his or her limited role in each offering.

In specific, the consultant would circulate for each major bond offering a request for proposals from all the credit rating agencies registered with the SEC. On the basis of these proposals, the consultant would select the agency best qualified to provide the most accurate rating for the bond offering from the perspective of investors. Once the consultant selects the credit rating agency for the bond offering, the agency would negotiate a fee with the bond issuer on the basis of the size and complexity of the offering.

Under this approach, the credit rating agency would be chosen by a neutral third party representing the interests of all investors. The choice would be based on the relative expertise of that agency to provide the most accurate rating. Thus the proposed system would avoid the potential conflicts involved when the agency is chosen by the issuer or one set of investors. Yet it would promote competition among credit rating agencies, which would have an incentive to develop expertise in specific types of bond offerings. Furthermore, the proposed system would not require any government authority to set fees for credit ratings.

IV. Toward a Middle Tier

Earlier in this chapter, I suggested what the parameters should be for the government and private tiers of mortgage securitization. In this section, I review the proposals for a middle tier of mortgage securitization, below the government tier and above the normal private tier. These proposals are aimed at creating a middle tier with higher-quality MBS than most private deals, but without a government guarantee or subsidy. We begin by analyzing the proposal for "covered" bonds, backed by both a mortgage pool on a bank's balance sheet and the financial resources of the bank itself.

---

19. Section 939F(b) of Dodd-Frank Act.

Covered Bonds

A covered bond is a debt instrument secured by a perfected interest in a specific pool of collateral—usually composed of high-quality mortgages and other assets—which is held in a separate account on the balance sheet of a bank. In the event of a problem with the pool, the bondholder first has recourse to the assets in the pool. Moreover, if those assets are insufficient to satisfy the bondholder's claims, he or she has another claim on the bank for the difference. Hence covered bonds are said to be "dual recourse."

In most covered bonds, the underlying pool of assets is dynamic, not static. The bank sponsor must regularly monitor the assets in the pool. If any asset becomes nonperforming, the bank must replace it with a performing asset in compliance with the eligibility criteria for the pool. For example, if the pool holds a mortgage that defaults, the bank must replace that mortgage with one meeting the loan-to-value ratio for the pool. In addition, the separate pool of assets underlying a covered bond is typically over-collateralized: holding more assets than the value of the covered bonds issued by the pool. Over-collateralization provides a cushion to investors in the covered bonds if most of the assets in the pool prepay or the pool suffers a large number of defaults.

The market for covered bonds is centered in Europe. At the end of 2009, there were €529 billion in covered bonds outstanding, of which more than 80 percent were based on high-quality mortgages (European Covered Bond Council 2010, pp. 375–77). Covered bonds have been sold by banks recently in other countries such as Canada, Australia, and New Zealand. In most countries, the terms and conditions of covered bonds are governed by a specific national statute.

In the United States, by contrast, covered bonds were sold by only two banks: Washington Mutual in 2006 and Bank of America in 2007. After 2007, no covered bonds have been sold in the United States, which has no specific legislation on this subject. In 2009 Representative Scott Garrett (R-N.J.) introduced legislation authorizing the sale of covered bonds by FDIC-insured banks.[20] However, that legislation was opposed by the FDIC, which in 2008 issued a restrictive policy statement on covered bonds (FDIC 2008).

BENEFITS OF COVERED BONDS

Covered bonds offer several potential benefits for banks. First, they help to diversify the sources of bank funding. Covered bonds tend to have larger maturities than other financing options such as advances from the Federal Home Loan Bank. In addition, covered bonds reportedly appeal to a different type of investor than most bond offerings. These are conservative investors that

20. H.R. 5823, 111th Cong., 2nd sess., July 22, 2010.

are attracted to the high-quality collateral and double recourse of covered bonds (Kashkari 2008).

Second, covered bonds reduce the moral hazards and agency costs inherent in the "originate-to-distribute" model. Since the collateral of covered bonds remains on the balance sheet of the bank sponsor, it has a strong incentive to demand reliable documentation and ensure that borrowers have the ability to repay. Moreover, as the bank sponsor must replace defaulting mortgages supporting covered bonds, it will likely insist on substantial down payments for these mortgages, since negative home equity is the best predictor of defaults on home mortgages.

Finally, it is easier to modify mortgages supporting covered bonds than mortgages securitized through other legal vehicles. Because covered bonds expressly allow the bank sponsor to replace troubled mortgages in the pool, these can be removed and modified without the consent of bondholders. By contrast, most securitizations must comply with the complex rules for real estate mortgage investment conduits (REMICs), which are based on a passive model. If a substantial portion of a REMIC's assets is "significantly modified," it may be subject to a penalty tax for active management.

LIMITATIONS OF COVERED BONDS

Despite these potential benefits, covered bonds will probably not be a significant driver of mortgage volume in the United States. Since covered bonds remain on the balance sheet of the sponsoring banks, they are limited by the size of the bank's balance sheet and the amount of its regulatory capital. In contrast to other forms of mortgage securitization, covered bonds do not allow a bank to sell its mortgages each month and use the proceeds to make new mortgages.

The sale of covered bonds is further constrained by the FDIC, which limits them to 4 percent of an insured bank's total liabilities. The FDIC (2008, p. 43757) explains its rationale for this limit as follows: "The larger the balance of secured liabilities on the balance sheet, the smaller the value of assets that are available to satisfy depositors and general creditors, and consequently the greater the potential loss to the Deposit Insurance Fund." In other words, the claims of covered bondholders to the assets in the separate account at the bank sponsor, including any over-collateralization, are probably senior to the claims of the FDIC if the bank becomes insolvent.

In my view, the FDIC's concerns about covered bonds are well founded. If a large portion of a bank's assets is backed by its covered bonds, many of its best assets would go to holders of these bonds in the event of the bank's insolvency. As a result, a substantial portion of the insolvent bank's losses would have to be absorbed by the federal government. Moreover, the holders of covered bonds usually have a specific right to mortgages other than those initially in the pool supporting the bonds—because of the bank's obligation to replace any defaulting mortgages in the pool with other performing mortgages from the bank's portfolio. In European parlance, the holders of covered bonds would have a "floating charge" on all the performing mortgages owned by the bank if it becomes insolvent.

In theory, Congress could limit the rights of covered bondholders to the mortgages actually held in the pool supporting those bonds at the time the sponsoring bank became insolvent. In practice, such legislation would severely undermine the attraction of covered bonds to conservative investors, who are looking for the broadest backing for their bonds. In fact, legislation in European countries has expressly enshrined the rights of covered bondholders over everyone else, despite the general trend to insist that a bank's bondholders incur some losses if it fails. In Germany, for example, if a bank fails, its losses must be absorbed partly by its bondholders—except for the holders of covered bonds who are fully protected (Hughes 2010, p. 17).

Covered bonds not only shift losses from large bondholders to taxpayers, but also promote a serious form of moral hazard if holders of covered bonds do not suffer any losses when the sponsoring bank fails. Without a significant chance of a loss, holders of covered bonds will have no incentive to monitor the bank's financial condition or pressure bank management to avoid excessive risks. Without market discipline exercised by sophisticated investors, these difficult tasks will be left primarily to bank examiners.

Qualified Residential Mortgages

While covered bonds are not likely to become a third tier in the mortgage securitization market, qualified residential mortgages (QRMs) will almost surely become one—higher quality than the rest of the private tier, but without a government guarantee or subsidy. QRMs are the product of a legislative compromise in the Dodd-Frank Act: it generally imposes a risk retention requirement on originators and securitizers in MBS deals, but directs federal regulators to exempt QRMs from this requirement.

In enacting the risk retention requirement, Congress was responding to widespread concerns about the originate-to-distribute model, which led to so many problems during the financial crisis. Since originators planned to sell their mortgages quickly to the secondary market, they did not have enough incentive to gather the proper documents and conduct due diligence on the borrower's ability to repay. Similarly, if banks sponsoring MBS deals sold all tranches to the investing public, they did not have sufficient incentive to make sure that these deals were designed to withstand possible downturns in home prices.

To realign these incentives, Congress wanted mortgage originators and securitizes to have "skin in the game"—that is, to retain an economic interest in the mortgages and MBS they sold. In specific, section 941 (c) of the Dodd-Frank

Act directs the federal banking agencies to adopt joint regulations requiring any "securitizer" to retain an economic interest "not less than 5 percent of the credit risk" of an asset-backed security. In an apparent drafting ambiguity, section 941 (d) of the act also directs these agencies "to allocate risk retention obligations between a securitizer and originator" according to criteria specified in the statute.

Nevertheless, Congress was worried that the strict application of a risk retention requirement would dramatically decrease the volume of mortgage originations and securitization. After originating and selling mortgages, for example, small brokers might not be able to hold capital reserves against potential losses. Therefore, Congress gave the federal banking agencies broad discretion to define QRMs that would be exempt from the risk retention requirement. As directed by Congress, these agencies have published a study on this requirement, which concludes that it should be customized to each type of asset-backed securities deal (Federal Reserve 2010b). In April 2011 these agencies proposed detailed rules defining the QRMs exempted from the risk retention requirement.

NARROW DEFINITION OF QRMs

The Dodd-Frank Act includes a long list of factors to be considered by the federal banking agencies in defining QRMs. These factors generally involve product features and underwriting standards that have historically been associated with relatively low levels of mortgage defaults. According to the act, however, QRMs will not encompass any mortgage directly or indirectly guaranteed or insured by the federal government; such mortgages are categorically excluded from the risk retention requirement.

Thus the regulators face a dilemma. On the one hand, if they define QRMs narrowly, they are likely to reduce the volume of home mortgages in the private sector due to the expansive application of the risk retention requirement. On the other hand, if they adopt a broad definition of QRMs, they will likely increase the level of defaults for such mortgages since they will not be backed by the federal government and will not be subject to any risk retention requirement.

In my view, the federal regulators should opt for a narrow definition of QRMs. Risk retention is a critical protection for investors in home mortgages; it aligns their interests with those of originators and securitizers. If both groups have no skin in the game for QRMs, this exemption should be defined quite narrowly to include high down payment requirements. While Wells Fargo has suggested a down payment requirement of at least 30 percent of the home purchase price, a 20 percent requirement would seem sufficient in light of Canada's experience. A 20 percent requirement was included in the QRM definition proposed by the regulators in April 2011.[21]

21. FDIC (2011). See SEC Release no. 34-64148 (March 30, 2011).

Moreover, the definition of QRMs should be narrow because it affects other significant rules governing the securitization of private mortgages. Most important, before passage of the Dodd-Frank Act, the FDIC proposed a safe harbor—agreeing not to reclaim mortgages previously transferred to an SPE by an insolvent bank under specified conditions. One proposed condition was that the bank sponsoring the SPE should retain at least 5 percent of the credit risk of the securities issued by the SPE (FDIC 2010b). Shortly after passage of the Dodd-Frank Act, the FDIC adopted this proposal as a permanent safe harbor with a major caveat: once the federal agencies define QRMs, a securitization based only on QRMs would no longer have to comply with the risk retention requirement in order to take advantage of this FDIC safe harbor (FDIC 2010a).

Similarly, before passage of the Dodd-Frank Act, the SEC proposed significant revisions to its existing rules for "shelf registrations" of asset-backed securities, which allow the public offering of such securities on a continuous or delayed basis without SEC review of the offering documents for each transaction. Under existing SEC rules, shelf registration is available to asset-backed securities only if they are rated investment grade. On May 3, 2010, the SEC proposed replacing this ratings condition for shelf registration with four new criteria. One of those criteria is that the sponsor of the asset-backed securities offerings must retain a 5 percent economic interest in the securities.[22] However, this criterion would likely be dropped for securities backed solely by QRMs once they are defined by the federal banking agencies.

In sum, mortgage securities based on QRMs could be offered quickly through shelf registrations, without any risk retention requirements for originators or securitizers. If the bank sponsoring such mortgage securities later becomes insolvent, the FDIC would not seek to attach the mortgages underlying these securities. Because of these regulatory advantages, QRMs have the potential to crowd out all other mortgages in the private sector. This is a potentially dangerous situation: QRMs will become popular due to what appears to be a federal seal of approval, yet they will not have federal guarantees or many regulatory protections. Thus it is critical that the regulators adopt the 20 percent down payment requirement for QRMs despite the vocal opposition to their proposal from the real estate industry (Protess 2011).

QRMs for Fannie and Freddie

Although the risk retention requirement does not apply to mortgages insured or guaranteed by federal agencies, it does apply to conforming mortgages purchased by Fannie Mae or Freddie Mac; Congress expressly declined to define

22. SEC Release nos. 33-9117, 34-6185 (April 7, 2010). See also SEC Release no. 33-9165 (December 16, 2010).

these two institutions as federal agencies for this purpose. As a result, executives at these two corporations have been pushing for QRMs to include all conforming mortgages sold to them. In response, the regulators have proposed that QRMs categorically include all conforming mortgages sold to Fannie Mae and Freddie Mac as long as these institutions are in federal conservatorship (and therefore such mortgages are effectively guaranteed by the federal government). In my view, QRMs should not indefinitely include all home mortgages sold to these two institutions; rather, the definition of QRMs should be narrowed over time to help phase out the role of Fannie Mae and Freddie Mac, as suggested in the third section of this chapter.

An indefinite QRM designation for all conforming mortgages sold to Fannie Mae and Freddie Mac not only would exempt their originators from the risk retention requirement of the Dodd-Frank Act, but also would offer these originators a highly liquid market for disposing of their mortgages. In practice, the combination would reinforce the originate-to-distribute model that proved so disastrous during the financial crisis. If conforming mortgages sold to these two corporations were categorically considered QRMs, then almost all privately issued mortgages would be structured to fit within this category. Why would any broker or bank establish a reserve for potential losses and take the bankruptcy risk involved with private securitization of its mortgages, instead of just selling all of its mortgages to Fannie Mae and Freddie Mac? In addition, conforming mortgages for these two institutions can meet their 20 percent down payment requirement by an actual down payment of 10 percent together with 10 percent in private mortgage insurance (Benson and Woellert 2011).

As discussed in the second section of this chapter, the current domination of the private market for mortgage securitization by these two corporations, even if needed temporarily, involves significant long-term costs. The U.S. Treasury has already infused $145 billion to cover losses at Fannie Mae and Freddie Mac and should be reluctant to increase this price tag by effectively guaranteeing home mortgages where the originator is exempt from the risk retention requirement. Moreover, if we want to focus government subsidies for homeownership on helping needy families, the role of these two corporations should be gradually replaced with private securitization vehicles for middle- and high-income families. Yet an indefinite QRM designation for conforming mortgages bought by Fannie Mae and Freddie Mac would expand their role.

To address these long-term concerns while recognizing the current fragility of the U.S. housing market, the federal regulators should develop a multistage definition of QRMs as applied to conforming mortgages sold to Fannie Mae and Freddie Mac. In specific, the definition should cover such conforming mortgages up to $625,000 for 2012, $600,000 for 2013, and so forth until the size limit falls to $350,000 or $400,000. At that time, Fannie Mae and Freddie

Mac should be replaced by Ginnie Mae as the securitizer of newly originated mortgages with federal subsidies based primarily on family income. In that manner, the definition of QRM would facilitate the gradual phasing out of the role played by Fannie Mae and Freddie Mac in the private mortgage market.

LONG-TERM MORTGAGES AND PREPAYMENT PENALTIES

Similarly, the definition of QRMs should be used to promote the continuation of long-term, fixed-rate mortgages in the United States by taking a more realistic approach to prepayment penalties. Americans have become accustomed to having ready access to thirty-year mortgages with a fixed interest rate and no prepayment penalties. But the United States is an international exception for good reason: it is very difficult and costly for any financial institution to manage effectively the asymmetrical risks inherent in a thirty-year, fixed-rate mortgage without any prepayment penalties.

In most countries, financial institutions offer only adjustable-rate mortgages: although they often have terms of more than twenty years, the interest rate adjusts on a yearly basis or more frequently. While France and Germany do offer long-term mortgages at fixed interest rates, they impose stiff penalties on early prepayment of these mortgages. Canada presents a third approach—long-term mortgages, but with rates and other terms that are effectively renegotiated every five or ten years (Wachter and Lea 2010).

If private lenders offer thirty-year, fixed-rate mortgages with no prepayment penalties, they face an asymmetrical set of risks that cannot be easily eliminated through financial management. If interest rates rise, the payments by borrowers on these long-term mortgages will not be sufficient to cover their short-term funding costs and generate a reasonable profit. However, if interest rates fall, these same lenders will not enjoy large spreads between continued high payments on mortgages and lower interest rates on short-term funding, because many borrowers will prepay their mortgages and refinance them at the lower current rates.

In the view of the mortgage bankers, the challenge of managing these asymmetrical risks should be met by having a federally backed agency buy and expressly guarantee fixed-rate, thirty-year mortgages without prepayment penalties. However, this just means shifting the significant risks associated with such mortgages from the private to the public sector. In 2000–04, for example, Fannie Mae and Freddie Mac ran into serious accounting problems when they tried to hedge against these risks (Pozen 2010, pp. 34–36).

We should not continue broad-based government guarantees of home mortgages primarily to prevent prepayment penalties for all long-term mortgages. A better approach would be for federal regulators to allow prepayment penalties for home mortgages with long terms if they meet the conditions of QRMs. The conditional acceptance of prepayment penalties in QRMs would set a powerful precedent for the rest of the private market for home mortgages in the United States.

In addressing prepayment penalties for QRMs, regulators should take their lead from the standards for "qualified mortgages" in sections 1414 and 1431 of the Dodd-Frank Act. These sections forbid prepayment penalties in subprime and high-cost mortgages, since home buyers should be able to switch easily out of these onerous mortgages. By contrast, these sections allow prepayment penalties—up to 3 percent for the initial three years of a mortgage—in fixed-rate mortgages of high quality without excessive fees. Although the regulators generally tried to keep QRM standards consistent with those for qualified mortgages, the proposed criteria for QRMs exclude all home mortgages with prepayment penalties.[23]

OTHER ASPECTS OF QRMS

The risk retention requirement of the Dodd-Frank Act applies to all originators of mortgages that sell them into the secondary market and the securitizers that transform these mortgages into MBS. Thus, in defining QRMs, federal regulators should adopt criteria that would help to standardize home mortgages and simplify securitization structures in the United States. In addition, the criteria should require language in the governing documents of MBS that would facilitate the modification of mortgages in the securitized pools.

In countries such as Denmark, the terms and conditions of home mortgages are highly standardized. This makes it less expensive to originate mortgages and easier to package them into securities. In fact, almost every home mortgage in Denmark is securitized in the same format (IMF 2007). Although such a high degree of standardization would be beneficial, the American mortgage market is probably too complex for the "one size fits all" approach of Denmark. Nevertheless, the federal regulators should delineate two or three standardized forms for home mortgages that would clearly qualify as QRMs. Since QRMs are so important to originators and securitizers of mortgages, these standardized forms would become widely accepted in the U.S. mortgage market.

In this same vein, federal regulators should limit the availability of the QRM exemption to relatively simple structures for mortgage securitization. For example, the risk retention requirement should apply to mortgages transformed into securities only if the securities are based on a single pool of actual mortgages (rather than on a pool of MBS or CDOs) with fewer than four tranches of securities. Such a simplified structure would be easier to evaluate by credit rating agencies and would be more attractive to investors burned by complex structures during the financial crisis.

23. SEC Release no. 34-64148 (March 30, 2011), pp. 63–64, 72.

Several senators and representatives have asked federal regulators, in defining the QRM exemption, to address the problems involving servicers of securitized pools.[24] If these servicers are affiliated with the sponsors of these pools, investors cannot rely on them to resolve disputes in a fair manner. Similarly, if these servicers own subordinated tranches of MBS they are servicing, they have a serious conflict of interest. In response, the proposed definition of QRM includes strong protections against conflicts of interest of mortgage servicers and more flexibility for them in reworking second mortgage liens.[25]

Even a truly independent servicer will be challenged by requests from borrowers to reduce the payment of principal or interest on mortgages in the pool. Servicers have often refused to consent to such mortgage modifications because they are not expressly authorized by the governing documents of the pool (Hunt 2006). To provide guidance in these situations, the QRM definition should require the governing documents of the relevant MBS pool specifically to authorize an independent servicer to agree to such mortgage modifications if the servicer reasonably believes that they will likely increase the returns from those mortgages to the pool.

Conclusions

To promote homeownership, the United States provides a broad range of government subsidies to home mortgages. Yet the link between these subsidies and homeownership is weak. Without most of these subsidies, the homeownership rate is higher in other industrial countries with similar legal systems, such as Australia, Canada, and the United Kingdom.

Assuming, as this chapter does, that the United States will continue to support some concept of homeownership, Congress should target government subsidies for home mortgages to households meeting both of two criteria: they cannot afford to buy a home without these mortgage subsidies, and, with these subsidies, they have the ability to meet the monthly payments on the home's mortgage. This combination would spread the social benefits of homeownership among more Americans, without imposing the social costs of mortgage defaults on individual homeowners and their neighbors.

The current government subsidies for homeownership in the United States are poorly designed to meet these two tests and are also very expensive. To promote more homeownership at a lower budget expense, Congress should reduce and reshape the current government subsidies for homeownership and adopt various measures to revive the private market for mortgage securitization.

24. Letter from Senator Robert Menendez et al. to HUD Secretary Shaun Donovan et al., March 3, 2011.

25. FDIC (2011). See SEC Release no. 34-64148 (March 30, 2011).

The tax deduction for mortgage interest is available only to taxpayers who itemize deductions, and this deduction is most valuable to taxpayers in the highest income tax bracket. But these are precisely the households least likely to buy homes mainly because of a tax benefit. To maximize the impact of tax expenditures on the homeownership rate, Congress should transform the interest deduction into a tax credit for interest paid on mortgages. Such a tax credit would be more attractive than a tax deduction to a household with modest income that is on the fence about buying a home.

Alternatively, Congress should lower the maximum mortgage eligible for the interest deduction from $1 million to $500,000 per household, as recently recommended by the co-chairs of the President's Deficit Commission. In addition, Congress should enact two other proposals made by the co-chairs of that commission: eliminate interest deductions for mortgages on second homes and for home equity loans. Neither increases the rate of homeownership, and both are costly from a budget perspective.

As Congress tries to increase the rate of homeownership through the tax code, it should revise federal and state laws to minimize the rate of mortgage defaults. Most important, Congress should gradually raise the minimum down payment on all home mortgages insured through federal agencies like the FHA and the VA, which currently range from zero to 3.5 percent of the home purchase price. With such minimum down payments, the home equity of borrowers will turn negative as soon as housing prices fall. And negative equity is the key driver of mortgage defaults.

Congress should also override the laws of certain states that inhibit lenders from attaching a borrower's personal assets when trying to collect a deficiency after a mortgage foreclosure. Such state laws encourage borrowers to buy homes with minimal down payments because they can simply walk away from a mortgage without any personal liability. If, in a specific case, a borrower does not have the ability to pay a deficiency after a mortgage foreclosure, he or she can choose to file for bankruptcy. The bankruptcy judge would then be in the best position to evaluate the borrower's ability to pay a foreclosure deficiency claim relative to his or her overall financial situation.

More generally, Congress should gradually switch the criteria for federal programs for mortgage insurance away from the amount of the home's price to the annual income of the borrower. It makes no sense to provide government-subsidized mortgage insurance for a $500,000 home to a professional couple with $500,000 in annual income. A household should be eligible for government mortgage insurance if household income is below a reasonable level—for example, below the median income level for the metropolitan area.

To securitize home mortgages insured by the federal government, we already have a federal agency—Ginnie Mae—that has operated successfully for many years. If Congress decides to expand its federal subsidies for home mortgages, it should do so directly through on-budget appropriations. Further, if Congress wants the federal government to support the securitization of other types of home mortgages, it should use Ginnie Mae—with accurate pricing of its guarantees that are reflected on the federal budget. Ginnie Mae is a much more efficient way to securitize home mortgages than Fannie Mae or Freddie Mac. Most of the government subsidies implicit in the special privileges of these two corporations went to their shareholders and executives, not homeowners.

Some have argued that Fannie Mae and Freddie Mac should survive in order to attract enough capital to meet the needs of the home mortgage market. But this argument is weak if the federal government is already subsidizing home mortgages for those households whose needs are not being met by the normal workings of the capital markets. Others have argued that Fannie Mae and Freddie Mac should survive in order to buy mortgages and MBS in financial crisis when those markets become illiquid. But this episodic role was performed well in the recent financial crisis by the Federal Reserve Board, which is in a better position to evaluate the need for such buying relative to the overall liquidity of the debt markets.

The strongest argument for the survival of Fannie Mae and Freddie Mac is the recent demise of the private market for mortgage securitization in the United States. Although its demise was the result of abuses before the financial crisis, its revival is now stymied in large part by the tremendous expansion of the activities of these two corporations. With two aggressive buyers and securitizers of home mortgages, controlled and financed by the U.S. Treasury, it would be very difficult for a private player to succeed in the market for mortgage securitization. Therefore, the federal government should gradually reduce the role of these two corporations as it implements measures to correct the past abuses in the private securitization process.

Federal regulators should begin by adopting capital requirements for bank sponsors of MBS that reflect the actual allocation of risks between the bank and other parties. Before the financial crisis, bank sponsors allocated almost no capital to support their obligations to sponsored MBS pools and their investors. This was wrong. But it is also wrong to impose on a bank a capital charge for all of the assets securitized as MBS as if they are still owned 100 percent by the bank. This capital charge does not reflect the realities of mortgage securitization and will deter most banks from engaging in the process.

In addition, federal regulators should encourage simpler designs and more detailed disclosures for MBS deals. Both of these objectives are already being pursued by federal regulators; they can reinforce these objectives by putting appropriate criteria into the definition of QRMs. The criteria for QRMs not only will define the exemption for the risk retention requirement but also will be incorporated into other exemptions by the SEC and the federal banking agencies. As a result, the criteria for QRMs will establish strong precedents that are likely to pervade the whole market for conventional mortgages.

Most important, the QRM definition should require a down payment of at least 20 percent of the purchase price. This requirement is part of the QRM proposal, recently published by federal regulators; they will have to resist strong pressures from representatives of the real estate industry who will lobby for lower down payment requirements. Nor should regulators indefinitely include as QRMs all home mortgages sold to Fannie Mae and Freddie Mac. The categorical QRM status of such mortgages should be gradually downsized on a reasonable time schedule.

At the same time, federal regulators should use the definition of QRMs to promote the continuation of long-term, fixed-rate mortgages in the private market. The United States is the only country in the world offering thirty-year, fixed-rate mortgages without any prepayment penalties. However, such mortgages are not financially viable absent a government subsidy. If interest rates rise sharply, the yield on these fixed-rate mortgages will likely drop below the deposit rates paid by mortgage lenders. However, if interest rates fall sharply, borrowers will prepay quickly and refinance into mortgages with lower fixed rates. To allow lenders to protect themselves against these asymmetrical risks, the regulators should follow the Dodd-Frank approach to qualifying mortgages, which is to allow QRMs to have prepayment penalties for the initial three years on home mortgages if they meet other high-quality standards.

Similarly, regulators should build into the QRM definition a few standardized formats for conventional home mortgages. Such standardization would reduce the costs of securitization and would increase the transparency of the process to investors as well as credit rating agencies. The standard terms and conditions of all QRMs should include a requirement that the servicer of any MBS pool must be independent of the pool's sponsors and underwriters and that the servicer must be expressly authorized to approve modifications of mortgages in the pools under certain conditions. For example, the servicer might be required to find that the mortgage modification would reasonably increase the total return of the mortgage to the pool. In addition, as recently proposed, the QRM criteria should protect against conflicts of interest by mortgage servicers.

In short, the United States is gradually moving toward a three-tier system for home mortgages and their securitization. The first tier, which is currently dominant, will consist of mortgages insured and securitized through government-subsidized programs. Congress should reduce the scope and cost of this first tier by tying these subsidies more effectively to the promotion of homeownership. The second tier will be the QRMs, which should become popular once they are defined by regulators in final rules. The regulators should limit QRMs to home mortgages meeting high standards for quality and securitized through relatively simple and transparent structures. The third tier will be all the remaining home mortgages in the United States, which will not qualify for government subsidies and will not meet the exemptive criteria for QRMs. This third tier will expand if appropriate reforms are implemented on the private securitization of conventional mortgages.

References

American Securitization Forum. 2008. "Restoring Confidence in the Securitization Markets." New York (December 3).

Bank of America–Merrill Lynch. 2010. "The Mortgage Credit Roundup, October Remittance." November 9.

Benson, Clea, and Lorraine Woellert. 2011. "Dodd-Frank Mortgage Risk-Retention Rule May Reinforce Role of Fannie Mae." *Bloomberg,* March 30.

Campbell, John Y., Stefano Giglio, and Parag Pathak. Forthcoming. "Forced Sales and House Prices." *American Economic Review.*

Capozza, Dennis, Richard Green, and Patric Hendershott. 1996. "Taxes, Mortgage Borrowing, and Residential Land Prices." In *Economic Effects of Fundamental Tax Reform,* edited by Henry J. Aaron and William G. Gale, ch. 5. Brookings.

Coulson, N. Edward, Seok-Joon Hwang, and Susumu Imai. 2001. "The Value of Owner-Occupation in Neighborhoods." Working Paper. Pennsylvania State University.

Currie, Antony. 2010. "BlackRock Paves Way to Reshape Mortgage Market." *Reuters Breakingviews,* November 5.

ElBoghdady, Dina. 2007. "No Money Down Disappearing as Mortgage Option." *Washington Post,* August 5.

European Covered Bond Council. 2010. *ECBC Covered Bond Fact Book.* Brussels.

FDIC (Federal Deposit Insurance Corporation). 2008. "Covered Bond Policy Statement, August 4, 2008." *Federal Register* 73 (July 28): 43754–59.

———. 2009. "12 CFR 325, RIN 3064-AD48: Modifications to GAAP; Consolidation of Asset-Backed Commercial Paper, etc." Washington (December 15).

———. 2010a. "FDIC Board Approves Final Rule Regarding Safe Harbor Protection for Securitizations." Press release. Washington (September 27).

———. 2010b. "FDIC Notice of Proposed Rulemaking, Treatment by the FDIC as Conservator or Receiver of Financial Assets Transferred by an Insured Depository Institution in Connection with a Securitization or Participation." *Federal Register* 75 (May 17): 27471.

———. 2011. "FDIC Chairman Sheila Blair's Statement Credit Risk Retention Notice of Proposed Rulemaking." Press release. Washington (March 29).

Federal Reserve. 2010a. "Joint Advance Notice of Proposed Rulemaking Regarding Alternatives to the Use of Credit Ratings in the Risk-Based Capital Guidelines." *Federal Register* 75 (August 25): 52283.

———. 2010b. "Report to Congress on Risk Retention." Washington (November).

FHFA (Federal Housing Finance Agency). 2010. *Conservator's Report on the Enterprise's Financial Performance.* Washington.

GAO (Government Accountability Office). 2005. "Rural Housing Services: Overview of Program Issues." GAO-05-382T. Washington (March 10).

Ghent, Andra C., and Marianna Kudiyak. 2010. "Recourse and Residential Mortgage Default: Theory and Evidence from U.S. States." Working Paper. Federal Reserve of Richmond (June 10).

Glaeser, Edward L., and Jesse M. Shapiro. 2003. "The Benefits of the Home Mortgage Interest Deduction." *Tax Policy and Economy* 17 (August): 37–82.

Green, Richard, and Kerry Vandell. 1999. "Giving Households Credit: How Changes in the U.S. Tax Code Could Promote Homeownership." *Regional Science and Urban Economics* 29, no. 4: 419–44.

Haviv, Julie. 2010. "U.S. Mortgage Bond Issuance Leaps Year to Date." *Reuters,* September 30.

Hilber, Christian, and Tracy Turner. 2010. "The Mortgage Interest Deduction and Its Impact on Homeownership Decisions." Cambridge, Mass.: National Bureau of Economic Research (August 12).

HUD (Department of Housing and Urban Development). 2010. "Annual Report to Congress Regarding the Financial Status of the FHA Mutual Mortgage Insurance Fund Fiscal Year 2010." Washington (November 15).

Hughes, Jennifer. 2010. "Covered Bonds Reach $356 Billion as Investors Seek Safe Havens." *Financial Times,* December 30, p. 17.

Hunt, John. 2006. "Loan Modification Restrictions in Subprime Securitization Pooling and Servicing Documents from 2006: Final Results." University of California, Davis, School of Law.

IMF (International Monetary Fund). 2007. "The Danish Mortgage Market: A Comparative Analysis." Country Report 07/123. Washington.

Joint Tax Committee. 2010. "Estimate of Federal Tax Expenditures for Fiscal Years 2010–2014." JCS-3-10. Washington: U.S. Congress (December 21).

Kalita, Mitra, and Nick Timiraos. 2010. "Homeowner Perks under Fire." *Wall Street Journal,* December 16.

Kashkari, Neil. 2008. "Can Covered Bonds Compete with Fannie and Freddie?" Remarks at the American Enterprise Institute. Washington, September 19 (aei.org/event/1789).

Kopecki, Dawn. 2009. "Mortgage Bankers Push for New Federal Loan Guarantee Program." *Bloomberg,* September 21.

Krugman, Paul. 2008. "Home Not-So-Sweet Home." *New York Times,* June 23.

Lascelles, Eric. 2010. "Canadian Mortgage Market Primer." *TD Securities,* June 17.

McLean, Bethany, and Joe Nocera. 2010. *All the Devils Are Here: The Hidden History of the Financial Crisis.* New York: Portfolio Hardcover/Penguin.

OFHEO (Office of Federal Housing Enterprise Oversight). 2008. *2008 Report to Congress.* Washington (April 15).

Passmore, Wayne. 2003. "The GSE Implicit Subsidy and the Value of Government Ambiguity." Finance and Economic Discussion Series. Washington: Federal Reserve Board (December).

Pollock, Alex, and Michael Lea. 2010. Testimony at a hearing comparing international housing finance systems before the Subcommittee on Security and International Trade and Finance of Senate Banking, Housing and Urban Affairs Committee, September 29.

Poterba, James, and Todd Sinai. 2008. "Tax Expenditures for Owner-Occupied Housing." *American Economic Review: Papers and Proceedings* 98, no. 2: 84–89.

Pozen, Robert. 2010. *Too Big to Save? How to Fix the U.S. Financial System.* Hoboken, N.J.: Wiley.

President's Deficit Commission. 2010. "Proposals by the Co-chairs." Washington (November).

Protess, Ben. 2011. "FDIC Proposes Rule to Tie Banks to Mortgage Risk." *New York Times: DealBook,* March 29 (dealbook.nytimes.com/2011/03/29).

SEC (Securities and Exchange Commission). 2011. "Disclosure for Asset-Backed Securities." Washington (January 20).

Shiller, Robert. 2008. *The Subprime Solution.* Princeton University Press.

Wachter, Susan, and Michael Lea. 2010. Testimony before the U.S. Senate, Committee on Banking, Housing, and Urban Affairs, Subcommittee on Security and International Trade and Finance, September 29.

Woellert, Lorraine, and John Gittelsohn. 2010. "Fannie-Freddie Fix at $160 Billion with $1 Trillion Worst Case." *Bloomberg,* June 14.

4

The Government's Role in the Housing Finance System: Where Do We Go from Here?

KAREN DYNAN AND TED GAYER

It is time to commit to a future housing finance system for the United States, as the current uncertainty surrounding this issue is likely deterring the recovery of the housing market and the broader economy. Returning to the system in place before the financial crisis is not a suitable option, as the government-sponsored enterprises (GSEs) Fannie Mae and Freddie Mac created significant problems that contributed to the crisis. Their precrisis activities also left the taxpayers with an enormous burden: as of early 2011, more than $100 billion had been put toward rescuing the GSEs, and the total cost may be up to several times that when all is said and done.

In this chapter, we discuss the weaknesses of the precrisis GSE model and lay out the broad outlines of a new housing finance model that attempts to address these problems. The new system includes a limited role for government that consists of providing credit guarantees for qualifying mortgage securities in normal times and becoming more expansive in times of mortgage market distress. It also attempts to reduce the incentives for excessive risk taking embedded in the old system. This feature is essential to creating a stable and robust mortgage finance system, which, over the long run, can help to foster economic growth.

We thank Martin Baily, Richard Herring, Dwight Jaffee, and Phill Swagel for helpful comments and Jean Marie Callan and John Soroushian for excellent research assistance.

Figure 4-1. *Home Prices, 2000–10*

Home price index (January 2000 = 100)

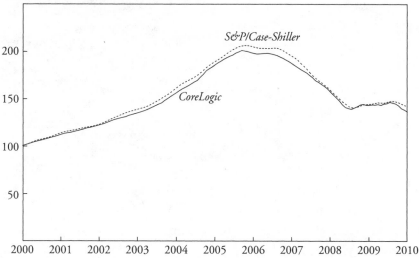

Sources: Standard and Poor's; CoreLogic/Haver Analytics.

The Housing Market and the Timing of Housing Finance Reform

The timing of GSE reform must take account of the weakness of the housing market recovery to date. As shown in figure 4-1, after dropping 32 percent from their peak value in April 2006 to their trough value in May 2009, home prices stabilized and even recovered a bit (rising 5 percent relative to the trough) by June 2010. However, this firming of home prices was in large part due to an enormous amount of government intervention in the housing market. The federal government supported demand for housing through an $8,000 housing tax credit for first-time home buyers (a program that ran from January 1, 2009, to September 30, 2010) and a $6,500 housing tax credit for repeat home buyers (which ran from November 7, 2009, to September 30, 2010). Demand was also supported by a drop in mortgage rates spurred by the Federal Reserve's purchase of $1.25 trillion of mortgage-related securities in 2009 and early 2010. Home prices were also likely bolstered by factors restricting the supply of homes coming to market, such as government efforts to forestall lender sales of distressed homes through various foreclosure prevention programs, including, most notably, the Home Affordable Modification Program (HAMP).

The underlying weakness in the housing market has fundamentally stemmed from an oversupply of homes that arose as a result of excessive construction

Figure 4-2. *Vacancies, 2000–10*

Percent

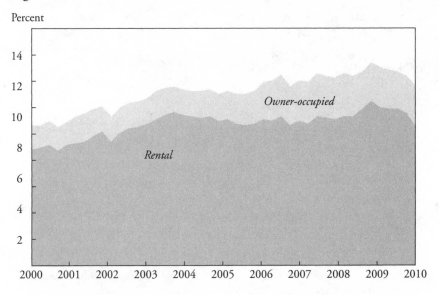

Sources: Census Bureau; Haver Analytics.

during the housing boom in the early to mid-2000s and the softness in house-hold formation that has prevailed since the recession began (see Shulyatyeva 2010). Figure 4-2 shows the vacancy rate for both owner-occupied and rental housing. When home prices peaked in the second quarter of 2006, the rental vacancy rate was 9.6 percent, and the owner-occupied vacancy rate was 2.2 per-cent—close to their averages since 2000. Vacancies proceeded to climb consider-ably, with the rental vacancy rate reaching 11.1 percent in the third quarter of 2009 and the owner-occupied vacancy rate reaching 2.9 in the first quarter of 2008 and again in the fourth quarter of 2008. (The differential timing of the increase in vacancy rates for rentals versus owner-occupied housing could be due to the home buyer tax credit, which incentivized renters to become buyers.)

After the various government programs either expired or played out, home prices resumed their downward trend. Since June 2010, home prices have expe-rienced five consecutive monthly declines, receding 3 percent. The evidence thus suggests that the various interventions have not remedied the fundamental prob-lem of an excess supply of homes. The rental vacancy rate currently stands at 9.4 percent, and the owner-occupied rate is at 2.7 percent; the latter remains notice-ably elevated compared with its average since 2000 of 2.1 percent.

The extremely low level of construction represents further evidence that the housing market is still working off excess supply. Single-family housing starts,

Figure 4-3. *Single-Family Housing Starts, 2000–10*

Thousands of starts

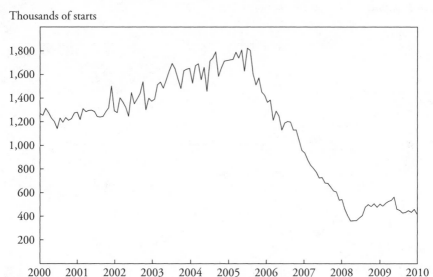

Sources: Census Bureau; Haver Analytics.

shown in figure 4-3, peaked at an annual rate of approximately 1.8 million in January 2006 before dropping precipitously—and nearly continuously—over the next thirty-six months, reaching a low of 360,000 in January 2009. The subsequent pattern was similar to that of home prices, with housing starts increasing modestly over the next fifteen months before leveling off and beginning to decline anew. At an annual rate of 417,000 in December 2010, the rate of housing starts was noticeably above its trough, but still only a fraction of the monthly average since 2000 of 1.16 million units (annual rate).

The protracted adjustment of the housing market is contributing to the softness of the recovery in the broader economy. Figure 4-4 shows the percentage point contribution of residential investment to annualized real GDP growth. The weakness in residential investment has been both persistent and severe. Since the beginning of the recession in the fourth quarter of 2007, declines in residential investment subtracted from real GDP growth for seven consecutive quarters. For comparison, the average number of quarters of negative contributions of residential investment to GDP growth across all recessions between 1947 and 2001 is three. In addition, the level of residential investment declined nearly 40 percent from its level when the recession started. For comparison, the average cumulative drop in residential investment across all recessions between 1947 and 2001 was approximately 8 percent (Hamilton 2010).

Figure 4-4. *Contribution of Private Residential Investment
to Percentage Change in Real GDP, 2000–10*

Percentage points

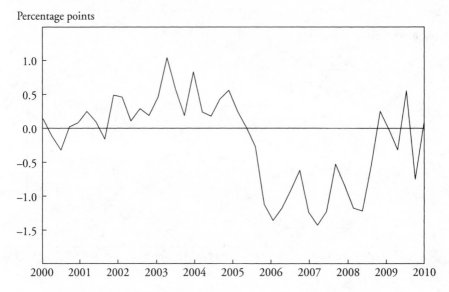

Sources: Bureau of Economic Affairs; Haver Analytics.

The drop in home prices also contributed to the depth of the recession and
the weakness of the recovery through its impact on housing wealth. According to the Flow of Funds Accounts, the value of residential assets held by the
household sector dropped from $22.7 trillion in the fourth quarter of 2006 to
$16.5 trillion in the first quarter of 2009, before recovering to $17.2 trillion
more recently. Historically, declines in wealth have dampened consumer spending, with a $1 decline in wealth associated with a reduction in the level of spend-
ing on the order of $0.03 to $0.05 (see Gramlich 2002). Historical relationships
thus imply that the $6 trillion net decline in housing wealth since its peak should
have led to a decline in consumer spending of $180 billion to $300 billion. This
calculation implies that wealth effects should have trimmed 2 to 3 percent off of
the prerecession level of nominal consumption.

A key policy question is whether the precarious state of the housing market—and the threat it poses to a robust and sustained economic recovery—
suggests that reform of the GSEs should happen quickly or slowly. As can be
seen from figure 4-5, the federal government's credit guarantees, provided in
large part through the GSEs, are lending enormous support to the mortgage
market. Over the first three quarters of 2010, GSE-backed mortgages constituted 62 percent of mortgage originations. Mortgages insured by the Federal

Figure 4-5. *Share of Originations, 2000–10*

Percent

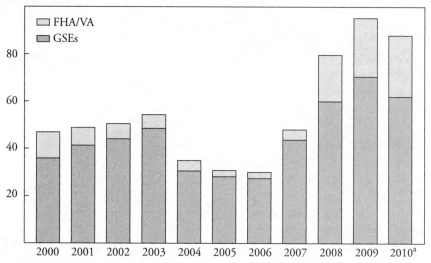

Source: Inside Mortgage Finance, October 29, 2010.
a. Through third quarter.

Housing Administration (FHA) and the Veterans Administration (VA) constituted an additional 26 percent of mortgage originations. This 88 percent share
of the market for originations is down slightly from 95 percent in 2009, but is
approximately double the share that prevailed from 2000 through 2007. While
this substantial degree of support may be inhibiting the recovery of the private
mortgage market, an excessively quick and disorderly transition could lead to a
pullback in the supply of mortgage credit that could further weaken the demand
for housing.

The GSEs are also playing a role in the government's foreclosure policy
efforts. For example, they are facilitating modifications of GSE-guaranteed loans
under the HAMP workouts and allowing high loan-to-value GSE-guaranteed
loans to be refinanced under the Home Affordable Refinance Program (HARP).
Again, policymakers face a trade-off. On the one hand, because it takes time
to evaluate mortgages for these programs, the efforts may be slowing down the
necessary transition of distressed mortgages that are fundamentally unsustain-
able over the long run. On the other hand, the programs are preventing at least
some unnecessary foreclosures, so an abrupt cessation of GSE activities in this
area would increase mortgage distress and exacerbate the supply problems in the
housing market.

All told, these considerations argue for a steady transition to a new U.S. system of housing finance. The specific timing depends on the feature under consideration. Ideally, activities directly related to the supply of mortgage credit should be accomplished relatively soon—perhaps within a year—especially given the desirability of expeditiously returning the demand side of the housing market to normal conditions. But a longer time frame, perhaps several years, should be allowed for the complete unwinding of all of the activities of the GSEs, both because they play a role in mitigating foreclosure and because dealing with their existing assets and obligations will be complicated and is not a critical factor for the housing market outlook.[1]

The issue of the appropriate speed of transition is separate from the question of the appropriate time line for developing and committing to a new housing finance system. The question of what the new system will look like is one source of uncertainty that is likely deterring the recovery by inhibiting the ability of businesses and households to plan and move forward. For example, anecdotal reports suggest that mortgage lending has been held back by a lack of information about what rules and regulations will apply to the new mortgages. Thus, while a gradual transition to the new housing finance system may be desirable, there are reasons to lay out a clearly defined vision for mortgage finance as soon as possible.

Activities of the GSEs

Prior to being taken into conservatorship in September 2008, Fannie Mae and Freddie Mac were owned by private shareholders. They also had congressional charters that both granted them certain privileges and assigned them a public mission to "provide liquidity, stability, and affordability" to the housing market. As part of this mission, 1992 legislation established "affordable housing goals" that specified what fractions of each enterprise's mortgage acquisitions should finance housing units occupied by low- and moderate-income families, by very low-income families, and by families living in underserved areas.

The GSEs have traditionally pursued two main lines of activity. The first line of activity is pooling certain types of mortgages into guaranteed mortgage-backed securities (MBS). Often these securities are created as part of a swap arrangement with the financial institutions that originated the loans: the originating institution essentially trades a group of loans for a security that pays regular dividends corresponding to the mortgage payments associated with the underlying loans.

---

1. Broadly speaking, the government either could retain these obligations and allow them to run off over time or could sell them off—perhaps through an auction—to a private entity. Either approach would induce taxpayer losses.

The guarantee assures payment even if the borrowers default; however, it does not protect holders from risks to the value of the security stemming from market interest rates changing and (relatedly) from borrowers refinancing and prepaying their loans. In exchange for the credit guarantee, the originating financial institution in a swap arrangement typically pays guarantee fees in the form of an upfront payment as well as regular ongoing payments over the life of the security. The GSEs also purchase mortgages directly from financial institutions for the purpose of producing guaranteed MBS; in these cases, the guarantee fee shows up implicitly as part of the price paid for the loans.

By charter, the GSEs are restricted to purchasing so-called conforming loans. These loans must be below a certain limit at origination; loans above this value are known as jumbo loans. The conforming loan limit increased annually with average home prices, reaching $417,000 for one-unit loans in 2008, at which point new legislation increased it temporarily to up to $729,750 in certain high-cost areas. Traditionally, conforming loans had to have a loan-to-value ratio no higher than 80 percent or else carry mortgage insurance that effectively reduces the risk to that of a similar loan with an 80 percent loan-to-value ratio.

The GSE guarantee fees are negotiated privately with loan originators. They vary by type of mortgage, by originator, and over time. Many factors influence the guarantee fees charged, including the expected cost of providing the guarantee, administrative expenses, competitive conditions in the market for bearing mortgage risk, and the GSEs' target return on capital. In the years leading up to the crisis, guarantee fees averaged around 21 basis points at both GSEs. Analysis by the GSEs' current regulator has found that guarantee fees have provided a cross-subsidization from lower-risk loans to higher-risk loans (see FHFA 2010b).

Freddie Mac began to securitize conforming loans in the early 1970s, and Fannie Mae followed suit around 1980. GSE mortgage-backed securities held by investors about doubled during the 1990s, reaching $1.3 trillion by 2000, and then increased more than threefold over the subsequent decade to reach close to $4 trillion in 2009 (see figure 4-6). As a share of GDP, outstanding GSE mortgage-backed securities climbed from 13 percent in 2000 to 28 percent in 2009. Notwithstanding the growth in their MBS during the mortgage boom of the early 2000s, the GSEs accounted for only about half of mortgage originations prior to the financial crisis, with the flourishing private secondary mortgage market providing financing to an enormous amount of nonconforming loans.

A second important activity pursued by the GSEs in the years leading up to the financial crisis was to hold large portfolios of assets that generated income for the agencies and their shareholders. By charter, the GSEs were restricted to holding assets that had some link to their mission of supporting the conforming mortgage market. However, this left a fairly wide range of permissible assets, including whole mortgage loans, their own mortgage-backed securities, and

Figure 4-6. *Mortgage-Backed Securities Outstanding, 1971–2007*

Millions of dollars

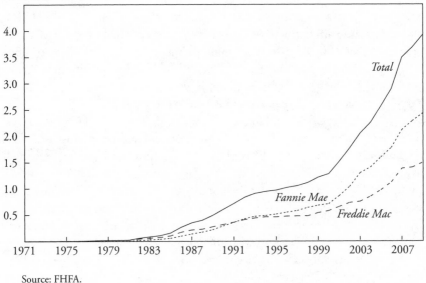

Source: FHFA.

private-label MBS backed by various types of nonconforming loan products, including subprime and near-prime mortgages.[2]

For many years, the GSE portfolios generated high returns. A key factor contributing to their profitability was their ability to finance their portfolios on relatively inexpensive terms because investors perceived GSE obligations to have an "implicit" federal guarantee. While rates on GSE debt never fell as low as rates on comparable-maturity Treasury debt, the GSEs were able to borrow at rates 20 to 45 basis points lower than large bank holding companies (Bernanke 2007).

Although the U.S. Code specified that the agencies "[do] not carry the full faith and credit of the Federal Government," the perception of an implicit guarantee was fed by their public mission as well as by certain charter-granted advantages that suggested they had a special relationship with the government. For example, the agencies had $2.25 billion lines of credit with the U.S. Treasury, and they were exempt from state and local taxes. Their obligations were classified

2. The charters are not specific about exactly what types of private-label securities can be held but do offer some general restrictions on quality. For example, Fannie Mae's charter states, "The operations of the corporation under this section shall be confined, so far as practicable, to mortgages which are deemed by the corporation to be of such quality, type, and class as to meet, generally, the purchase standards imposed by private institutional mortgage investors."

Figure 4-7. *Total Retained Mortgage Portfolio, 1971–2007*

Millions of dollars

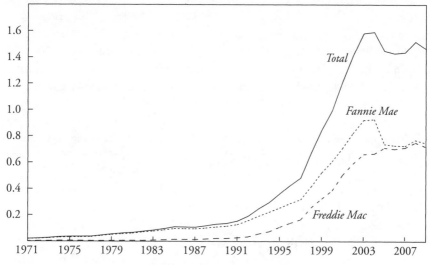

Source: FHFA.

as "government securities," which, among other things, meant that they were eligible for unlimited investment by financial institutions insured by the Federal Deposit Insurance Corporation (FDIC) and that they were exempt from the registration and reporting requirements of the Securities and Exchange Commission. In addition, until the summer of 2008, there was no resolution process for addressing an insolvent GSE.

The GSEs' ability to borrow cheaply fostered growth in their portfolios. As shown in figure 4-7, the combined portfolios of the GSEs rose from $0.1 trillion (equivalent to 2 percent of GDP) in 1990 to $1 trillion (equivalent to 10 percent of GDP) in 2000. They continued to grow over the first half of the last decade, topping out at $1.6 billion (equivalent to 13 percent of GDP) in 2004, before receding a bit in more recent years. This growth, in turn, reinforced the perceived implicit guarantee, as the agencies became increasingly viewed as too big to fail without creating systemic risk to the financial system.

The risk associated with the GSEs' portfolios depends not only on the amount of assets held but, of course, on the type of assets held. To the degree that the GSEs were holding their own MBS or conforming whole loans that they would otherwise securitize and guarantee, they were not taking on additional credit risk. The return on these assets did vary with other factors: any increase in market interest rates would decrease the value of the mortgage assets that the GSEs held on their balance sheets, and a decrease in mortgage interest rates would spur demand for refinancing, leading to prepayment of the mortgage assets on their balance sheets. Even though the GSEs engaged in substantial hedging of these risks, many critics of the GSEs in the early 2000s pointed to these risks as the most likely source of a potential systemic problem (see, for example, Frame and White 2005). The riskiness of the GSEs' portfolios also depended on the amount of private-label mortgage-backed securities held (particularly those backed by nonprime loans), for which the GSEs were taking on credit risk in addition to other types of risk.

Information about the composition of the GSEs' portfolios is somewhat limited, particularly prior to the last few years. However, the available evidence suggests that the portfolios of both GSEs shifted toward riskier assets in the early 2000s. As shown in the top panel of table 4-1, Fannie Mae's holdings of private-label MBS about tripled between 2000 and 2004 (the year in which such holdings peaked), with essentially all of the growth accounted for by a rise in holdings of subprime and alt-A MBS. Private-label MBS accounted for about one-quarter of the growth in Fannie Mae's overall portfolio and reached a peak share of around 11 percent of total assets in the middle of the decade. Most of the remainder of the growth in Fannie Mae's portfolio over this period was attributable to an expansion of holdings of whole loans. Detailed information about these loans is not available, but the fact that the rise was concentrated in fixed-rate single-family loans not insured by the FHA or VA suggests that it was not driven by higher holdings of nonprime loans, as most nonprime loans had adjustable rates.

As shown in the bottom panel of table 4-1, Freddie Mac's portfolio moved more aggressively toward higher-risk loans in the early 2000s. Its holdings of private-label MBS increased nearly sixfold between 2000 and 2005 (the year in which these holdings peaked). This expansion accounted for almost two-thirds of the growth in the overall portfolio over this period, and, at the peak, the private-label MBS holdings represented about one-third of total assets. Most of the remainder of the growth in Freddie Mac's portfolio in the early 2000s was accounted for by the growth in holdings of its own MBS.

The lower cost of borrowing associated with the GSEs' implicit guarantee was not the only factor incentivizing the GSEs to amass these portfolios. For example, assets associated with riskier loan products were desirable not only because they produced high returns but also because they frequently counted toward the GSEs' affordable housing goals. The incentive to take risk was also reinforced by the weakness of their precrisis regulator, the Office of Federal Housing Enterprise Oversight (OFHEO). OFHEO had limited control over the GSEs' capital standards, as 1992 legislation had largely defined how these standards should be set. OFHEO was widely viewed as understaffed and underfunded, perhaps

Table 4-1. *Details of the Retained Mortgage Portfolio of Fannie Mae and Freddie Mac, 2000–09*

Millions of dollars

		Whole loans						Mortgage-backed securities						
		Single-family						Private-label[a]						
		Conventional												
Year and institution	Total retained mortgage portfolio	Fixed-rate	Adjustable rate	Seconds	Total FHA, VA, and USDA rural development programs	Multi-family	Total	Subprime	Alt-A	Other[b]	Total	Own[c]	Other agency[d]	Other[e]
Fannie Mae														
2000	607,731	125,786	13,244	480	4,763	8,361	152,634				34,266	351,066	57,058	12,707
2001	706,347	140,454	10,427	917	5,069	10,538	167,405				29,175	431,776	61,718	16,273
2002	820,627	282,899	12,142	416	6,404	21,383	323,244	9,404	3,925	14,828	28,157	380,383	48,345	40,498
2003	919,589	335,812	19,155	233	7,284	35,149	397,633	29,175	8,812	8,992	46,979	405,922	37,975	31,080
2004	925,194	307,048	38,350	177	10,112	44,470	400,157	74,657	25,610	8,542	108,809	344,404	41,763	30,061
2005	736,803	261,214	38,331	220	15,036	51,879	366,680	47,110	33,051	6,754	86,915	234,451	31,041	17,716
2006	726,434	255,490	46,820	287	20,106	60,342	383,045	46,876	35,124	15,281	97,281	199,644	32,038	14,426
2007	723,620	240,090	43,278	261	28,202	91,746	403,577	32,040	32,475	30,295	94,810	180,163	33,038	12,032
2008	767,989	223,881	44,157	215	43,799	117,441	429,493	24,551	27,858	30,997	83,406	228,950	34,900	-8,760
2009	745,271	208,915	34,602	213	52,399	120,414	416,543	20,527	24,505	30,312	75,344	220,245	42,667	-9,528
Freddie Mac														
2000	385,451	39,537	2,125	9	1,200	16,369	59,240				35,997	246,209	37,294	6,711
2001	503,769	38,267	1,073	5	964	22,483	62,792				42,336	308,427	76,827	13,387
2002	589,899	33,821	1,321	3	705	28,036	63,886				70,752	341,287	83,707	30,267
2003	660,531	25,889	871	1	513	32,996	60,270				107,301	393,135		22,536
2004	664,582	22,055	990	0	344	37,971	61,360			166,411	166,411	356,698	59,715	20,398
2005	709,503	19,238	903	0	255	41,085	61,481			231,594	231,594	361,324	44,626	10,478
2006	710,002	19,211	1,233	0	196	45,207	65,847	122,099	35,369	67,163	224,631	354,262	45,385	9,877
2007	710,042	21,578	2,700	0	311	57,569	82,158	101,325	30,063	87,526	218,914	356,970	47,836	4,164
2008	748,747	36,071	2,136	0	548	72,721	111,476	74,851	25,067	85,123	185,041	424,524	70,852	-43,146
2009	716,974	50,980	2,310	0	1,588	83,938	138,816	61,574	21,439	80,803	163,816	374,615	66,171	-26,444

Source: FHFA.

a. Fannie Mae private-label MBS were not available before 2002. Freddie Mac subprime and Alt-A MBS were not available before 2006. Other private-label MBS were not available before 2004.

b. Includes other single-family securities, including manufactured housing, and multifamily securities.

c. Fannie Mae holdings of Fannie Mae MBS in top panel; Freddie Mac holdings of Freddie Mac MBS in lower panel.

d. Fannie Mae holdings of Freddie Mac and Ginnie Mae MBS in top panel; Freddie Mac holdings of Fannie Mae and Ginnie Mae MBS in lower panel.

e. Includes unamortized premiums, discounts, deferred adjustments, and fair-value adjustments on securities and loans and mortgage revenue bonds.

in part because its budget was determined by an annual appropriations process. Although some members of Congress introduced legislation aimed at increasing oversight and reducing the perception of an implicit guarantee, the overall appetite among policymakers for strengthening OFHEO was tempered by support for the GSEs' public mission as well as the agencies' extensive lobbying efforts.

A lack of market discipline also promoted excessive risk taking by the GSEs. Market discipline was low in part because of the widespread perception among investors that the federal government stood behind the GSEs' obligations. However, even in the absence of the implicit guarantee, market participants would have had trouble determining how much risk was being taken on because of the limited financial reporting requirements imposed on the agencies.

In sum, both the guarantee business and the portfolio business posed risks to the GSEs, and, to the degree that the agencies became "too big to fail," the activities posed risks to the taxpayers. The fees charged to provide the credit guarantees included with the GSEs' mortgage-backed securities, in principle, could cover the potential costs associated with the guarantees, but only if they were set correctly. Returns on the portfolio depended on both the costs of financing the portfolio and the risks associated with the assets held. As to the degree to which these activities were providing social benefits that offset the potential costs, the evidence suggests that the benefits to borrowers historically have been limited. Most studies suggest that the lower borrowing rates available to the GSEs to finance their portfolios translated into only modestly lower mortgage interest rates for borrowers (see GAO 1996; Naranjo and Toevs 2002; González-Rivera 2001; Passmore, Sherlund, and Burgess 2005; Lehnert, Passmore, and Sherlund 2008). Lehnert, Passmore, and Sherlund (2008) also conclude that GSE portfolio purchases did not have a meaningful stabilizing effect on the supply of mortgage credit. Further, as discussed below, there is scant evidence that GSE activities significantly contributed to the supply of affordable housing for low- and moderate-income households.

MBS Credit Risk and Portfolio Systemic Risk

GSE losses in recent years stemmed largely from credit losses, not from interest rate risk or prepayment risk associated with their portfolio holdings. Figure 4-8 shows the delinquency rate for mortgages backed by Fannie Mae and Freddie Mac. The initial decline in home prices in late 2006 through 2007 primarily led to distress among nonprime loans. By early 2008, however, the ninety-plus-day delinquency rate for GSEs began increasing, reaching a peak of 5.59 percent of Fannie loans and 4.20 percent of Freddie loans in February 2010. These delinquencies ultimately led to defaults and credit-related losses. As shown in the top panel of figure 4-9, Fannie Mae saw persistent credit-related losses from the first

Figure 4-8. *Delinquency Rates of Government-Sponsored Enterprises, 2006–10*

Percent

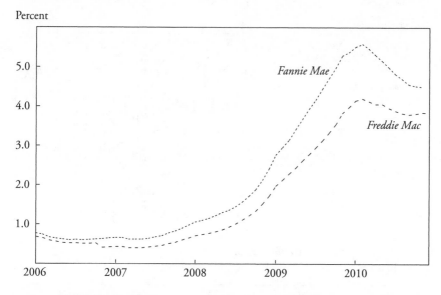

Sources: Fannie Mae; Freddie Mac.

quarter of 2007 through the most recent quarter. These losses were severe, with quarterly losses of $21 billion, $19 billion, and $22 billion, in the first, second, and third quarters of 2009, respectively. As shown in the bottom panel of figure 4-9, Freddie Mac also saw persistent and severe credit losses. Quarterly credit-related losses for Freddie Mac started in the second quarter of 2006 and have continued ever since. The credit-related losses peaked at about $9 billion in the first quarter of 2009.

The GSEs also incurred losses related to their portfolio holdings of private-label mortgage-backed securities, which, as discussed earlier, were heavily concentrated among nonprime mortgages. These losses have been large—a total of $150 billion for Fannie and $90 billion for Freddie since the beginning of 2007. The available data do not allow for a precise comparison of how such losses compare with those related to the credit guarantees when all is said and done, but it is worth noting that the outstanding value of GSE-guaranteed mortgages was at least ten times as large as GSE holdings of private-label MBS in the years leading up to the mortgage crisis. For the losses to be comparable, the net loss rate on these holdings would have to be ten times as high as that on the GSE-guaranteed mortgages.

In a direct sense, though, the failure of the GSEs stemmed from a different aspect of the portfolios. The portfolios were financed largely through short-term

Figure 4-9. *Losses of Government-Sponsored Enterprises, 2006–10*

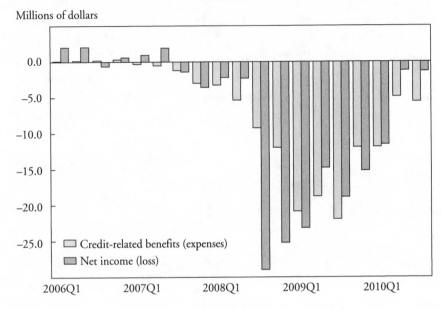

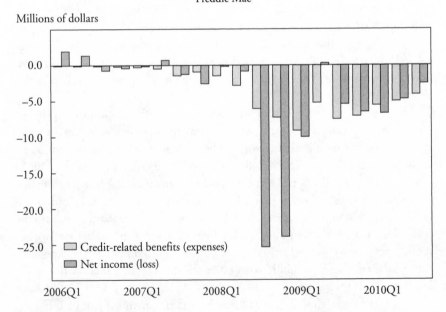

Sources: Fannie Mae; Freddie Mac.

borrowing by the GSEs (at reduced rates due to the implicit subsidy). This reliance on short-term borrowing to finance long-term assets set up the conditions for a classic bank run. The persistent and severe credit losses of the GSEs ate into their capital, which, coupled with expected enormous future losses, led to a mounting loss of confidence by the GSE debt holders in mid-2008, increasing the cost at which the GSEs were able to borrow. Left unchecked, this loss of confidence could ultimately have resulted in a run on GSE debt and an inability of the GSEs to finance their operations. Legislation establishing a stronger regulator—the Federal Housing Finance Agency (FHFA)—and effectively granting the U.S. Treasury the ability to bail out the GSEs was enacted on July 30, 2008, with the goal of providing reassurance to investors. However, investor confidence continued to deteriorate in subsequent weeks, as evidenced by further declines in share prices. Amid strong evidence that the agencies were in fact insolvent, the federal government decided to forestall any possibility of a run by placing the GSEs into conservatorship.[3]

GSE Reform

Any effort to lay out the contours of a new housing finance system needs to take into account the underlying weaknesses of the old system. Before laying out our proposal for reform, we first outline the problems with the existing GSE structure.

Fundamental Problems with the Existing GSE Structure

First and foremost among the problems is that the conflation of the GSEs' private and public roles is financially and fundamentally unsound. The implicit government backstop incentivized the GSEs to take on excessive risk. Because their debt was perceived as backed by the federal government, they were able to engage in a massive amount of arbitrage by borrowing at low rates and purchasing mortgage products with higher yields for their portfolios. By July 2008, their retained portfolios amounted to $1.6 trillion. While the source of the GSEs systemic risk was their retained portfolios, their guaranteeing of securities exposed them to an enormous amount of credit risk, amounting to a notional liability of $3.7 trillion by July 2008. Thus the future structure of mortgage finance should prevent the conflation of public goals and private goals within any one entity. Any public goals for mortgage finance should be provided explicitly by the federal government.

---

3. For further discussion of this episode, see Swagel (2009) and Hancock and Passmore (2010). Debt yields did not spike further over this period, suggesting that the market expected the government to step in ultimately (at some cost to shareholders).

Another problem with the precrisis GSE model arose from how the two primary public goals of the agencies interacted with each other. The GSEs were to provide liquidity in mortgage markets by purchasing and securitizing mortgages and then selling them with a credit guarantee attached. And they were to promote affordable housing by subsidizing mortgages for low- and moderate-income families. As it turned out, the pairing of these two goals was a key factor behind the GSEs' substantial credit losses.

On some levels, these goals are consistent. The GSEs provide liquidity in the mortgage market by providing credit guarantees for MBS. Mortgage-backed securities are thus made safer and easier to value for investors. This enhanced liquidity passes through in (small) part to borrowers through lower mortgage interest rates. Lower borrowing costs for home buyers can promote affordable housing goals, to the extent that low- and moderate-income families qualify for GSE mortgages.

However, the pricing of the guarantee is critical to whether the government is simply resolving a market failure through the GSEs or providing an out-and-out subsidy to investors (and borrowers, to the extent there is a pass-through to lower rates). In principle, a lack of liquidity in the secondary mortgage market can be addressed by charging an actuarially fair premium for the credit guarantee. The standard economic argument for insurance markets is that risk-averse individuals will want to insure fully against a possible loss of income if offered the actuarially fair premium. Indeed, as risk aversion increases, so does the willingness to pay an amount above the actuarially fair premium. The economic justification for a government role in providing insurance is that private insurers will fail to pool risk appropriately when the risk of default is not independent across the insured people, as is the case when housing markets are subject to price shocks that drive aggregate waves of default. The government role here is to pool the credit risk through a nationwide guarantee, thus providing liquidity to—and limiting the volatility of—the secondary mortgage market, but to do so while charging at least the actuarially fair premium (which accounts not only for the expected defaults in normal times but also for the tail risk of widespread and severe credit defaults).

However, the coexistence of a public goal of providing liquidity to mortgage markets and a public goal of promoting affordable housing leads to pressures to subsidize the guarantees by charging premiums that are less than actuarially fair. Charging less than the actuarially fair premium amounts to a subsidy—primarily to investors and secondarily to home buyers. Even if society desires to subsidize the purchase of homes, there are more direct and explicit ways to do so than underpricing the government guarantee of credit risk, such as through a tax credit for purchasing a house, direct housing vouchers, a tax credit that promotes saving for a down payment on a house, or even a direct and explicit government subsidy to reduce the mortgage interest rate for qualified borrowers. Moreover, these alternatives are less risky. The GSEs became insolvent largely because they increased their risk exposure by guaranteeing securities with lower credit scores and higher loan-to-value ratios during the mortgage credit boom, without charging commensurately higher guarantee fees (FHFA 2010a). The degree to which the GSEs' decisions to pursue this business strategy reflected direct pressure to subsidize housing as opposed to a desire to maintain market share and profitability so as to meet obligations to shareholders is unclear. However, even under the latter motivation, a combination of lax regulation, the perception of an implicit guarantee, and a lack of market discipline—all fostered in part by a public interest in subsidizing homeownership—allowed the GSEs to pursue this strategy.

As for the benefits of assigning the GSEs an affordable housing mission, the available evidence suggests that the GSEs—despite meeting their affordable housing goals—had only limited effects on the supply of affordable housing (Congressional Budget Office 2010). In a case study of underserved markets in the Cleveland area, Freeman, Galster, and Malega (2006) find little relationship between the degree of GSE secondary market purchases of mortgages and home price appreciation. Gabriel and Rosenthal (2005) present evidence suggesting that almost all of the sizable increase in homeownership in the 1990s can be attributed to household characteristics rather than to policies to lift credit barriers. Bostic and Gabriel (2006), in a study of the effects of GSE activities on homeownership rates, vacancy rates, and median home values in California, find only limited evidence of improved housing market performance. Other studies suggesting that the GSEs have not had a significant or sizable impact on homeownership among low-income and other underserved families include Feldman (2002) and Ambrose and Thibodeau (2004).

Separating out the Affordable Housing Mission

A nimble policy would accurately price the credit guarantee and then explicitly cross-subsidize from low-risk (or high-income) families to high-risk (or low-income) families. But the experience of recent years has demonstrated that such a policy is difficult—if not impossible—to achieve within a single entity (or two single entities), as the inherent difficulties and opaqueness of accurately pricing risk, combined with the political pressures that favor implicit cross-subsidizing, lead to mispricing the guarantee (thus leading to credit losses), while also failing to achieve housing support for low- and middle-income families. The goal of supporting affordable housing should therefore be detached from whatever entity is providing the credit guarantee and instead pursued through the tax code, or the Department of Housing and Urban Development, whether by expanding FHA programs or by providing direct, explicitly funded assistance to targeted borrowers.

Restrictions on Portfolio Holdings

The reform of the housing finance system should also address whether the entities that replace the securitization and guarantee activities of the GSEs should be allowed to hold portfolios. One consideration is whether such portfolios would serve a public purpose. Without the affordable housing goals, the entities succeeding the GSEs would not need to rely on portfolios in order to hold difficult-to-securitize multifamily mortgages or private securities backed by nonprime mortgages. In addition, as discussed earlier, analysis of primary and secondary market spreads suggests that the portfolios did not buffer mortgage originators from financial market shocks (Lehnert, Passmore, and Sherlund 2008).

The next consideration would be whether portfolios, even if they did not provide benefits, would present risks to the taxpayers. The key issue here is whether the portfolios would come to represent a systemic risk, as they did under the precrisis GSE model. The likelihood of this happening depends on the degree to which perceptions of an implicit guarantee on the debt of the new entities (that is, the means through which their portfolios would be financed) can be contained. These perceptions, in turn, hinge on whether the new structure includes features suggesting that the new entities, like the GSEs, have special privileges (including lower capital standards) or a special relationship with the federal government and whether the new entities (either by design or because of economies of scale) have the potential to become so large that they are viewed as too big to fail. All told, then, the degree to which the portfolios are restricted in size (or composition) should depend on the degree to which the entities replacing the GSEs' guarantee and securitization activities will be able to borrow at submarket rates. As we discuss below, our proposal calls for a more competitive market structure (subject to a narrowly defined guarantee), in which financial institutions—subject to capital requirements—can supply government-guaranteed securities, which thus should require fewer limits on portfolios.

Pricing the Credit Guarantee

Under our proposal, the government would provide credit guarantees on mortgage-backed securities, funded by a premium that is at least actuarially fair. Unlike the implicit government guarantee on the GSEs' obligations, this would be an explicit government guarantee, recorded in the federal budget.

We note, though, that the existence of an economic justification for a government role in guaranteeing credit risk does not necessarily make it good policy. As the recent experience of the GSEs makes clear, while the borrowing they did to maintain their portfolio holdings ultimately triggered the government takeover, the main source of their losses was related to credit. Advocates of fully privatizing the housing finance system are in effect arguing that the cost of government failure—in the form of political pressure to underprice the credit guarantee—trumps the benefits to be gained from addressing the market failure of the illiquidity stemming from the inability to pool the dependent credit risk.

Some argue that the benefits of addressing the market failure are small. Indeed, as noted earlier, the available evidence suggests that GSE guarantees have resulted in only modestly lower mortgage interest rates (and only for qualified mortgages) under normal mortgage market conditions. However, a key point is that the most important benefits from making credit guarantees available accrue during times of extreme market stress. In such times, the price demanded by investors to take on credit risk might soar, leading mortgage credit to become prohibitively expensive and, in turn, hurting the prospects for economic activity and leading to yet more market distress.

Of course, the recent episode has painfully illustrated that the costs of government failure can be immense. However, even if the lesson were that the risk of repeating such failure trumps all other considerations, it is not clear that policymakers can in practice eliminate the notion that they will stand behind at least some portion of the mortgage market going forward. Given the massive amount of government intervention in financial markets over the past three years, and especially given the efforts by the Treasury, the FHA, and the Federal Reserve to provide a government backstop for mortgages, investors are highly likely to assume an ongoing implicit—and possibly expansive—guarantee. And while the Dodd-Frank legislation aimed to address the problem of too big to fail, recent history suggests that an implicit guarantee could still extend to the largest financial institutions, which would encourage them to take on further mortgage credit risk.

With this inevitable moral hazard in place, the best outcome, then, is to make the guarantee explicit and limited, so as to minimize the risk of government failure. An essential feature of such a model is to price the guarantee correctly. Having just experienced a financial crisis that revealed a widespread inability to price sophisticated financial instruments accurately, we recognize the difficulty of this task. However, we offer two possible approaches. One strategy would be to set a fixed price ex ante that would more than cover the expected losses (including those associated with the tail risk of widespread defaults). By design, this price should be high enough such that take-up is limited to a fairly small share of the market under normal conditions. In periods of market stress, the guarantees would become more attractive to investors and market share would increase. Thus the relatively high price would both protect taxpayers and prevent sharp contractions in the supply of mortgage credit that have the potential to turn an episode of market stress into a wholesale financial crisis.

A second, and related, option would be for the government to choose explicitly the target share of mortgage credit that is guaranteed under normal conditions ex ante and to allow the price to be determined by auctioning the fixed number of guarantees. The government would simultaneously establish an above-market price (known as a "safety valve"), in which more guarantees could be purchased from the government. The safety valve price would not bind during times of normal market conditions, but it would mitigate the chances of disruption in the mortgage finance market. If conditions deteriorate in the private mortgage market, the safety valve price would increasingly bind, and thus the take-up for the government guarantee would increase. Similarly, as credit conditions again improve, the take-up for the government guarantee would decrease, as the safety valve price would be seen as too expensive for most market participants. Once the safety valve price is no longer binding, the share of government-backed mortgage credit would again return to the fairly small market share target.[4]

Under either approach, an essential feature of our proposal is to limit the government guarantee to easily priced "plain vanilla" high-quality mortgages. In light of the events of the past few years, we should have great skepticism about the ability of the government or the private sector to price accurately the risk of heterogeneous mortgages and mortgage-backed securities. We thus propose that eligible mortgages be restricted to those meeting simple parameters, such as a maximum cumulative loan-to-value ratio, fully documented income statements, and a minimum credit score.[5] Given the difficulty of monitoring underwriting and accurately pricing heterogeneous mortgage products, such a restriction is needed in order to limit the risk exposure of taxpayers. Under the approach where the government sets a price for credit guarantees ex ante, restricting the guarantee to a relatively homogeneous pool of securities is needed to mitigate the risk of mispricing the guarantee. Under the auction approach, the restrictions mitigate the potential for adverse selection where imperfect information allows investors to purchase the guarantee only for what they know to be riskier mortgages.

Our proposal for a government guarantee of only plain vanilla mortgages is grounded in the behavioral economics approach to regulation. Whereas others

---

4. The potential for government guarantees to serve as a backstop is also discussed by Scharfstein and Sunderam (chapter 7 of this volume) and by the Department of the Treasury and Department of Housing and Urban Development (2011). The backstop feature of our proposal differs from the one in these papers because we advocate for establishing a market mechanism for the backstop, rather than relying on regulatory determination of when to increase or decrease the government's market share. By preestablishing a quantity and a safety valve price, we aim to remove the political influences that can lead to government-subsidized guarantees during normal credit conditions and to persistent crowding out of the private sector after a crisis.

5. In light of the problems engendered by the GSEs relaxing their underwriting standards during the mortgage boom, such parameters should not be able to change with market conditions.

have promoted simple, default mortgages to protect borrowers from harming themselves due to their inability to distinguish among complex loan products (see, for example, Barr, Mullainathan, and Shafir 2009), our plan would protect taxpayers from regulators' inability to price properly the credit risk associated with a government guarantee fee.

More thought is needed to determine the optimal share of mortgages that would be covered by government guarantees under normal market conditions. Too small a share might restrict the ability of the entities providing the guarantee to ramp up their operations under times of market distress. That said, we advocate a share that is small enough such that the private mortgage finance market is able to redevelop and flourish (certainly the guarantees should account for less than a quarter of the market under normal conditions).[6]

Providing the government guarantee to only a narrow range of mortgage products would admittedly limit the number of borrowers who benefit. For example, a maximum cumulative loan-to-value ratio is akin to requiring a down payment, which would be a challenge for many lower-income households. Bucks and others (2009) find that the median net worth of families in the lowest fifth of the income distribution was $8,100 in 2007—not close to being enough for a 10 percent down payment on the median home in 2007 (the value of which was around $247,900).

As we discuss above, the GSEs' efforts to support affordable housing appear to have had limited impact (Congressional Budget Office 2010), and we believe that more effective and efficient support in this area could be delivered through the Department of Housing and Urban Development, either by expanding the FHA programs or by providing direct, explicitly funded assistance to targeted borrowers. With regard to the question of down payments in particular, although low- or no-equity loans have the potential to provide important benefits to low-income households, the mortgage crisis has demonstrated that they also have the potential to impose tremendous costs on these households if home prices depreciate. Thus government support would be better targeted at helping low-income households save for a down payment through tax credits or matched-savings programs (like individual development accounts) than at providing loans that require no down payment.

For qualifying mortgages, the guarantee would lower mortgage interest rates relative to a system with no guarantee because it would enhance the liquidity

6. Advocates of more widespread guarantees often argue that the thirty-year, fixed-rate mortgage would not exist in the absence of government guarantees and that such mortgages are integral to the financial security of many American families. While it is true that thirty-year, fixed-rate mortgages are not prevalent in other countries (which also lack entities like GSEs), it is unclear that their existence hinges on government guarantees, as the precrisis private market was able to provide jumbo thirty-year, fixed-rate mortgages without government guarantees.

of the associated MBS. However, having actuarially fair pricing is likely to raise mortgage interest rates relative to what they would be under the precrisis model. Together with the restrictions on scope, this higher pricing would reduce the market share of these loans, particularly during a credit boom. We view this as an upside, not a downside, of our proposal. It means that the government's role in the housing finance system will not exacerbate booms and their associated risks, like it did under the GSE model. It also means that the government will have more available resources to help should a boom lead to a crisis where credit markets seize up.[7]

In sum, our proposal provides some liquidity that increases the supply of mortgage credit in normal times, but the main purpose of the guarantees is to avert and mitigate a credit crisis.

Market Structure

The limits placed on eligibility for the government guarantee help to address the separate issue of market structure—how many and which entities would be able to offer the guarantee. A public utility model would allow only a few, highly regulated, private entities (for example, reconstituted Fannie and Freddie) to securitize and sell MBS with the federal guarantee. A more competitive model would allow many private financial institutions—subject to their capital requirements—to securitize and sell MBS with the federal guarantee.[8] A competitive model with numerous firms would mitigate the too-big-to-fail risk that was present with Fannie and Freddie. One drawback of the more competitive model involves the potential difficulty of monitoring underwriting and pricing the MBS credit risk. This could expose the government to higher risk. The existence of many securitizers might also limit the amount of liquidity associated with the guaranteed MBS market to the extent that the MBS of different institutions are not viewed as interchangeable.[9]

The trade-offs between the public and private production of a public good are fairly well established within the economics literature (see, for example, Hart, Shleifer, and Vishny 1996). The balance typically hinges on whether it is possible to address the quality concerns with private production through a

---

7. Of course, an important complement to the reforms suggested here is to regulate nonqualifying mortgages more tightly so as to limit credit booms.

8. See Congressional Budget Office (2010) for descriptions of the different market structure models.

9. Hall and Woodward (2009) argue that seemingly small differences in the amount of information provided by Fannie Mae and Freddie Mac about their MBS led to a small but noticeable difference in their pricing. Moreover, Freddie's MBS, for which investors had more information, had the higher price, because the information effectively made those securities less homogeneous from the perspective of investors.

complete and enforceable contract. For some public goods, it is nearly impossible to specify in advance every possible contingency. As Hart, Shleifer, and Vishny (1996, p. 3) write, a "government would not contract out the conduct of its foreign policy because unforeseen contingencies are a key part of foreign policy, and a private contractor would have enormous power to maximize its own wealth . . . without violating the letter of the contract." However, for relatively routine activities (such as snow removal), incomplete contracts are not a serious impediment to private production.

Thus a key consideration for the question of how many entities should replace the GSE securitization activities, as well as the degree to which these entities should be allowed to compete privately versus being subject to greater government restrictions, depends on the scope of the guarantee. Given that our proposal restricts the availability of the government guarantee to only MBS that contain plain vanilla, high-quality mortgages, it is consistent with many institutions being allowed to participate in the market. The restriction mitigates concerns about the limited ability of both the government and investors to monitor individual firms; it also enhances the liquidity benefit of the guarantees because the resulting securities are more likely to be viewed as homogeneous.[10]

Conclusion

This chapter calls for a significant overhaul of the U.S. housing finance system. We propose that the government have a limited role that consists of providing credit guarantees on mortgages, which provides some benefit to the mortgage market under normal conditions and, even more important, reduces the likelihood that periods of market strain will evolve into a credit crisis. A key feature of the plan is that the guarantees would be limited to high-quality mortgages that meet certain simple parameters specifying a maximum cumulative loan-to-value ratio, a minimum credit score, and a minimum degree of income documentation. Restricting the guarantee to plain vanilla mortgages enhances the odds that the guarantee can be priced in an actuarially fair way so as to limit the risk to taxpayers. The guarantee is designed to apply to a small market share during times of normal credit conditions, but also to provide for a ramping up of government involvement in the secondary market as credit conditions deteriorate. The affordable housing mission of the GSEs would be transferred to other parts

10. Our proposal to rely on a competitive market to provide the government guarantee is similar to what Marron and Swagel (2010) propose. We differ from them in not requiring financial institutions to take a first-loss position on any MBS credit losses. Our requirement that the guarantee be limited to plain vanilla mortgages and our above-market, safety valve pricing structure both would presumably be consistent with their plan, although they do not specifically support (or reject) these components.

of the government, increasing transparency and removing pressures and incentives to underprice the guarantee. Relative to the precrisis system (all else equal) mortgage interest rates on loans covered by the guarantee would be somewhat higher and the market share of these loans would be smaller. But, unlike the precrisis system, this role for government would be less likely to exacerbate credit booms and their costs.

In terms of market structure, we propose that private financial institutions be allowed to issue mortgage-backed securities with the government guarantees. Because the guarantees would be restricted to mortgages that meet simple criteria, the costs of monitoring would not be large, implying that many firms can participate in the activity in a relatively competitive environment (that is, the heavy regulation associated with a public utility model of housing finance would not be needed). The well-defined restrictions on qualified mortgages also mean that the resulting MBS would be more likely to be viewed as interchangeable, which would enhance market liquidity.

References

Ambrose, Brent W., and Thomas G. Thibodeau. 2004. "Have the GSE Affordable Housing Goals Increased the Supply of Mortgage Credit?" *Regional Science and Urban Economics* 34, no. 3: 263–73.

Barr, Michael S., Sendhil Mullainathan, and Eldar Shafir. 2009. "The Case for Behaviorally Informed Regulation." In *New Perspectives on Regulation,* edited by David Moss and John Cisternino, pp. 25–61. Cambridge, Mass.: Tobin Project.

Bernanke, Ben S. 2007. "GSE Portfolios, Systemic Risk, and Affordable Housing." Remarks before the Annual Convention and Techworld. Independent Community of Bankers of America, Honolulu, Hawaii, March 6.

Bostic, Raphael W., and Stuart A. Gabriel. 2006. "Do the GSEs Matter to Low-Income Housing Markets? An Assessment of the Effects of the GSE Loan Purchase Goals on California Housing Outcomes." *Journal of Urban Economics* 59, no. 3: 458–75.

Bucks, Brian K., Arthur B. Kennickell, Traci L. Mach, and Kevin B. Moore. 2009. "Changes in U.S. Family Finances from 2004 to 2007: Evidence from the Survey of Consumer Finances." *Federal Reserve Bulletin* 95 (February): A1–A56.

Congressional Budget Office. 2010. "Fannie Mae, Freddie Mac, and the Federal Role in the Secondary Mortgage Market." Washington (December).

Department of the Treasury and Department of Housing and Urban Development. 2011. *Reforming America's Housing Finance Market: A Report to Congress.* Washington.

Feldman, Ron J. 2002. "Mortgage Rates, Homeownership Rates, and Government-Sponsored Enterprises." *The Region [2001 annual report issue]* (April): 5–23.

FHFA (Federal Housing Finance Agency). 2010a. "Data on the Risk Characteristics and Performance of Single-Family Mortgages Originated from 2001 through 2008 and Financed in the Secondary Market." Washington (September).

————. 2010b. "Fannie Mae and Freddie Mac Single-Family Guarantee Fees in 2008 and 2009." Washington (July).

Frame, W. Scott, and Lawrence J. White. 2005. "Fussing and Fuming over Fannie and Freddie: How Much Smoke, How Much Fire?" *Journal of Economic Perspectives* 19, no. 2 (Spring): 159–84.

Freeman, Lance, George Galster, and Ron Malega. 2006. "The Impact of Secondary Mortgage Market and GSE Purchases on Underserved Neighborhood Housing Markets: A Cleveland Case Study." *Urban Affairs Review* 42, no. 2: 193–223.

Gabriel, Stuart, and Stuart Rosenthal. 2005. "Homeownership in the 1980s and 1990s: Aggregate Trends and Racial Gaps." *Journal of Urban Economics* 57, no. 1: 101–27.

GAO (Government Accountability Office). 1996. "Housing Enterprises: Potential Impacts of Severing Government Sponsorship." GAO/GGD-96-120. Washington.

González-Rivera, Gloria. 2001. "Linkages between Secondary and Primary Markets for Mortgages." *Journal of Fixed Income* 11, no. 1: 29–36.

Gramlich, Edward M. 2002. "Consumption and the Wealth Effect: The United States and the United Kingdom." Remarks before the International Bond Congress. London, February 20.

Hall, Robert, and Susan Woodward. 2009. "What to Do about Fannie Mae and Freddie?" *WordPress,* January 28.

Hamilton, James. 2010. "Looking Back at the Great Recession." *EconoMonitor,* December 29.

Hancock, Diana, and Wayne Passmore. 2010. "An Analysis of Government Guarantees and the Functioning of Asset-Backed Securities Markets." Finance and Economics Discussion Series 2010-46. Washington: Federal Reserve Board.

Hart, Oliver, Andrei Shleifer, and Robert W. Vishny. 1996. "The Proper Scope of Government: Theory and an Application to Prisons." NBER Working Paper 5744. Cambridge, Mass.: National Bureau of Economic Research.

Lehnert, Andreas, Wayne Passmore, and Shane M. Sherlund. 2008. "GSEs, Mortgage Rates, and Secondary Market Activities." *Journal of Real Estate Finance and Economics* 36, no. 3 (April): 343–63.

Marron, Donald, and Phillip Swagel. 2010. "Whither Fannie and Freddie? A Proposal for Reforming the Housing GSEs." Washington: Economic Policies for the 21st Century (May).

Naranjo, Andy, and Alden L. Toevs. 2002. "The Effects of Purchases of Mortgages and Securitization by Government-Sponsored Enterprises on Mortgage Yield Spreads and Volatility." *Journal of Real Estate Finance and Economics* 25, no. 2-3: 173–96.

Passmore, Wayne, Shane M. Sherlund, and Gillian Burgess. 2005. "The Effect of Housing Government-Sponsored Enterprises on Mortgage Rates." *Real Estate Economics* 33, no. 3 (Fall): 427–63.

Shulyatyeva, Yelena. 2010. "Back to Living with Mom and Dad." *BNP Paribas U.S. Daily Economic Spotlight,* September 24.

Swagel, Phillip. 2009. "The Financial Crisis: An Inside View." *Brookings Papers on Economic Activity* (Spring): 1–63.

5

Eliminating the GSEs as Part of Comprehensive Housing Finance Reform

PETER J. WALLISON

In the wake of the financial crisis of 2008, the government-sponsored enter-prises (GSEs) Fannie Mae and Freddie Mac have become insolvent corpora-tions operating under the control of the federal government, yet still mainstays of the U.S. housing finance system. There is general agreement in Congress, ranging from Jeb Hensarling on the right to Barney Frank on the left,[1] that Fan-nie and Freddie should be eliminated. There is much less agreement on what should replace them or indeed whether they should be replaced at all. This chapter argues that Fannie and Freddie should be eliminated and not replaced because the U.S. housing finance system would function well without them, or any other government financial support, and the removal of any government role in housing finance would free the U.S. taxpayers from the costs of yet another massive bailout in the future. However, because of the central role of the GSEs in the current housing finance system, removing them from that system without a replacement is complicated and depends on factors that do not exist today.

Accordingly, in this chapter I argue that the GSEs—or indeed any replace-ments serving a similar purpose—are no longer necessary, discuss why a con-tinuing role for government in the housing finance system would be faulty

---

1. Kudlow (2010). Frank stated, "I hope by next year we'll have abolished Fannie and Fred-die. . . . It was a great mistake to push lower-income people into housing they couldn't afford and couldn't really handle once they had it." He then added, "I had been too sanguine about Fannie and Freddie."

public policy, detail how the housing finance system should be reformed so it will function without any government support, and explain how the GSEs can be eliminated or privatized without serious disruption of housing finance.[2]

U.S. Government's Financial Support for Housing

The U.S. government's involvement with housing finance began in 1934 with the creation of the Federal Housing Administration (FHA), which had authority to insure mortgages up to 100 percent of the loan amount. At the time, there was no national market for mortgages, many local and regional differences in mortgage terms, very low loan-to-value (LTV) ratios of 50 to 60 percent, and a homeownership rate of less than 44 percent. Mortgages tended to be relatively short term, with bullet payments at the end. If a mortgage could not be refinanced at the end of its term—and many in the Depression could not be— it was foreclosed. The purpose of the FHA was to overcome the reluctance of banks and others to make mortgage loans during this period. Over time, the FHA had a major role in standardizing mortgage terms, increasing acceptable LTV ratios to approximately 80 percent, and encouraging the development of mortgages that amortized over multiyear periods (Vandell 1995).

Although the FHA could overcome the reluctance of lenders to make long-term mortgage loans, it could not provide them with the necessary liquidity. That role fell to Fannie Mae, which was originally chartered in 1938 to buy mortgages that had been FHA insured. By purchasing these loans, Fannie Mae provided banks and other mortgage originators with the liquidity to make more mortgages and thus finance the growth of homeownership and the U.S. housing industry. By 1950, the homeownership rate in the United States had risen to 50 percent (Vandell 1995).

Savings and Loan Associations

During the Depression era, Congress also created the legal structure for a system of federal savings and loan associations, depository institutions that were limited to making loans for residential housing. Under a Federal Reserve rule known as Regulation Q, deposit interest rates had been capped since 1934. In 1966, in order to give the savings and loans an advantage over banks in competing for deposits—and thus to give a financial preference to housing—the Federal Reserve adjusted the cap so that savings and loans could pay one-quarter point more than banks for their deposits. The result was rapid growth in the savings and loan industry, which quadrupled in size between 1966 and 1979.

2. The arguments in this chapter are filled out in greater detail in Wallison, Pollock, and Pinto (2011), a white paper on reform of U.S. housing finance policy.

When the rise of money market mutual funds made it impossible for the federal government to continue to control deposit interest rates, Congress authorized the removal of deposit interest rate caps in the Monetary Control Act of 1980.[3] With the elimination of these rate restrictions, savings and loans that were holding low-interest-rate thirty-year mortgages became exposed to much higher market rates for their deposits, and large portions of the industry became insolvent. The losses far exceeded the amount in the savings and loan insurance fund, and the taxpayers eventually had to absorb a loss estimated at approximately $150 billion.

Government-Sponsored Enterprises

In 1968, for budgetary reasons, Fannie Mae was "privatized" in the sense that it was allowed to sell its equity shares to the public. This removed it from the federal budget, but Fannie retained sufficient ties to the government—including a congressional charter and a "mission" to establish and maintain a secondary market in mortgages—that it became a quasi-public, quasi-private company known as a government-sponsored enterprise. In 1970 Congress chartered an identical GSE, Freddie Mac, primarily to provide liquidity to the savings and loan industry in the way that Fannie was providing liquidity to banks and authorized both GSEs to buy conventional mortgages in addition to those insured by the FHA or other government agencies. The congressional charters of both GSEs required that they purchase only mortgages that would be acceptable investments for institutional investors.[4]

In 1992 Congress enacted Title XIII of the Housing and Community Development Act of 1992,[5] legislation intended to give low- and moderate-income borrowers better access to mortgage credit through Fannie Mae and Freddie Mac. The act authorized the Department of Housing and Urban Development (HUD) to establish affordable housing goals for the GSEs. These goals, which were increased substantially during the Clinton and second Bush administrations, required a certain percentage of all the loans that Fannie and Freddie bought to be loans to borrowers at or below the median income in the area in which they lived. This put Fannie and Freddie in direct competition with the

3. Depository Institutions Deregulation and Monetary Control Act of 1980, Pub. L. no. 96-221; 94 Stat. 132, effective March 31, 1980.

4. Section 1719 of Fannie Mae's charter states, "The operations of the corporation . . . shall be confined . . . to mortgages which are deemed by the corporation to be of such quality, type, and class as to meet, generally, the *purchase standards imposed by private institutional mortgage investors*" [emphasis added] (www.law.cornell.edu/uscode/html/uscode12/usc_sec_12_00001719—-000-.html).

5. Housing and Community Development Act of 1992, Pub. L. no. 102-550, 106 Stat. 3672, H.R. 5334, enacted October 28, 1992.

FHA. Under the requirements of HUD's affordable housing goals, by 2008 Fannie and Freddie held the credit risk—either through mortgages they retained in their portfolios or through mortgages they securitized—for 12 million subprime and Alt-A loans. This was about 40 percent of their single-family book of business. At the same time, the FHA had insured the credit risk for, and other government agencies held, about 5 million subprime and Alt-A loans (Pinto 2010b).

As a result of defaults on the subprime and other high-risk loans that they acquired under HUD's affordable housing requirements, Fannie and Freddie are now insolvent. Treasury has already contributed approximately $150 billion to cover their losses. Their regulator, the Federal Housing Finance Agency (FHFA), has projected that they will eventually require between $221 billion and $363 billion in government support. This may be optimistic and will depend heavily on the direction of home prices in the years ahead.

Federal Housing Administration

By the late 1970s, the role of the FHA had changed. Competition from the GSEs and private mortgage insurers had pushed the FHA out of the business of insuring middle-class mortgages; with the support of Congress, it began to concentrate increasingly on low-income borrowers and to see its role as an element of the government's social rather than its economic policy. During the 1960s and 1970s, to meet its social responsibilities, it significantly increased the LTVs of the mortgages it would insure and otherwise lowered its underwriting standards. Although this increased its credit risks, its losses were low because of the secular growth of housing values during this period. During the period of stagflation in the 1970s, however, and in the regional recessions of the 1980s, substantial losses began to show up at the FHA, requiring it to adopt tighter underwriting standards.

Still, as the government's authorized subprime lender, the FHA seems to believe that it has an obligation to accept significant losses in pursuit of its mandate. Its claim rate has been excessive for many decades. Over a thirty-five-year period (1975–2009), the agency's cumulative claim rate averaged 10.5 percent, and over 1992–2009 it averaged 10 percent. During the boom years of 1995–2003, the claim rate still averaged nearly 8 percent, while during the bust periods (1980–85 and 2005–08), it averaged 18 percent. For 2010–17, the FHA has projected an 8 percent average claim rate even with an expected 33 percent increase in home prices over 2011–20 (FHA 2000, 2010). Although the FHA's accounting is difficult to penetrate, and the agency claims that its losses are fully covered by the fees it charges for its insurance, a recent study by Barclays Capital suggests that the imbedded losses at the FHA are substantial: "We project cumulative default rates in the 20 percent area on average, with loss given default rates of 60 percent. This represents average losses of about 12 points, of which 8.5

points could flow back to taxpayers. On an original balance of $1.4 trillion, this translates to $130 billion" (Barclays Capital 2010).

By the 1980s, the operations of both the FHA and the GSEs had created the beginnings of a national market—even an international market—in mortgages. Terms had been standardized, and the technology of securitization had been sufficiently developed so that it was possible for many kinds of institutional investors—insurance companies, pension funds, and mutual funds as well as banks and other depositories—to hold the credit risk of conventional mortgages. Fannie and Freddie, which were perceived in the market as having the implicit backing of the U.S. government, provided an important bridge between mortgage originators and the ultimate investors by placing their guarantee on the securities that were backed by pools of mortgages (mortgage-backed securities, or MBS). This eliminated much of the risk for these investors and facilitated the sale of the GSEs' mortgage-backed securities.

At the same time, following their charter requirements, Fannie and Freddie established underwriting standards for down payments, debt-to-income ratios, borrower information, and mortgage quality that limited their risks and kept delinquencies and defaults at very low levels. However, the existence of the GSE guarantee created moral hazard, in which neither investors in the GSEs' mortgage-backed securities nor the buyers of their debt securities cared about the quality of the loans they were buying; this allowed Fannie and Freddie—responding to government requirements—to acquire vast numbers of subprime and Alt-A loans that were eventually the source of their downfall.

Finally, in the Housing and Economic Recovery Act of 2008 (HERA), which toughened the regulation of Fannie and Freddie, Congress also increased the conforming loan limit for the GSEs in areas with high housing costs. The new limits in high-cost areas had the effect of increasing the size of the mortgages that Fannie and Freddie could purchase, so that buyers of homes in the million dollar range could have access to the benefits conferred by eligibility for purchase by the GSEs.

From this brief survey, two facts stand out. The government role in housing finance has been successful in standardizing mortgage terms and creating a national market for mortgages, largely through the sale and distribution of mortgage-backed securities. This has drawn financial resources from institutional investors in the United States and around the world, supplementing the funds previously supplied primarily by banks and by savings and loans. But these benefits have come at a huge cost to U.S. taxpayers, who have supplied in the past and will have to supply in the future hundreds of billions of dollars to bail out the losses incurred by government in its financial support for housing. In addition, once the government gets involved in assisting housing finance, its role will expand over time.

Deficiencies of Government Financial Support for Housing

The massive government losses described above occurred because government agencies do not have either the incentives or the means to price accurately for the risks they are taking. Even if that were not true and the government could price for risk like an insurance company, political pressures would not allow a government agency to accumulate the reserves (as insurance companies do) during the good times that would be necessary to meet its obligations during the inevitable bad times. This has been shown not only by the experience of the FHA but also by that of the Federal Deposit Insurance Corporation (FDIC),[6] the National Flood Insurance Program,[7] and the Pension Benefit Guarantee Corporation (PBGC).[8] As a result, virtually every government intervention in the housing finance market has resulted in substantial losses for the taxpayers.

Many of the proposals making the rounds in Washington today rely on government guarantees of MBS issued by special companies formed for the purpose of securitizing mortgages. These are an obvious attempt to avoid the mistake of extending a government guarantee—implicit or explicit—to specific entities such as Fannie Mae and Freddie Mac. It is likely that the Obama

6. When the deposit insurance system was reformed in 1991 in response to the failure of the Federal Savings and Loan Insurance Corporation, Congress placed a limit on the size of the deposit insurance fund that the FDIC could accumulate to meet the demands of a future crisis. Since 1996, the FDIC has been prohibited by law from charging premiums to well-capitalized and stable institutions. As a result, between 1996 and 2006, institutions representing 98 percent of deposits paid no deposit insurance premiums. When the financial crisis hit in 2008, the FDIC's insurance fund was inadequate to meet the losses incurred by the FDIC. In 2009 FDIC chair Sheila Bair observed, "An important lesson going forward is we need to be building up these funds in good times so you can draw down upon them in bad times." Instead, once the bad times hit, the FDIC was forced to raise its premiums at the worst possible moment, thereby reinforcing the impact of the down cycle. Principle 2 will discuss in greater detail the need for countercyclical reserving policies. Center on Federal Financial Institutions (2005). See also Congressional Budget Office (2005). "Currently, 93 percent of FDIC-insured institutions, which hold 98 percent of insured deposits, pay nothing for deposit insurance."

7. As reported by Thomas Fink in *USA Today*, "FEMA Administrator Craig Fugate says the debt results partly from Congress restraining insurance rates to encourage the purchase of coverage, which is required for property owners with a federally backed mortgage. . . . 'It is not run as a business,' Fugate said. Congress' Government Accountability Office said in April that the program is 'by design, not actuarially sound' because it has no cash reserves to pay for catastrophes such as Katrina and sets rates that 'do not reflect actual flood risk.' Raising insurance rates or limiting coverage is hard. 'The board of directors of this program is Congress,' Fugate said. 'They are very responsive to individuals who are being adversely affected.'" Fink (2010).

8. As of the end of fiscal 2010, the Pension Benefit Guaranty Corporation reported a deficit of $23 billion. "In part, it is a result of the fact that the premiums PBGC charges are insufficient to pay for all the benefits that PBGC insures, and other factors." PBGC (2010).

administration's plan will embrace an idea like this. But it is an illusion to believe that the government will be taking fewer risks and suffering fewer losses if the government is only guaranteeing MBS. A government guarantee will eliminate investor concern about both the quality of the underlying loans and the financial capacity of the issuer. Like deposit insurance, this government role will create moral hazard; the buyers of the MBS will not be concerned about either the quality of the underlying mortgages or the financial condition of the issuers of the MBS. The government, in turn, to protect itself and the taxpayers, will have to rely on regulation of the issuing firm—whether a GSE or a wholly private entity—so that the issuer does not take excessive risk. As we have seen again and again, regulation has not worked to keep banks insured by the GSEs from taking risks, and there is no reason to believe that it will prevent the issuers of MBS from doing the same. Accordingly, any continuing government support for housing finance is highly likely to result in massive taxpayer losses and thus, as a matter of policy, should be rejected as a valid policy path.

Second, experience in the housing field shows that the benefits associated with government financial support cannot be effectively limited. Government financial support for housing is a subsidy from the taxpayers to the buyers and sellers of homes, no matter where in the process the government support is injected, and as such it confers a benefit on all home buyers and sellers who are eligible to receive it. Accordingly, it is difficult—and probably impossible over the long term—to limit the availability of this benefit. No matter where the line is drawn, there is always a group that is excluded. This inevitably produces political pressure to provide excluded groups with access to the benefits of government support. Because these groups are always more organized than the taxpayers, they are eventually able to gain support in Congress for inclusion within the eligible category. Thus, in 1992, Congress adopted affordable housing requirements for Fannie and Freddie, so that low-income and other borrowers who could not meet traditional mortgage standards would have access to the benefits that the GSEs conferred on the middle class. Similarly, in 2008, in the HERA,[9] Congress conferred the same benefits on high-income constituents by increasing the conforming loan limits of the GSEs so that they could buy mortgages on million dollar homes in areas where housing prices are especially high.

Thus, once a government subsidy program is established, it will expand to cover larger and larger portions of the population and will drive out all competing private sector activity, just as Fannie and Freddie drove all private competition out of the areas of the housing market where they were allowed to operate.

---

9. Housing and Economic Recovery Act of 2008, Pub. L. no. 110–289, H.R. 322, enacted July 30, 2008.

Arguments in Support of Government Involvement

Judging by the proposals that are circulating today in Washington, there is still a great deal of support for retaining some continuing role for Fannie and Freddie or for creating a new system in which the government will still be responsible for backing some portion of the housing finance market. Given the deficiencies and taxpayer losses associated with past government efforts, what arguments are advanced to support yet another program of government financial support for housing?

The easiest of these arguments to dismiss is the one most often cited—that government backing is necessary to assure that a thirty-year, fixed-rate mortgage is available for home buyers. This one is simply a myth. Jumbo fixed-rate, thirty-year mortgages, which by definition are not government backed, are freely available and advertised extensively on the Internet. A Google search for "jumbo thirty-year fixed-rate mortgage" turns up dozens of offers. They might be somewhat more expensive than a government-backed thirty-year, fixed-rate mortgage, but that is only true because the taxpayers are subsidizing the government-backed version. Why it makes sense for the taxpayers to subsidize a mortgage that people can freely get without taxpayer assistance is a mystery, particularly when that particular mortgage does not make much sense as a matter of public policy. It amortizes very slowly, so it does not create much equity in a home for many years, and at a time when we are finally recognizing the downside of leverage in homeownership, the thirty-year, fixed-rate mortgage encourages maximum homeowner leverage.

Another argument is that the mortgage market must be assured of a steady flow of funds; otherwise, the process of building homes will be slowed or interrupted for periods when mortgage money is not readily available. One has to wonder why the housing business deserves to be protected against changes in the availability of funds, when every other industry has to live with this cyclical problem. Moreover, the fact that housing finance has been protected all these years against the fluctuations that every other industry has to bear probably has something to do with the bubbles to which this industry seems particularly prone. Concern about the availability of funds is likely to reduce risk taking and speculation, which is something that, as a matter of policy, we ought to encourage.

A third argument—sometimes explicit and otherwise implicit—is that institutional investors will buy U.S. mortgages, or MBS backed by U.S. mortgages, only if they are supported by a government guarantee. This is probably the key reason for the support this idea enjoys in Washington, and it would certainly be true if the quality of the mortgages were low. But there is no reason why mortgages allowed into the securitization system should be of low quality. Until the introduction of the affordable housing requirements for Fannie and Freddie, the GSEs maintained high underwriting standards and never suffered substantial losses on the mortgages they held or guaranteed. Even in the current crisis, their delinquency rates among *prime* mortgages have been less than 3 percent, while their delinquency rates on the subprime and Alt-A loans they acquired because of the affordable housing goals have ranged from 13.3 to 17.3 percent (Pinto 2010a, chart 53). Accordingly, the key to a successful mortgage market is not providing a government guarantee—which will inevitably cause serious losses to the taxpayers—but ensuring that the mortgages made in the market are of prime quality.

Finally, the argument is made that only with government backing can we provide the concessionary rates or other benefits that will enable low-income families to become homeowners. This is true, but it does not mean that the entire housing market has to be government backed—only the portion that is targeted to low-income home buyers.

Weighing the Policy Arguments for and against Government Backing

If we weigh taxpayer losses in the balance, the policy arguments in favor of government involvement in housing finance seem weak indeed. Over the nearly seventy years that the government has been attempting to assist housing finance, the taxpayers have been called on to rescue one or another specially designed government program every time, and the costs—by the time the GSEs' and the FHA's losses have been added up—will have run into the hundreds of billions of dollars. We did get a nationwide mortgage market, a standardized mortgage, and an efficient system for turning a mortgage into a suitable and liquid investment for an institutional investor, but the costs for the taxpayer have been horrific.

In other important areas, government involvement in the housing finance system has also been a failure. First, as shown in table 5-1, prepared by Dwight Jaffee, the United States ranks last among a number of developed countries in terms of the average interest rate on residential mortgages. This is remarkable, considering that in most other developed countries there is no direct government backing of mortgages. Moreover, government financial backing has not succeeded in raising the U.S. homeownership rate over the long term. This rate reached 64 percent in 1964 and remained there for thirty years. The rate began to climb when Fannie and Freddie were making subprime and Alt-A loans under the affordable housing requirements imposed by Congress and administered by HUD, but since the insolvency of the GSEs (because of those very loans) and their inability to sustain affordable housing lending, U.S. homeownership rates seem to be returning to the historic rate of 64 percent. When considered among a large number of developed countries, the United States ranks seventeenth in homeownership (Pollock 2010), and among Jaffee's list of countries it ranks

Table 5-1. *Performance of Mortgage Markets in Europe and the United States, 2008[a]*

Percent

Country	Mortgage to GDP ratio (1)	Rate of owner occupancy (2)	Coefficient of co-variation housing starts (3)	Standard deviation of house price inflation (4)	Mortgage interest rate average level (5)	Mortgage interest rate average spread[b] (6)
Austria	25.3	57.0	8.3	2.6	5.12	0.66
Belgium	39.8	78.0	16.3	4.0	5.87	1.37
Denmark	95.3	54.0	40.8	6.1	5.96	1.41
Finland	47.5	59.0	11.0	3.4	4.5	0.05
France	35.9	57.4	16.4	5.5	4.93	0.53
Germany	46.1	43.2	30.1	0.8	5.27	0.97
Iceland	129.0	82.5	56.3	9.8	5.01	0.64
Ireland	80.0	74.5	35.8	11.5	4.69	0.22
Italy	19.8	80.0	47.0	3.1	5.25	0.64
Luxembourg	43.5	75.0	19.2	4.3	4.33	−0.16
Netherlands	99.1	57.0	10.2	5.5	5.17	0.77
Norway	55.7	77.0	21.1	5.0	6.54	1.61
Portugal	63.3	76.0	31.5	5.4	5.15	0.61
Spain	62.0	84.5	32.5	2.5	4.38	−0.09
Sweden	60.6	52.0	53.9	5.1	4.05	−0.49
United Kingdom	80.5	59.0	10.5	5.0	5.32	0.42
Euro average	61.5	66.6	27.6	5.0	5.10	0.57
U.S. average	83.6	67.8	24.9	5.5	6.57	1.82
U.S. rank (of 17)	4	9	9	4	1	1

Source: Jaffee (2010, p. 10).

a. Unless noted otherwise, the data are all from European Mortgage Federation (2008), an annual fact book that contains comprehensive mortgage and housing market data for 1998 to 2008 for the sixteen Western European countries and the United States. Statistical measures are computed with annual data by country for 1998–2008.

b. The mortgage interest rate spread (column 6) equals the mortgage interest rate (column 5) relative to the government bond rate of each country, derived from the International Financial Statistics of the International Monetary Fund.

ninth. In other words, U.S. taxpayers have received very little for the huge costs they have borne.

Accordingly, there seems to be an overwhelming policy argument against continuing any government role in support for housing finance. We have already realized all of the benefits we are likely to get from government involvement—a

Figure 5-1. *Home Price Index, 1890–2010*

Index (1890 = 100)

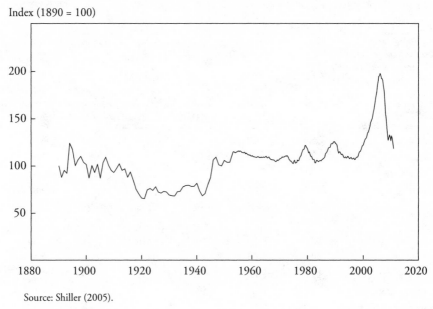

Source: Shiller (2005).

national mortgage market, standardized mortgages, and a workable system for bringing in funding from institutional investors—and it is likely that if we bring the government in again we will have another taxpayer catastrophe on our hands some years from now. The only remaining question is whether it will be possible to sustain a securitization system that allows institutional investors to support U.S. housing finance without a government guarantee on either mortgages or MBS.

A Housing Finance Market without a Government Role

How would the housing market function without government support? The best way to start this analysis is to contrast the current state of the housing market with what prevailed in the past. We are now in the midst of a continuing deflation of a massive housing bubble, by far the largest bubble in our history. Figure 5-1 shows its growth in relation to bubbles of the past and its subsequent deflation.

At least three housing bubbles are visible in this figure, one around 1980, another around 1990, and then the big one that started in about 1997, extended until 2007, and is now quickly deflating. Why were the two earlier bubbles so small and short-lived in comparison to the most recent and destructive one? As I noted earlier, by 2008 the GSEs were exposed to the credit risk of 12 million subprime and Alt-A loans, while the FHA and other government agencies

Table 5-2. *Number of Subprime and Alt-A Loans and Unpaid Principal,*
by Entity

Entity	Subprime and Alt-A loans (number)	Unpaid principal (dollars)
Fannie Mae and Freddie Mac	12 million	1.8 trillion
FHA and other federal entities[a]	5 million	0.6 trillion
Community Redevelopment Act and HUD programs	2.2 million	0.3 trillion
Total federal government	19.2 million	2.7 trillion
Other[b]	7.8 million	1.9 trillion
Total	27 million	4.6 trillion

Source: Pinto (2010b, p. 4).

a. Includes Veterans Administration, Federal Home Loan Bank, and others.

b. Includes subprime and Alt-A private-label MBS issued by Countrywide, Wall Street, and others.

accounted for an additional 5 million. According to Edward Pinto's research, approximately 2.2 million loans of this kind were also made by banks under the Community Reinvestment Act or by mortgage banks such as Countrywide under a HUD program that pledged them to reduce down payments and lower underwriting standards generally in order to assist low-income families to buy homes. All these weak and high-risk loans were, in one way or another, the result of government policies.

An additional 7.8 million loans were securitized by Countrywide and others, sold through Wall Street underwriters, and still outstanding before the financial crisis. In an important sense, these loans were also the government's responsibility, because the funds the government poured into subprime and Alt-A loans during the 1990s and the 2000s drove the growth of the bubble, which in turn made it possible for Countrywide and others to originate and sell the private-label MBS that formed about one-third of the weak and high-risk mortgages outstanding.

Thus approximately 27 million subprime and Alt-A loans were outstanding in the United States before the financial crisis—about half of all U.S. mortgages. Table 5-2 summarizes these numbers and the dollar amounts involved.

The earlier bubbles had a far different composition. The 1980 bubble occurred at a time when subprime mortgages were very rare and Alt-A mortgages were almost nonexistent. When that bubble collapsed, the foreclosure starts, according to Mortgage Bankers Association data, peaked at 0.87 percent in 1983.[10] When the 1990 bubble collapsed, subprime and other high-risk loans

10. Mortgage Bankers Association, National Delinquency Survey (www.mbaa.org/Research andForecasts/ProductsandSurveys/NationalDelinquencySurvey.htm).

were still few, and foreclosure starts peaked at 1.32 percent in 1994. However, in the 1997–2007 bubble, almost half of which consisted of subprime or otherwise weak and high-risk loans, foreclosure starts have thus far reached 5.3 percent in 2009, even though the government has established various programs to prevent or reduce foreclosures.

In other words, there is very strong evidence that if mortgages are of prime quality the likelihood of a large and long-lived bubble is much reduced. This leads to the conclusion that one way to assure that a securitization system for housing finance will work—without any government financial backing—is simply to ensure that the vast preponderance of mortgages, and all securitized mortgages, are of prime quality. Prime-quality mortgages are good investments. Historically, and even during the financial crisis, prime mortgages did not suffer high rates of delinquency. For this reason, after the markets return to normal, there should be no difficulty placing MBS based on prime-quality mortgages with institutional investors in the United States and around the world.

Regulation is necessary in this case because there is strong evidence in the history of housing bubbles that human nature creates repeating market failures. As a bubble grows, people come to believe that "this time it's different." Borrowers seek to keep their down payments and monthly payments low, with riskier loans and more leverage, while they try to buy homes that have become more expensive. Lenders believe that the increasing value of homes limits their risks even on riskier mortgages. Not seeing any increase in delinquencies while the bubble is growing (because higher home prices allow homeowners who cannot meet their mortgage obligations to sell or refinance the house), investors are willing to buy MBS backed by weak loans. As we have seen time and again, all these market participants are wrong. Inside the bubble, risks are growing substantially, and when the bubble finally deflates the losses can be so severe that, as we saw in 2008, a serious financial panic erupts. Appropriate regulation can break this cycle, by requiring all securitized mortgages to meet certain quality tests.

The necessary regulation would not be complicated. It would require all securitized mortgages to be of prime quality. This means that the borrower, among other requirements, has made a 10–20 percent down payment or, for a refinancing, has equity in the home of at least 20 percent, a debt-to-income ratio of no more than 38 percent, and a Fair Isaac Corporation (FICO) credit score of at least 660. The rules would be less stringent for loans held in the portfolios of banks and other financial institutions, but there would have to be disclosure of the quality of the mortgages outstanding so that participants in the market understand how many of the mortgages outstanding do not meet prime standards. This would allow them to estimate the severity of any subsequent downturn.

Correspondingly, given that the market share of nonprime loans tends to grow as a boom develops, these loans—characterized by low or no down payments, higher debt ratios, impaired credit, reduced or negative loan amortization, loans to investors or speculators, and other underwriting standards not present in prime loans—must be limited to a relatively small percentage of all mortgage loans. These loans would be deemed unsuitable to serve as collateral for private MBS, covered bonds, and Federal Home Loan Bank (FHLB) advances.[11] This provision would be enforced by the Securities and Exchange Commission in the case of securities and bonds and the FHFA in the case of FHLB advances.

Other requirements would be a one-page mortgage information form, signed by the borrower when the purchase price and terms are negotiated—not at the closing when there are pressures to proceed no matter what the costs. The form would describe, among other things, the major features of the mortgage and its costs under varying scenarios, its percentage of the borrower's monthly income, and special features such as prepayment fees, if any. The purpose of the form would be to make sure that the buyer understands the undertaking and its costs.

Regulation should also require countercyclical measures to address the growth of bubbles and suppress the tendency for bubbles to create weak mortgages. Such countermeasures would include an increase in down payments when housing prices have risen by a certain percentage in the local area. In addition, countercyclical loan loss reserves should be enforced by bank regulators, requiring banks during the good times to set aside reserves for the lean years. Under current accounting rules, banks only reserve for expected losses, not for the inevitability that the bad times will come. Better appraisal practices would also tend to reduce the growth of bubbles, because values would be based not solely on current prices, but on other factors as well.

Examples from Abroad

Regulation of this kind is what makes other housing finance systems work as well as they do. The United States is one of a very few developed countries that back residential mortgages. Most other countries in Europe and elsewhere rely on regulations that control mortgage quality to assure that their mortgage systems work (Barclays Capital 2010, fig. 3). A case in point is Denmark, where mortgage banks arrange for mortgages and take the credit risk, but the mortgage is funded in the open market, as part of a pool of mortgages of the same tenor. The quality of the mortgages that go into the system is strictly controlled, and because the mortgage banks assume the credit risk their interests are aligned with the buyers of the MBS issued by the mortgage pool. Germany has a covered bond system that also rests on regulations that strictly control the quality of the mortgages allowed into the cover system. Neither Denmark

---

11. Ginnie Mae securities backed by government agency loans would be exempt.

nor Germany backs any part of the mortgage financing system, which seems to work well because of the regulatory assurances of mortgage quality. In more than 200 years there has never been a failure of a mortgage bank in Denmark or a failure to meet covered bond obligations in Germany (Association of German Pfandbrief Banks n.d.).

Lending to Low-Income Borrowers

How would a social policy that provides government assistance for low-income families fare in this environment? The first point to note is that there is no internal inconsistency between a system that relies primarily on high-quality mortgages for steady functioning and a social policy that encourages concessionary loans to low-income borrowers. Unless a new system is set up by Congress, the FHA could continue to function as the insurer for loans to low-income borrowers. But certain restrictions would be necessary to protect the taxpayers, the borrowers, and the firms that are engaged in operating in the prime market.

First, all FHA commitments should be on budget, so that Congress and the taxpayers have an idea of the liabilities they and the FHA are assuming. The FHA's obligations are currently covered by the Federal Credit Reform Act, but its accounting is very complex and makes it difficult to determine something as simple as whether the FHA's assets exceed its liabilities. Second, while the quality standards for FHA mortgages would be lower than those in the prime market, the agency cannot be allowed to function with no standards. In other words, lower FICO scores would be expected, but there would have to be a minimum. Down payments could be much lower than for prime mortgages, but they could not be zero. Finally, the FHA should not compete with private originators or securitizers. They should be seen as two different markets. Among other things, a new law should restrict FHA loans to borrowers who are at or below 80 percent of the median income in the area in which they live and the size of any loan to 100 percent of the median home price in the area.

What to Do about the GSEs

The prior discussion has shown, I believe, that continuing a government role in housing finance is not necessary and is ill-advised from the standpoint of policy. To summarize, if only prime-quality mortgages are allowed into the securitization system, the delinquency and default rates on mortgages and MBS should be low enough—even under stressed conditions—that institutional investors will want to hold these instruments as investments. If a government guarantee is not required to make these instruments attractive, then there is no need for the GSEs or for any other system that requires a government guarantee. Although past government financial assistance for housing has not succeeded in raising the homeownership rate, reducing mortgage interest rates to the level of countries that do not involve the government in guaranteeing mortgages, or creating a stable market, it has had the effect of creating a standardized form of mortgage and a national market in mortgages—both of which were necessary for the development of a fully private market—so government involvement in the housing market has not been a total loss.

Eliminating government involvement in housing finance turns out to be good policy for other reasons that are equally important. Because government agencies have no effective way of pricing the risk they would be required to take—and in any event cannot for political reasons create the kinds of reserves against loss that are created by insurers—eliminating a system in which the government takes a financial risk by backing mortgages or MBS would likely save the taxpayers yet another major bailout at some time in the future. This would be true, it appears, whether the government is backing the issuers of the MBS—as was the case with the GSEs—or just the MBS; in both cases, government backing creates moral hazard that allows excessive risk taking by the issuers of the MBS that cannot be prevented by regulation.

Nevertheless, while it seems that a fully private market has significant advantages over a government-backed system—principally because it avoids the losses that seem to accompany the government's efforts to support housing finance—as of the time of this writing a robust private securitization system does not exist. There have been a few successful deals since the financial crisis, but by and large the private securitization market is still dormant and by some estimates 85 percent of the mortgage finance system in the United States today depends on the GSEs to supply liquidity. Under these circumstances, how can the system be converted to one that does not rely at all on Fannie and Freddie?

The first step is to await the development of a more robust private securitization market. This is not a cop-out; there is little or no chance that a decision on the GSEs' future will be reached during the next two years. The House of Representatives, controlled by the Republicans, may be prepared to adopt a timetable that ends with the elimination or privatization of the GSEs, but that plan will not be adopted in the Senate or approved by the administration, which is preparing its own proposal and is likely to propose a system that continues to have a government role in housing finance. Accordingly, there are at least two years, past the presidential elections of 2012, before any plan for Fannie and Freddie is likely to be adopted. By that time, there is a good chance that the private securitization market will have revived sufficiently so that it will look like a viable successor to Fannie and Freddie.

Assuming that a robust securitization market develops, the following steps would be a workable way to wind down the GSEs:

—Provide by law for a reduction in the GSEs' conforming loan limit by 20 percent of the previous year's cap each year, starting with the current general limit for one-unit properties of $417,000 and the high-cost-area limit of $729,750. If we assume an 80 percent LTV, the current limits allow mean home prices of more than $500,000 and $900,000, respectively. In contrast, according to the National Association of Realtors, the median U.S. house price is $171,300.

—Under this schedule of conforming loan reductions, the general limit for a one-unit property would decrease to $334,000 in year one, $267,000 in year two, and $214,000 in year three. The high-cost-area limit for a one-unit property would decrease to $584,000 in year one, $467,000 in year two, and $374,000 in year three.

—As the GSEs withdraw from markets larger than the conforming loan limits, private securitization will assume the role of providing a secondary market. If only prime mortgages are involved in these securitizations, the MBS should be attractive investments for banks, insurance companies, pension funds, mutual funds, and other institutional investors.

—At this point, the first formal review of the GSE transition would take place. If the transition is judged to be proceeding successfully, and unless the Congress votes to the contrary, the 20 percent annual reductions would continue through year five, reducing the general conforming loan limit to $171,200 and finally $136,960. The high-cost-area conforming loan limit would be reduced to $299,200 in year four and $240,800 in year five.

—Final termination or "sunset" of GSE status would take place at the end of year five.

—From the beginning of the wind-down period, the GSEs would be prohibited from adding to their portfolios of mortgages or MBS. These would be allowed to run off naturally, although if the market is strong enough they could be sold by the GSEs. The GSEs would not be permitted to hold loans or MBS in their portfolios, except for short periods as necessary to support MBS issuance.

—During the wind-down period, Fannie and Freddie would be allowed to buy only prime loans and, in order to prevent them from arbitraging their GSE status, to invest only in short-term Treasury bills.

—At the sunset date, a liquidating trust would be created containing all remaining mortgage assets, guarantee liabilities, and debt. The trust would hold Treasury securities to be liquidated if necessary to meet the trust's obligations. When the last mortgage has been refinanced or sold off by the trustee, the trust would be terminated, and any remaining Treasury securities would be returned to the Treasury. The GSE net worth shortfall would unjustly—but at this point unavoidably—be borne by taxpayers, including the Treasury's writing off of its preferred stock.

—All of Fannie and Freddie's intellectual property, systems, securitization platforms, goodwill, customer relationships, and organizational capital would be auctioned off in a termination or privatization. The proceeds would reduce the losses to the Treasury and the taxpayers.

Conclusion

The history of government support for housing finance shows that it invariably results in massive taxpayer losses, but produces very few of the benefits—such as increases in homeownership or lower interest rates for housing finance—that the government is seeking. Instead of basing the financing of housing on government backing, a robust system of housing finance can be based on ensuring the quality of mortgages. This is how other developed countries generally structure their residential finance systems, and in doing so they achieve better outcomes than the United States without any substantial taxpayer costs. Once this system has been adopted and rules are in place to ensure mortgage quality, Fannie and Freddie can be gradually withdrawn from the market by reducing the conforming loan limit over a period of years. As that happens, it is highly likely that the private sector will take over the areas from which the GSEs have withdrawn.

References

Association of German Pfandbrief Banks. n.d. "The Pfandbrief—A Safe Investment." Brochure. Berlin (www.hypverband.de/cms/bcenter.nsf/docsbykey/65192645/$file/Flyer+EN_Pfandbrief_a+safe+investment.pdf?openelement).

Barclays Capital. 2010. "U.S. Housing Finance: No Silver Bullet." London (December 13).

Center on Federal Financial Institutions. 2005. "Federal Deposit Insurance Corporation." Washington (August 10). (www.coffi.org/pubs/Summaries/FDIC%20Summary.pdf).

Congressional Budget Office. 2005. "Modifying Federal Deposit Insurance." Washington (May 9). (www.cbo.gov/ftpdocs/63xx/doc6342/05-09-DepositInsurance.pdf).

European Mortgage Federation. 2008. *European Covered Bond Fact Book 2008.* Brussels.

FHA (Federal Housing Administration). 2000. *Actuarial Review of the Mutual Mortgage Insurance Fund 2000.* Washington (http://portal.hud.gov/hudportal/HUD?src=/program_offices/housing/rmra/oe/rpts/actr/actrmenu).

————. 2010. *Actuarial Review of the Mutual Mortgage Insurance Fund 2010.* Washington (http://portal.hud.gov/hudportal/HUD?src=/program_offices/housing/rmra/oe/rpts/actr/actrmenu).

Fink, Thomas. 2010. "Huge Losses Put Federal Flood Insurance Plan in the Red." *USA Today,* August 26 (www.usatoday.com/news/nation/2010-08-25-flood-insurance_N.htm).

Jaffee, Dwight M. 2010. "Reforming the U.S. Mortgage Market through Private Market Incentives." Presentation at the Federal Reserve Bank of St. Louis, November 17 (http://faculty.haas.berkeley.edu/jaffee/Papers/JaffeeMortgageReform.pdf).

Kudlow, Larry. 2010. "Barney Frank Comes Home to the Facts." *GOPUSA,* August 23 (www.gopusa.com/commentary/2010/08/23/kudlow_barney_frank_comes_home_to_the_facts).

PBGC (Pension Benefit Guaranty Corporation). 2010. *2010 PBGC Annual Report.* Washington (November 12). (www.pbgc.gov/documents/ar2010.htm).

Pinto, Edward. 2010a. "Government Housing Policies in the Lead-up to the Financial Crisis: A Forensic Study." Washington: American Enterprise Institute (November 4). (www.aei.org/docLib/Government-Housing-Policies-Financial-Crisis-Pinto-102110.pdf).

———. 2010b. "Sizing Total Federal Government and Federal Agency Contributions to Subprime and Alt-A Loans in U.S. First Mortgage Market as of 6.30.08, Exhibit 2 with corrections through October 11, 2010." Washington: American Enterprise Institute. (www.aei.org/docLib/PintoFCICTriggersMemo.pdf).

Pollock, Alex J. 2010. Testimony before the Subcommittee on Security and International Trade and Finance, U.S. Senate Committee on Banking, Housing, and Urban Affairs, September 29 (www.aei.org/docLib/Testimony-Comparison-International-Housing-Finance-Systems-Pollock.pdf).

Shiller, Robert J. 2005. *Irrational Exuberance.* 2d ed. Princeton University Press.

Vandell, Kerry D. 1995. "FHA Restructuring Proposals: Alternatives and Implications." *Fannie Mae Housing Policy Debate* 6, no. 2: 299–387.

Wallison, Peter J., Alex J. Pollock, and Edward J. Pinto. 2011. "Taking the Government out of Housing Finance: Principles for Reforming the Housing Finance Market." Washington: American Enterprise Institute (January 20).

6

Catastrophic Mortgage Insurance and the Reform of Fannie Mae and Freddie Mac

DIANA HANCOCK AND WAYNE PASSMORE

Mortgage securitization has been tried several times in the United States, and each time it has failed amid a credit bust.[1] In what is now a familiar recurring history, during the credit boom, underwriting standards are violated and guarantees are inadequately funded; subsequently, defaults increase and investors in mortgage-backed securities attempt to dump their investments.[2] Ex post, the securitizers are taken to task for the methods they used to originate and sell bonds and for not looking out for the interests of bondholders.[3] In the most

The views expressed are the authors' and should not be interpreted as representing the views of the Federal Open Market Committee, its principals, the Board of Governors of the Federal Reserve System, or any other person associated with the Federal Reserve System. We thank Andrew Davidson, Karen Dynan, Skander Van den Heuvel, Trish Mosser, Richard Roll, David Torregros, Lawrence White, and various participants at the several meetings we attended between 2008 and 2010 for helpful comments. We also thank Melissa Hamilton and Benjamin Unterreiner for their research assistance.

1. For example, Snowden (1995, 2007) describes the farm mortgage debenture movement of the 1880s, and Snowden (2010) describes two types of mortgage-backed securities that were developed by mortgage guarantee companies and real estate bond houses in the 1920s.

2. White (2009) argues that investors purchased mortgage-backed bonds in the 1920s because they were reassured by the legalization of private mortgage insurance, approval of regulators, and favorable assessments by rating agencies.

3. In describing the situation during the mid-1920s, Snowden (2010, p. 19) indicates, "Real estate bond houses were excoriated for the methods they used to originate bonds and sell securities, and for abusing their position as fiscal agents for the bondholders."

severe cases, a federal emergency response to a mortgage crisis is mounted.[4] In effect, the government is "on the hook" to provide catastrophic insurance ex post when mortgage securitization markets go awry.[5]

The recent U.S. experience with mortgage securitization is no exception. During the credit boom in the early 2000s, the portion of the mortgage-backed securitization market not backed by the government-sponsored agencies, Fannie Mae and Freddie Mac, expanded at a rapid pace (left panel of figure 6-1). Indeed, in 2005 and 2006, nonagency issuance of mortgage-backed securities (MBS) exceeded that of agency MBS for the first time. During this period, there is mounting evidence that the inherent risks associated with high-risk mortgage products, such as no-money-down and stated-income mortgages, were not controlled through sound underwriting practices.[6] But in the presence of rapidly rising house prices, lax underwriting was masked by the ability of the borrower to refinance or quickly resell the property prior to defaulting on the mortgage. When home prices stalled or declined, however, there were much earlier defaults than initially expected on the mortgages that backed many nonagency MBS. Spreads on nonagency MBS "blew out," reaching very high levels before the issuance of all nonagency MBS ceased.[7]

Mortgages with principal amounts less than the conforming loan limit are eligible for purchase by Fannie Mae and Freddie Mac so long as they meet or exceed the underwriting criteria set by these government-sponsored enterprises (GSEs).[8] In turn, the GSEs guarantee the timely payment of principal and interest on agency MBS that are backed by the conforming mortgages they purchase. As of 2009, about $5.5 trillion of agency MBS were outstanding, of which $1 trillion were held by Fannie Mae and Freddie Mac in their portfolios.

4. Snowden (2010) describes the Federal Home Loan Bank system and the Home Owners' Loan Act that represented the federal response in the 1930s. More recently, Congress passed the Hope for Homeowners Act of 2008, the Housing and Economic Recovery Act of 2008, and the Dodd-Frank Wall Street Reform and Consumer Protection Act of 2010.

5. As Henry Paulson, secretary of the Treasury, told Congress during hearings about the government's bailout plan: "You're angry and I'm angry that taxpayers are on the hook. But guess what: they are already on the hook for the system we all let happen." See "When Fortune Frowned," *The Economist,* October 11, 2008, p. 7.

6. See, for example, Costello, Kelsch, and Pendley (2007); Keys and others (2010).

7. The private-label MBS market essentially disappeared except for "resecuritizations," which combined previously issued nonagency MBS into new securities.

8. The maximum growth in the conforming loan limit each year is set either by a formula related to the growth in average home prices or by Congress. The underwriting criteria is less well defined, but is generally taken to mean that the mortgage must have the same credit risk as an 80 percent loan-to-value mortgage made to a borrower with a good credit history. The GSEs, within some limits, risk-adjust their guarantee fees.

Figure 6-1. *Issuance of Mortgage-Backed Securities, Quarterly Data, 2000Q1–2010Q2*[a]

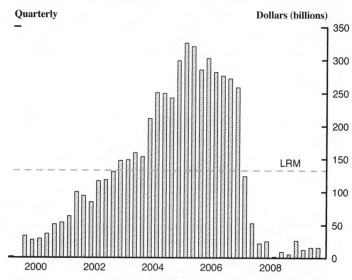

Nonagency MBS issuance

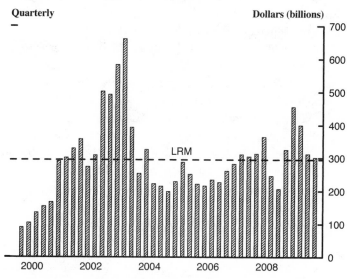

Agency MBS issuance

Source: Permission of Bloomberg.
a. LRM is the long-run mean (2000Q1–2010Q2).

As is now well understood, Fannie Mae and Freddie Mac posed a systemic risk to the U.S. financial system.[9] This risk arose mainly because market participants viewed the debt securities they issued to fund their respective portfolios as being "implicitly guaranteed" by the U.S. government. That is, investors assumed that the government would back the debt regardless of the financial condition of the GSEs. With this implicit government guarantee, the GSEs issued debt at a relatively low cost, operated without bondholder market discipline, and undertook excessive risks within their portfolios.

In July 2008 the short-term concerns of bondholders about the credit quality of mortgages backed by the GSEs as well as the credit quality of private-label MBS held in the portfolios of Fannie Mae and Freddie Mac led to difficulties in rolling over GSE debt. As a result, bondholders needed reassurance that the government stood behind Fannie Mae and Freddie Mac. On July 13, 2008, the Department of the Treasury and the Federal Reserve took actions to provide such reassurance until Congress could pass new GSE legislation.[10]

The new regulator created by Congress at the end of July—the Federal Housing Finance Agency (FHFA)—began an intensive examination of Fannie Mae and Freddie Mac. By September 2008, it determined that significant credit losses were embedded in GSE portfolios and that the quality of capital held by the GSEs was poor. The interaction of significant credit losses, poor control over credit underwriting for the mortgages held in the portfolios, bond investors' uncertainties about the quality of the portfolios, and the razor-thin capitalization of Fannie Mae and Freddie Mac led to the establishment of the GSE conservatorships on September 7, 2008.

If Fannie Mae and Freddie Mac had only been mortgage securitizers and had not held portfolios, these agencies likely would still have suffered from inadequate (and poor-quality) capital reserves relative to the credit losses suffered during the housing downturn and financial crisis (like most other financial institutions). However, the opaqueness of the on-balance-sheet portfolio and the difficulty of rolling over the short-term GSE debt were what led to the need for more immediate government actions during the summer of 2008. Perhaps the GSEs could have raised private capital to support their mortgage securitization operations had they not incurred the losses on the whole mortgages and the

9. For descriptions of the systemic risk posed by the GSEs, see Bernanke (2007); Greenspan (2004, 2005).

10. According to Paulson (2008), "GSE debt is held by financial institutions around the world. Its continued strength is important to maintaining confidence and stability in our financial system and our financial markets. Therefore, we must take steps to address the current situation as we move to a stronger regulatory structure." On July 13, the Board of Governors granted the Federal Reserve Bank of New York the authority to lend to Fannie Mae and Freddie Mac should such lending prove necessary. See www.federalreserve.gov/newsevents/press/other/20080713a.htm.

nonagency mortgage-backed securities that were held in their portfolios (and had there not been uncertainty and lack of transparency surrounding potential losses on such assets).[11]

Despite the insolvency of Fannie Mae and Freddie Mac, agency-backed mortgage securitization was fairly robust during the financial crisis, with the GSEs under conservatorship of their regulator and with Department of Treasury preferred stock agreements in place. As shown on the lower panel of figure 6-1, agency MBS issuance remained strong, falling only somewhat below its long-run mean of $300 billon per quarter in the second half of 2008. The GSEs were also generally successful in keeping MBS spreads (not shown) somewhat reasonable throughout the financial crisis (with the notable exception of some periods during the summer and fall of 2008). The different outcomes in the nonagency and agency MBS markets during the recent credit boom and bust suggest that the credibility of the guarantee provided by the securitizer (that is, the MBS issuer) is instrumental to realizing the benefits of securitization.

In this chapter we consider three interrelated questions: Why is mortgage securitization fragile? Would government provision of catastrophic insurance for mortgage credit likely improve financial stability? Is there a potential role for Fannie Mae and Freddie Mac to provide government-backed insurance for mortgage-backed instruments? The chapter is organized as follows. First we consider why mortgage securitization is fragile. Second we analyze how government-backed catastrophic insurance for prespecified mortgage-backed instruments might mitigate such fragility, whereas a private insurance market for such instruments is unlikely to do so. We then describe how Fannie Mae and Freddie Mac could be restructured, analogous to the current setup for the Federal Deposit Insurance Corporation (FDIC), to provide such catastrophic insurance.

Regardless of its institutional structure, a federally backed insurer of prespecified mortgage-backed instruments would provide greater financial stability and ensure that mortgage credit is provided at reasonable cost both in times of prosperity and during downturns. The *explicit* pricing of a government-backed guarantee would mitigate market distortions that have been created by *implicit* government guarantees during prosperity. Moreover, guarantee-sensitive investors would not engage in a run if they were certain that their money would be repaid with interest. For such reasons, Chairman Bernanke has argued, "If the GSEs were privatized, it would seem advisable to retain some means of providing government support to the mortgage securitization process during times of

---

11. During a financial crisis, capital is "slow moving" and time is needed for equity investors to assess the value of possible investors (see Acharya, Shin, and Yorulmazer 2009). Runs by short-term debt investors deprive financial firms of this needed time.

"turmoil," with "one possible approach being to create a bond insurer."[12] This chapter spells out the rationale for and details of such an approach.

Why Is Mortgage Securitization Fragile?

To understand who bears the credit risks of mortgage securitization during normal economic times in the United States, one must consider the roles of mortgage originators, typically depository institutions and mortgage-backed securitizers. We build on the model of Heuson, Passmore, and Sparks (2001), who use their model to describe GSE mortgage-backed securitization, and on Hancock and others (2005), who customize the model for bank capital requirements. Our analysis of loan market equilibriums shows that the additional liquidity provided by securitization may (or may not) lower primary mortgage rates, but such liquidity comes at a cost. More specifically, if guarantee-sensitive investors doubt the credit quality of mortgage-backed bonds, significant risk premiums can develop.[13] If a financial crisis ensues, mortgage securitization can disappear from the market entirely, leaving banks that originate just the highest-quality mortgages as the only source of credit.

The Mechanics of Mortgage Securitization

In the United States, mortgage securitization is segmented by type of loan, size of loan, and riskiness of the borrower. Each market segment (for example, conforming mortgages, subprime mortgages, and "prime jumbo" mortgages) is typically characterized by uniform pricing; that is, risk-based pricing usually occurs across market segments, but only to a limited extent within market segments. Originators generally do not further segment the market because doing so would involve significant underwriting expense.[14] Moreover, uniform pricing may lead

12. See Bernanke (2008a). This idea is described briefly in Hancock and Passmore (2009). See also Hancock and Passmore (2010).

13. Hancock and Passmore (2010) argue that the same logic applies to asset-backed securitization more generally. Our analysis is similar in spirit to Gorton (2009) and Gorton and Metrick (2009) who develop the analogy that investor runs in the shadow banking industry are similar to retail depositor runs in the banking era prior to creation of the Federal Reserve. In their view, banks create "informationally insensitive" debt (for example, deposits) that appeals to retail depositors because there is no need to invest in due diligence. In the shadow banking system, investment banks use repurchase (repo) transactions, which use short maturities, collateral, and haircuts to appeal to a broad range of investors. Similarly, Shleifer and Vishny (2009) show how banks cater to uninformed "investor sentiment" using securitization, but the net result is a less stable financial system.

14. Steinbach (1998) argues that mortgage pricing maintains an element of cross-subsidization (and thus uniform pricing) because collateral risk is more dominant than credit risk and collateral risk cannot be forecast with precision. In GSE mortgage securitization, the recent advent of the

an originator who has the option of holding a mortgage in its own portfolio to withhold safer mortgages from a pool. By "cherry picking" the safer mortgages, the originator avoids paying a securitizer (or an insurer) the guarantee fee, which is often an average fee for a pool.[15]

For mortgage-backed securitization, Heuson, Passmore, and Sparks (2001) show that the securitizer must guard against buying a relatively high proportion of higher-risk mortgages from originators who have a "first-mover" advantage. This means that the mortgage securitizer will set a tougher underwriting standard than will mortgage originators, who can both underwrite and hold mortgage credit risk.[16] Moreover, Cutts, Van Order, and Zorn (2001) note that the practice of uniform pricing and the resulting concern over adverse selection cause mortgage guarantors, such as Freddie Mac and Fannie Mae, to set a maximum level of risk they are willing to accept and to enforce it through tighter underwriting standards.

Adverse selection is a concern in all lending markets, and the first-mover advantage for originators holds true for all forms of mortgage securitization.[17] When securitization is an option, financial institutions, such as banks, have three strategies. The first is an "originate-and-hold" strategy, where the financial institution bears the credit risk of an asset and funds its loans on the balance sheet, using a mix of deposits, Federal Home Loan Bank (FHLB) advances, and perhaps covered bonds. The second is a "swap-and-hold" strategy, where the

---

GSEs' loan-level pricing adjustments suggests that for more extreme credit scores and loan-to-value ratios, the GSEs feel that they can further divide the conforming loan market segment. However, part of this price differentiation might reflect the demise of the private-label securitizers, who in the past had been in a position to cream skim any perceived mispricing of loans by the GSEs. In addition, the recent financial turmoil has perhaps made the dispersion of risks within the market for prime-conforming borrowers more distinct and measurable.

15. Calem, Henderson, and Liles (2010) find substantial evidence of cream skimming in subprime mortgage securitizations. They attribute their results to asymmetric information, but also believe that a breakdown of due diligence—an explanation consistent with the model presented here—is also a possibility.

16. A "first-mover" argument is distinct from an argument that relies on information asymmetries. The former reflects market structure (that is, the originator has the right to pick first), whereas the latter represents information (that is, the originator has better knowledge of the underlying risks than the securitizer). Passmore and Sparks (1996) show that a situation where the originator has better information than the mortgage securitizer has can also lead to tighter underwriting standards by the securitizer. The trade-off between the selection advantages of mortgage originators because of information asymmetries and the lower costs of financing and controlling risks in the secondary mortgage market is also discussed in Van Order (2000).

17. The examples provided are taken from the mortgage markets. For a description of secondary market financing and the automobile market and the important role of a government backstop (more specifically, the Term Asset-Backed Securities Loan Facility), see Johnson, Pence, and Vine (2010).

financial institution purchases a guarantee to cover the credit risk of the mortgage and simultaneously swaps the mortgage for a guaranteed MBS. These MBS are funded using the institution's balance sheet. Finally, the financial institution might employ a "swap-and-sell" strategy, where it purchases a guarantee to cover the credit risks associated with the mortgage and swaps the mortgage for a guaranteed MBS that it simultaneously sells into the secondary market (where guarantee-sensitive investors fund the mortgage). The second and third strategies are securitization-based strategies.

In principle, one might separate the guarantee provided for a mortgage from the conversion of the mortgage into MBS. For example, in U.S. mortgage markets, the Federal Housing Administration (FHA) guarantees a mortgage and the Government National Mortgage Association (Ginnie Mae) may or may not convert the mortgage into a security. The financial institution has the option of either holding the guaranteed FHA mortgages in its portfolio or holding the Ginnie Mae securities in its portfolio.

However, in the model below, the value of a securitizer's guarantee is that it provides liquidity for MBS because, if the guarantee is credible, the MBS can be sold to and traded among guarantee-sensitive investors in all market conditions—good and bad. At its best, securitization is the process of making illiquid mortgages liquid; that is, the holders of the securities know—without performing substantial due diligence on the underlying mortgages—that such securities can be readily traded in active secondary markets at fair market values over the lives of the securities. Therefore, our model applies directly to mortgage securitization rather than simply to the pricing of mortgage guarantees.

The Decision Problem for Financial Institutions

We begin by comparing the originate-and-hold strategy (where the financial institution holds the mortgage on its balance sheet) with the swap-and-hold strategy (where it holds the MBS on its balance sheet). In either case, the financial institution uses the same mix of liabilities to fund the mortgage on its balance sheet.

Figure 6-2 presents the industry supply curve for a given segment of the mortgage market (for example, the prime conforming mortgage segment).[18] On the vertical axis of the figure is the interest rate for the mortgage extended to the household. On the horizontal axis is the probability that a borrower will *not* default, q, in the mortgage market segment, which ranges from 0 to 1. Borrowers with higher probabilities of *not* defaulting (that is, those closer to 1 in the right corner of the figure) have the *lowest* credit risks. The marginal cost of bearing

---

18. As discussed earlier, risk-based pricing occurs across loan segments, but not within a loan segment.

Figure 6-2. *Financial Institution Funding of Mortgage Portfolios and Securitization*

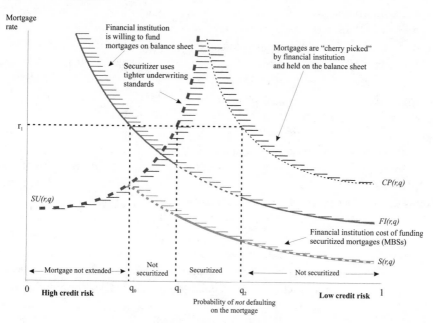

Source: Authors' calculation.

borrower credit risks declines as q increases, so the lowest rate that a lender is willing to accept falls as the probability of *not* defaulting on a mortgage rises.[19]

The line $FI(r,q)$—solid and dashed—represents the locus of zero economic profit combinations of mortgage rates (r) and credit risks (q) from using liabilities (including insured deposits and FHLB advances) to fund mortgages using the originate-and-hold strategy.[20] At any given interest rate, the financial institution is willing to use its liabilities to fund all mortgages with credit risk equal

19. Focusing on the portfolio decision in the absence of capital requirements, a risk-neutral originator will offer a loan if $qr + (1-q)rd \geq rf$, where r is the interest rate received by the lender if the borrower does not default, rd is the expected return to the lender if the borrower does default, and rf is the expected return on an alternative investment. Rewriting this expression in terms of an equality and solving for r, it can be demonstrated that the inverse supply function for mortgages is decreasing in q and rd, but increasing in rf. See Heuson, Passmore, and Sparks (2001, p. 340).

20. The $FI(r,q)$ line incorporates the market's risk-sensitive capital requirement, which covers credit risks of the funding institution. This marginal cost curve with respect to credit risk implicitly assumes that other marginal costs of loan financing do not vary with respect to credit risk. Thus the curvature simply reflects the effective cost of capital to back the credit risk (or an equivalent credit guarantee).

to, or less than, the credit risks represented by this line, denoted as the set of all points to the right of $FI(r,q)$, indicated by the cross-hatches.

An important part of this economic profit is the illiquidity premium embedded in whole mortgages. If the financial institution needs to sell or finance a whole mortgage, it requires due diligence from a sophisticated investor. This process is costly and time-consuming, meaning that whole mortgages are often sold at a substantial discount if the institution needs to raise funds quickly. Similarly, if the whole mortgage is pledged for a repo transaction, the financing is only available with a substantial haircut.

The line $S(r,q)$—solid and dashed—is the locus of zero economic profit combinations of mortgage rates and credit risks if the financial institution uses the swap-and-hold strategy. In this case, the institution is willing to fund all MBS with credit risks equal to, or less than, the credit risks represented by this line (indicated by the cross-hatches). As portrayed in figure 6-2, the MBS yield a liquidity benefit to the financial institution, measured by the distance between $FI(r,q)$ and $S(r,q)$. If the guarantee offered by a securitizer is *credible* among market participants, then the securities backed by the whole mortgages are easily transacted and can be sold to guarantee-sensitive investors. The financial institution would prefer to use its liabilities to fund MBS, all things equal, rather than mortgages.

The mortgages that a financial institution will keep in its portfolio are all those with credit risks that are equal to, or less than, those to the right of the dashed line $CP(r,q)$, indicated by cross-hatches. Changes in an institution's underwriting standards (that is, the quality of mortgages that are cherry picked) are represented by movements of the $CP(r,q)$ dashed line.

In the course of maximizing profits, a mortgage securitizer must offset the mortgage originators' first-mover advantage (the cherry picking) to earn a target rate of return and to avoid being stuck with "lemons." Thus the securitizer generally sets a higher standard for credit risk than does the mortgage originator. This higher standard does not necessarily ensure that the securitizer's average credit risk is lower than the originator's average credit risk on the mortgages because the originator can pool the lemons (mortgages that have a higher credit risk than allowed under the securitizer's underwriting standards) and the cherries (mortgages that are very low risk and are not sold to the securitizer).[21]

In figure 6-2, the credit standard of the securitizer is represented by the dashed line $SU(r,q)$. The securitizer will only purchase, securitize, or rate mortgages with credit risks equal to, or less than, those represented by this line. That is, only mortgages to the right of $SU(r,q)$—indicated by cross-hatches—are

21. See Hancock and others (2005) for a discussion of this pooling equilibrium in the context of meeting financial institution capital requirements.

securitized. The line $SU(r,q)$ slopes upward because the originator is more likely to cherry pick mortgages when mortgage rates are higher, which provides an incentive to the securitizer to tighten its underwriting standards.

Changes in underwriting standards by the securitizer, other than those due to changes in mortgage rates, are represented by shifts of the $SU(r,q)$ line. (The line shifts to the right when the underwriting standard is tightened.) Such changes are, of course, linked to the financial institution's underwriting standards as well as to any exogenous events that change the securitizer's target rate of return on its equity. As the originator removes more low-risk loans from the flow of mortgages into the pools of collateral backing a securitization, the securitizer has to tighten its lending standards to guard against adverse selection when taking mortgages out of the remaining pool of mortgages. These actions reduce the gap between the $SU(r,q)$ and $CP(r,q)$ lines.[22]

When the mortgage rate is r_1, loan originators (financial institutions) only want to *sell* loans with credit risks between 0 and q_2 because they are engaging in cherry picking vis-à-vis the securitizers.[23] Moreover, because of this cherry-picking activity, the mortgage securitizer wants to avoid lemons and only wants to guarantee mortgages with credit risks between q_1 and 1 to create marketable securities. High-quality mortgages originated by a financial institution (that is, mortgages with credit risks lower than q_2 and therefore to the right of q_2) are placed in the institution's own investment portfolio. As a result, the effective industry supply curve (used to determine r_1) for mortgage credit risks of a given type of product is represented by the solid segments of the $FI(r,q)$ and the $S(r,q)$ lines.[24]

The Effect of Guarantee-Sensitive Investor Participation on Financial Institution Funding Costs

The implicit, or conjectural, government guarantees that are presumed to be present for GSEs and large financial institutions, sometimes referred to as too-big-to-fail (TBTF) status, can provide competitive advantages because a much broader range of investors—guarantee-sensitive investors—will purchase the debt issued, or the securities guaranteed, by such institutions. GSEs and large financial institutions can, in essence, convert loans (for example, mortgages)

22. During 2005 through 2007, mortgage originators' underwriting standards fell, and Fannie Mae and Freddie Mac did not respond by tightening underwriting standards. Despite misgivings of the risk managers at the GSEs, Fannie Mae and Freddie Mac both bought into the view that mortgage risks were more manageable than they had been in the past.
23. The $CP(r,q)$ line at q_2 is determined by the originator's comparison of the marginal profit derived from holding the mortgage loan to the price offered by the securitizer for selling the loan.
24. The supply curve is downward sloping because the originators and guarantors require the same risk-adjusted return on all loans. As risk falls, the nominal rate of return needed to hit the target rate of return falls.

made to borrowers into a relatively risk-free investment for a broader range of investors. The target investor is one who desires an investment that is so free of credit risk that the yields should be close to those offered on sovereign debt. If such "guarantee-sensitive" investors are willing to buy a financial instrument, the liquidity of the instrument is greatly enhanced. Such investors, however, are likely to reason that they can quickly dispose of their holdings in a liquid market if they smell trouble ahead. Indeed, guarantee-sensitive investors are prone to run in a manner similar to what retail depositors did before the establishment of government-provided deposit insurance.[25]

Runs by guarantee-sensitive investors have significant spillovers to other parts of the financial system. When credit conditions deteriorate and capital becomes dear, liquidity can dry up as uncertainty about future returns becomes pervasive. Large financial institutions become vulnerable to runs if they depend heavily on funding from guarantee-sensitive investors. As a result of this uncertainty, very large banks, as well as other large financial institutions (including Fannie Mae and Freddie Mac during the most recent crisis), hoard capital even in the face of likely profitable investments.[26] Financial turmoil results in real economic effects since otherwise productive investments are not made because money cannot be reallocated.

Consider a model with two types of investors: (1) sophisticated investors, who are willing to invest in due diligence, and (2) guarantee-sensitive investors, who are unwilling or unable to take such actions and only hold securities they perceive as risk free. [27] Let $1 - \alpha$ denote the share of a bank's liabilities sold to

25. Uninformed investors often play an instrumental role in models of liquidity runs. For example, uninformed investors may rely on past price movements to infer asset volatilities and thereby induce "liquidity runs" (Brunnermeier and Pedersen 2008). The idea that during 2007 and 2008 the "shadow banking system" experienced a run similar to that of a banking panic and that additional government involvement is needed to avoid such panics has been advanced by a variety of observers. See Bernanke (2008b); Gorton (2009); Kashyap, Rajan, and Stein (2008); He and Xiong (2009). As emphasized by Hanson, Kashyap, and Stein (2011), the current theories of runs on financial institutions (based on asset fire sales and credit crunches) are based on socially excessive balance sheet shrinkage and the existence of deposit insurance. As pointed out by Pozsar and others (2010), one of the main contributors to financial stress in the shadow banking system is the lack of access to public sources of insurance. Covitz, Liang, and Suarez (2009) examine the structure of special-purpose vehicles and their reliance on short-term funding and argue that the problems in these markets resemble a bank-like run.

26. For examples of models of deleveraging and hoarding during a financial crisis, see Adrian and Shin (2008); Geanakoplos (2009).

27. Our model assumes that the guarantee-sensitive investor is unwilling to pay others to perform due diligence as well. In principle, a credible nongovernment bond insurer or a credit rating agency could undertake the necessary due diligence and, in conjunction with a government bond insurer who bears the catastrophic risk, provide market discipline. However, to date, guarantee-sensitive investors are unwilling to pay (or are able to "free ride" on the work of others) for such analysis or structuring (as illustrated by the prevalence of the "issuer pays" model used by the credit

sophisticated investors (which is very small) and α be the proportion sold to guarantee-sensitive investors. The cost of funds for a TBTF bank (or a GSE) would be as follows:

$$(6\text{-}1) \qquad r_f = (1 - \alpha)(r_T + \varepsilon) + \alpha r_T,$$

where r_f is the cost of funds and r_T is the yield on a risk-free security (for example, a Treasury bill). Sophisticated investors charge a risk premium, ε, because they understand that the financial institution is not directly backed by the government. In contrast, guarantee-sensitive investors perceive that the government implicitly or explicitly guarantees the financial institution and either lack the resources or do not want to make the investments to undertake due diligence. Financial institutions desire to expand the proportion of their funding that comes from guarantee-sensitive investors because it is lower cost than funding operations relying solely on more sophisticated investors.

The overall cost of funds for a TBTF financial institution is slightly higher than the risk-free rate. As long as the yield on deposits and securities offered by a TBTF bank is perceived as slightly better than a Treasury yield, the liability will attract guarantee-sensitive investors because they perceive the liability to be risk free. As a result, the financial institution is able to attract extensive funding from a broader range of investors.[28]

Similarly, mortgage-backed securities appeal to guarantee-sensitive investors if the securitizer's guarantee is viewed as credible, and this appeal lessens the effect of the liquidity discount applied by market participants to the securities backed by the securitizer. The expected return on the MBS is the following:

$$(6\text{-}2) \qquad r_{MBS} = (1 - \alpha)(c - \varsigma) + \alpha c,$$

where c is the coupon offered on the MBS and ς is the credit and liquidity discount imposed by sophisticated investors.

If we assume that a TBTF financial institution is the marginal investor in the MBS market, then the spread of MBS to the bank's cost of funds is as follows:

$$(6\text{-}3) \qquad r_{MBS} - r_f = c - r_T - (1 - \alpha)(\varepsilon + \varsigma),$$

---

rating agency). Thus it seems likely that, for guarantee-sensitive investors to bear this cost, there would have to be a legislative mandate requiring a structure for securitizations that effectively creates institutions to perform due diligence on behalf of such investors and collects funds to cover the costs. There are a variety of financial architectures that might accomplish this goal.

28. The supply-demand imbalance for safe assets (that is, the supply of safe assets is dwarfed by the demand for safe assets) and its role in the recent financial crisis are described in Caballero (2009).

which implies that the TBTF financial institution can raise its return by increasing the proportion of guarantee-sensitive investors in its funding mix.

We model guarantee-sensitive investors as those who can only observe the average risk of an activity. (In the model that follows, depending on the discussion, the average risk will be either that of securitization overall or that of the institutions that are securitizing.) In normal times, such investors expect to earn slightly more than the Treasury rate (as described above). During a financial crisis, however, many guarantee-sensitive investors withdraw from the market *unless the asset or institution backing the asset is explicitly backed by the government.* We model this "flight to quality" by altering the cost of funds of sophisticated and guarantee-sensitive investors as the risk of the TBTF's portfolio rises:

$$
\begin{array}{ll}
\text{If } q > q_{min} & \text{then } \kappa = 0; \\
\text{If } q \leq q_{min} & \text{then } \kappa = 1; \\
(6\text{-}4) \qquad \omega_S = \omega_{G-S}(1 - \alpha)(r_T + \varepsilon) + \kappa D(q_{min}) & \omega_{G-S} = (1 - \kappa)\alpha r_T
\end{array}
$$

where the average cost of funds to the TBTF institution is $\omega_S + \omega_{G-S}$, and q_{min} is implicitly defined by the average risk of the activity (given an average credit risk, one can define the most risky borrower associated with that average, given a distribution of borrowers by level of credit risk).[29] As the average credit risk of the activity that is acceptable to the guarantee-sensitive investors declines, a breakpoint is reached where such investors are unwilling to fund the TBTF financial institution and the cost of raising funds from sophisticated investors rises. The institution's cost of funds becomes whatever the market will bear— that is, $D(q_{min})$, where D is the demand for mortgages given the credit risk. The same structure can be used to model guarantee-sensitive investors in MBS—as guarantee-sensitive investors perceive that the risk of the MBS guaranteed by the MBS securitizer is increasing, a breakpoint is reached where no guarantee-sensitive investors are willing to hold the MBS and only sophisticated investors who extract the maximum possible return are willing to hold the financial institution's MBS.

The potential for guarantee-sensitive investors to run limits the average risk of the TBTF institution's portfolio. The TBTF institution's average credit risk without this discontinuity in its cost of funds (as shown in figure 6-2) is as follows:

$$
(6\text{-}5) \qquad q_A = \int_{q_0}^{q_1} qf(q) + \int_{q_2}^{1} qf(q).
$$

---

29. Recall that our measure of risk is the odds of not defaulting on the mortgage. Thus when q_{min} is equal to 0, the borrower is certain to default, whereas when q_{min} is equal to 1, the borrower is certain to pay back the mortgage.

With the discontinuity, the TBTF institution's average credit risk, shown in figure 6-3, is as follows:

(6-6)
$$q_{A_{min}} = \int_{q_{min}}^{q_1} q f(q) + \int_{q_2}^{1} q f(q),$$

where the average credit risk is the same or smaller once the discontinuity is imposed. As the risk tolerance of the guarantee-sensitive investor decreases, q_{min} increases and the average credit risk of the financial institution's portfolio decreases (that is, q_{min} moves to the right in figure 6-3).

Loan Market Equilibriums without Guarantee-Sensitive Investors

We first examine potential mortgage market equilibriums assuming that all providers of funds to financial institutions are either sophisticated investors or insured depositors. As a result, there is no "kink" in the financial institution's cost of funds. The top and bottom panels of figure 6-4 show demand curves, D_1 in the top panel (D_2 in the bottom panel), that rank borrowers in each mortgage market segment by the maximum interest rate they are willing to pay for a loan. Because mortgage default is costly for borrowers, when high interest rates prevail, only borrowers with high odds of not defaulting stay in the pool of loan applicants.[30] This means that the demand curve slopes upward. (Note that the probability of *not* defaulting on a loan is on the horizontal axis.)

The equilibrium mortgage rate for a mortgage market segment is determined by where the demand curve for that segment crosses the industry supply curve.[31] In the top panel of figure 6-4, the financial institution's marginal cost of covering the credit and liquidity risks associated with mortgages (for the lowest-quality borrower) sets the mortgage rate in the primary loan market. In the bottom panel of figure 6-4, the marginal borrower had his or her mortgage securitized. In this case, the securitizer's cost of guaranteeing mortgages, combined with the liquidity benefits associated with such securitization, sets the interest rate in the

30. In an adverse selection model (such as proposed by Stiglitz and Weiss 1981), as loan rates rise, lower-risk borrowers drop out of the pool of potential borrowers. It is assumed that borrowers with higher default risks have higher expected returns. In our model, however, the project is a household purchase and the associated benefits are not related to a household's potential to earn income (and thus its default probability), so higher rates increase household costs without any offsetting effects on household revenues.

31. As noted earlier, the model presented here is a version of Heuson, Passmore, and Sparks (2001). More generally, the underwriting standards of market participants—depositories and securitizers alike—may change as interest rates change (that is, the black vertical dashed lines may move to the left or to the right). Also note that while the equilibrium may appear to yield positive profits for the financial institution, the fixed costs associated with loan underwriting activities are not explicitly accounted for, nor is the distribution of borrowers across types of credit risk. Both of these factors would need to be modeled to assess the total profitability of the originator.

Figure 6-3. *Financial Institution Funding with Guarantee-Sensitive Funding*

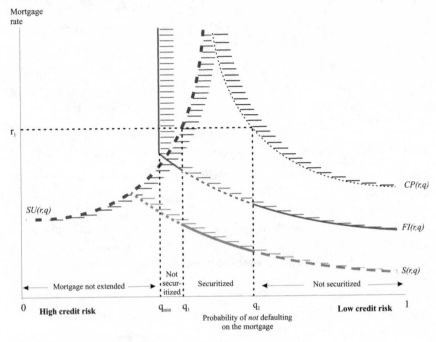

Source: Authors' calculation.

primary mortgage market, instead of the liquidity premium associated with holding the whole loan directly. Assuming that the financial institution and the loan guarantor assess credit risk in the same manner, the difference for the financial institution between the originate-and-hold and the swap-and-hold strategies is the additional liquidity (and associated lower trading and funding costs) from holding the loan as an asset-backed security. This additional liquidity may or may not result in a lower interest rate for the borrower. This suggests the following proposition:[32]

> *Proposition 1. Securitization may or may not lower primary market mortgage rates.*

Loan Market Equilibriums with Guarantee-Sensitive Investors: Funding Risk Premiums

Once guarantee-sensitive investors become part of the investor base, significant funding risk premiums can arise in the primary mortgage market that reflect

32. This result was established in Heuson, Passmore, and Sparks (2001).

Figure 6-4. *Equilibrium Mortgage Rates without Guarantee-Sensitive Investor Funding*

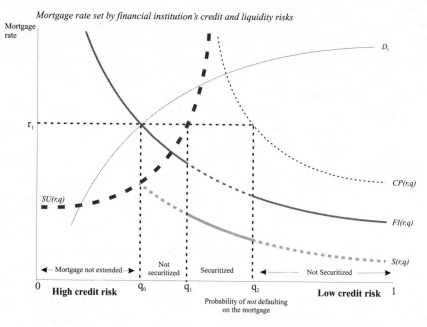

Mortgage rate set by financial institution's credit and liquidity risks

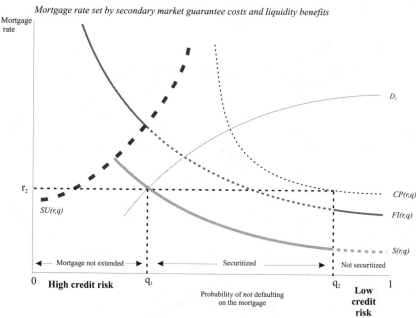

Mortgage rate set by secondary market guarantee costs and liquidity benefits

Source: Authors' calculation.

the conditions underlying the financing of mortgages and not the liquidity of the mortgages being financed. For example, if the financial institution relies on uninsured brokered deposits at the margin, the funding costs of the institution might be prone to increase rapidly in response to a run by guarantee-sensitive investors (for example, by using brokered deposits or repurchase agreements, known as repos) should the average credit quality of the financial institution's mortgage portfolio fall below the guarantee-sensitive investors' tolerance for risk.

As shown in the example provided in the top panel of figure 6-5, interest rates in the primary mortgage market rise from r_1 to r_R and the credit quality of the marginal mortgage borrower rises from q_0 to q_{min} because the financial institution adjusts its pricing to reflect the risks of the run by guarantee-sensitive investors.

Such funding risk premiums might be mitigated by securitization. As shown in the bottom panel in figure 6-5, the mortgage extended to the marginal borrower is swapped for a mortgage-backed security. If guarantee-sensitive investors distinguish between the credit quality of the underlying mortgages and the credit quality of the securitizer, then the average credit risks of the financial institution might be viewed as significantly lower when it holds MBS. (This is the case shown in the bottom panel.) However, if the credibility of the mortgage securitizer is called into question, then the guarantee-sensitive investors might view the average risk of the financial institution as equal to, or perhaps even greater than, the risk of its underlying mortgage portfolio. This suggests the following proposition:

Proposition 2. Securitization has the potential to remove significant funding risk premiums from the primary mortgage market if (1) financial institutions rely heavily on uninsured investors for funding and (2) the guarantee against credit defaults provided by the securitizer is credible.

In the United States, most guarantee-sensitive investors in financial institutions are insured depositors. In addition to insured deposits, most financial institutions use Federal Home Loan Bank advances for their funding needs. These advances are effectively backstopped by the federal government. The combination of insured deposits and FHLB advances means that, for most banks in the United States, funding sources are stable regardless of changes in the perceptions of credit risk. Only the largest of the financial institutions—including the largest banks—in the United States rely heavily on uninsured and nonguaranteed sources of funding. (Of course, these large institutions also extend the majority of mortgages to consumers.) Thus, except for the largest banks (which extensively use securitized assets in repurchase transactions), the primary advantage of securitization is the liquidity advantage derived from the ability to sell a mortgage quickly and not the funding cost advantages.

Figure 6-5. *Equilibrium Mortgage Rates with Guarantee-Sensitive Investor Funding*

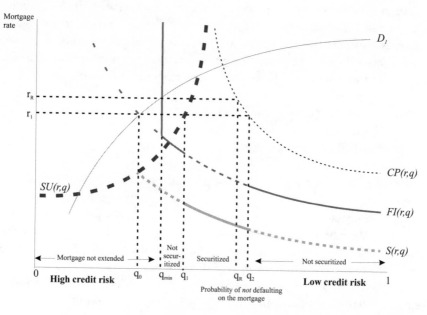

Mortgage rate set by secondary market guarantee costs and liquidity benefits

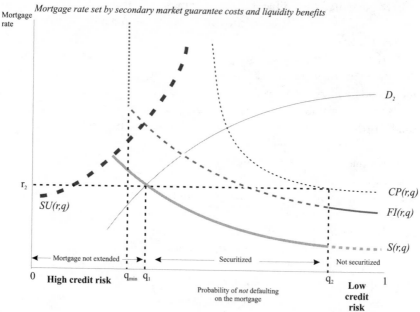

Source: Authors' calculation.

Originate-and-Hold Versus Swap-and-Sell Strategies

Guarantee-sensitive investors can also influence a financial institution's ability to sell a mortgage asset quickly. Indeed, the credibility of the securitizer's guarantee is instrumental to selling an MBS quickly into a deep and liquid market. To illustrate the guarantee-sensitive investor's influence on the investor base for MBS, we compare the originate-and-hold strategy with the swap-and-sell strategy, while assuming that the supply of funding for banks is stable (that is, there is no "kink" in the financial institution's cost of funds) because it consists of only insured deposits (see figure 6-6).

Suppose MBS are sold into a secondary market and purchased by investors—some of whom are guarantee-sensitive investors. These MBS investors rely on the securitizer's guarantee. If the average credit risk of the securitizer's guaranteed mortgages falls below the guarantee-sensitive investors' tolerance for risk, then these investors run. In the top and bottom panels of figure 6-6, $S(r,q)$ has a "kink" that reflects the possibility of a run by guarantee-sensitive investors. In these panels, $FI(r,q)$ represents funding costs when whole mortgages are funded using the financial institution's insured deposits, while $S(r,q)$ represents funding costs when MBS are funded by the financial institution. The liquidity advantage of securitization increases the return from holding MBS so long as the securitizer's guarantee is credible, but securitizing the mortgage lowers the return sharply should the guarantee-sensitive investors come to doubt the guarantee of the securitizer.

As shown in the top panel of figure 6-6, if the marginal borrower is funded directly by the financial institution as a whole mortgage, then the conditions in the secondary market do not affect the interest rate in the primary loan market. Since the financial institution holds the marginal loan as a whole mortgage, no funding risk premium is embedded in the mortgage rate, since funding is provided only by insured depositors.

In contrast, if the marginal borrower's mortgage is securitized, then the financial institution gains a liquidity premium by holding the mortgage as an MBS (bottom panel). But the presence of guarantee-sensitive investors creates an offsetting liquidity risk premium that raises the mortgage rate in the primary market relative to what the rate would have been had such investors not been concerned about the *average* credit risk of the securitizer. The mortgage rate increases from r_2 to r_R, and the credit quality of the marginal borrower increases from q_1 to q_{min}. As a result, a smaller portion of the mortgage market segment is securitized. As was the case when the financial institution was funded directly by uninsured retail investors, when MBS are funded by insured financial institutions, the credibility of the guarantee provided by the securitizer is instrumental to realizing the benefits of securitization. This suggests the following proposition:

Figure 6-6. *Equilibrium Mortgage Rates with Deposit Insurance and MBS Purchases by Guarantee-Sensitive Investors*

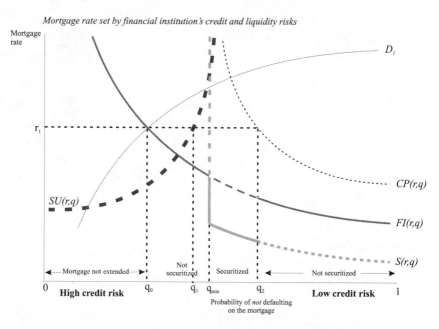

Mortgage rate set by financial institution's credit and liquidity risks

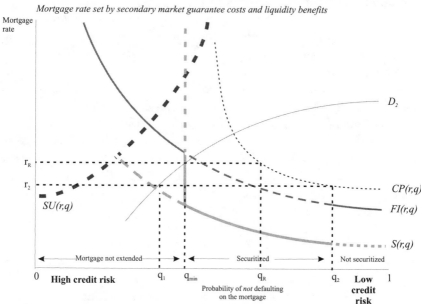

Mortgage rate set by secondary market guarantee costs and liquidity benefits

Source: Authors' calculation.

Proposition 3. If the credibility of the guarantee of a securitizer becomes questioned by guarantee-sensitive investors, then the possibility that market conditions for selling MBS into secondary markets will deteriorate quickly can increase mortgage rates in primary mortgage markets and decrease the extent of securitization.

Financial Crisis and Securitization

The shifting of the risk tolerance of guarantee-sensitive investors and of the average risk of mortgage portfolios provides a way to characterize a financial crisis. All things equal, as guarantee-sensitive investors' average risk tolerance decreases—represented by a shift of the vertical portion of the zero profit function to the right—lending to higher-risk borrowers decreases first, the proportion of securitized mortgages decreases second, and finally the proportion of low-risk mortgages that originators cherry pick and keep in their portfolios diminishes (as demonstrated in figures 6-4 and 6-5). This process of shifting the vertical portion of the zero profit function to the right in figures 6-4 and 6-5 is one way to portray how a run by guarantee-sensitive investors results in the collapse of private-label mortgage securitizations during a financial crisis.

Prior to the recent financial crisis, many dubious financial structures for nonagency MBS were created for the purpose of selling guarantee-sensitive investors highly rated securities. As the high risks associated with such structures were revealed through higher-than-expected losses, guarantee-sensitive investors fled these markets and dumped the securities. Nearly the only nonagency mortgage credit extended during this panic consisted of low-risk mortgages that financial institutions were willing to fund and hold in their portfolios. As illustrated in the top panel of figure 6-7, mortgage rates increase from r_{R1} to r_{R2} and the credit quality of the marginal borrower increases from q_{min1} to q_{min2}. When a run occurs, securitization disappears from the mortgage market.

Our model can also describe the strength of government-backed mortgage securitization during the crisis. The GSE guarantee of MBS was generally perceived to be credible by guarantee-sensitive investors, and thus GSE mortgage securitization remained robust. Indeed, during 2007 and 2008, investor uncertainty about the asset quality of whole mortgages and private-label MBS, which were held mainly at the largest financial institutions, caused the capital costs of financial institutions to rise sharply. This phenomenon is represented by the $FI(r,q)$ line shifting even farther up relative to $S(r,q)$. As a result, financial institutions found it too costly to hold even the safest mortgages (as illustrated in the bottom panel of figure 6-7). Thus, during the crisis, almost all mortgages in the conforming prime market were guaranteed by Fannie Mae and Freddie

Figure 6-7. *Description of the Recent Financial Crisis*

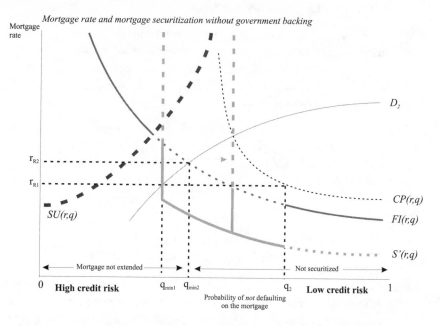

Mortgage rate and mortgage securitization without government backing

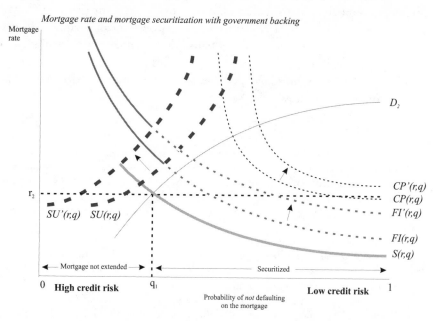

Mortgage rate and mortgage securitization with government backing

Source: Authors' calculation.

Mac, and many of the resulting MBS were eventually sold into the secondary market.[33] This suggests the following propositions:

> *Proposition 4a. If the guarantees for MBS are not trusted by guarantee-sensitive investors, then the only mortgages that are provided during a financial crisis are low-risk mortgages that the financial institutions are willing to hold in their own portfolios. The primary mortgage rates become high because of a substantial funding risk premium.*

> *Proposition 4b. As uncertainty about the credit quality of mortgages and MBS in financial institution portfolios increases, mortgages for which there remains a credible (for example, government-backed) secondary market securitizer are more likely to be securitized, and primary mortgage rates on such mortgages remain stable.*

Would Government Provision of Catastrophic Insurance for Mortgage Credit Likely Improve Financial Stability?

Our analysis of loan market equilibriums shows that the additional liquidity provided by securitization may (or may not) lower primary mortgage rates, but such liquidity comes at a cost. More specifically, if guarantee-sensitive investors doubt the credit quality of MBS, then significant risk premiums can develop.[34] If a financial crisis ensues, securitization can disappear from the mortgage market entirely, leaving banks that originate just the highest-quality mortgages as the only source of credit. This abrupt increase in lending standards can tighten mortgage credit, exacerbate home price declines, and impinge on economic growth.

---

33. According to the GSE regulator, the Federal Housing Finance Agency, Fannie Mae and Freddie Mac guaranteed about 73 percent of all new mortgage originations in 2008. Most of the mortgages not guaranteed by these entities were FHA mortgages. Mortgage originators often hold onto much of the GSE-guaranteed MBS during times of market turmoil because of liquidity concerns, but generally sell off the MBS to fund other assets during times when markets appear to be functioning normally.

34. Government-sponsored enterprises are dominated by the government when it comes to providing liquidity. The government guarantee is less likely to be in doubt (unlike say Fannie Mae's and Freddie Mac's backing, which came into question in 2008). Similarly, the portfolio of a GSE can only create liquidity during a relatively mild financial crisis because the GSE must itself issue debt to engage in asset purchases (unlike a central bank). Thus, during the financial turmoil in 1998, the GSEs purchased substantial quantities of MBS and issued a lot of debt. These strategies succeeded because these actions would have been undertaken by any profit-maximizing financial institution with access to an implicit government guarantee (see Lehnert, Passmore, and Sherlund 2008).

Credibility of Private Catastrophic Insurance for Mortgage-Backed Instruments

A private provider of catastrophic insurance for mortgage-backed instruments would have to solve an intertemporal problem to match a smooth flow of annual premium receipts to a highly uneven flow of annual loss payments (see Jaffee and Russell 1997). With a highly variable and lumpy payout pattern, it is not feasible for an insurer to pay today's losses out of today's premiums. By its nature, the contract of catastrophic insurance requires the seller to have access to a large pool of (liquid) capital to cover potential losses in every year in which the insurance contract stands.[35]

Market participants deem some catastrophic risks as uninsurable. Because aggregate U.S. home prices are likely to be correlated with the price of a global market index, insurance payouts on mortgage-backed instruments are not likely to be diversifiable. Because of the undiversifiable nature of expected payouts, the risk premiums necessary to induce investors to hold even a small fraction of their portfolio in catastrophic bonds that are designed to provide liquid capital to a private provider of catastrophic insurance for mortgage credit would likely be large. The magnitude of the U.S. housing market compared with other financial markets suggests that a capital market solution that would provide sufficient (liquid) capital to the catastrophic insurer would be expensive and lack credibility.

The government has a comparative advantage in providing catastrophic insurance for mortgage-backed instruments because private providers of insurance that guarantee payment of principle and interest do not have the power of taxation.[36] A private provider of guarantees (for example, MBS insurance) is constrained by its access to capital and its accumulated reserves in the scale of unconditional guarantees that it can offer.

The foregoing features of the catastrophic risks related to mortgage-backed instruments suggest that the private provision of guarantees associated with mortgage-backed instruments would not be credible in a severe housing downturn. Accordingly, guarantees for mortgage-related instruments provided by private entities would not necessarily stem a run by guarantee-sensitive investors, and the market failure we have identified would remain. Consequently, catastrophic risk insurance provided by the government (and financed using an explicit optimal

35. Jaffee and Russell (1997) argue that a private insurer with a large accumulation of liquid capital to cover potential payouts can become a hostile takeover target. Such takeovers may reflect either the myopic behavior of stock market investors or the agency-cost aspects of surplus cash reserves.

36. For a discussion of the U.S. experience with government provision of catastrophic insurance, see Jaffee (2008). If the government does not charge risk-based premiums for catastrophic insurance, then subsidies are created.

risk-based premium) would allow for guaranteed mortgage-backed instruments that dominate the best that can be offered without such insurance and would never do worse.[37] In addition, the government provision of catastrophic insurance for mortgage-backed instruments would avoid the "sudden stop" in the provision of mortgage credit that can exacerbate a severe housing downturn. Hence, government-backed insurance for mortgage instruments, so long as it is available under all market conditions, resolves some of the problems associated with systemic risk and implicit government guarantees and thus enhances financial stability.

Other Potential Benefits Associated with Government-Backed Catastrophic Insurance for Mortgage Instruments

Explicit, rather than implicit, guarantees lower the competitive advantage of size. Too-big-to-fail perceptions can lower the funding costs for the largest financial institutions because guarantee-sensitive investors in financial institution debt (including MBS) presume that the government will not let a very large financial institution fail. Because the government would provide catastrophic insurance on mortgage instruments to all financial institutions on equal terms (that is, at the same risk-based prices), one of the competitive advantages that result from size would be removed. Indeed, the proposed government-backed catastrophic insurer of mortgage-backed instruments would substitute the (limited) market oversight by guarantee-sensitive investors with government risk management and oversight.

Like deposit insurance, government-backed catastrophic insurance on mortgage instruments would encourage guarantee-sensitive investors to be involved in financing a wide variety of mortgage-backed instruments, rather than simply focusing on financial products provided by institutions that are perceived as implicitly backed by the government.

Long-maturity debt issuance and hedging are facilitated. Government-insured mortgage-backed instruments would enhance the ability of financial institutions to issue and hedge long-term debt.[38] Government-backed MBS (and also government-backed covered bonds) of long duration could be issued to guarantee-sensitive investors in almost all financial market conditions. Such instruments would entail no credit risk and could be easily hedged against

37. See Diamond and Dybvig (1983) for a discussion of government deposit insurance in a Nash equilibrium context. For a discussion of the challenges of pricing such insurance, see Pennacchi (2000, 2005, 2006, 2009).

38. However, as pointed out by Huberman and Repullo (2010), this ability to issue longer-term debt might undermine the market discipline imposed by shorter-term debt holders on financial institutions. The government-backed insurer of catastrophic risks associated with mortgage-backed instruments would need to have the ability to monitor the behavior of the financial institutions ex post (similar to the monitoring currently undertaken by Fannie Mae and Freddie Mac) to ensure that the underwriting conditions for use of the government guarantee were followed.

interest risk, thereby resolving some of the problems associated with the interest rate risks of mortgage contracts (particularly the thirty-year mortgage contract). Like the current MBS market, mortgage-backed instruments with government catastrophic mortgage insurance could potentially be distributed using a "to be announced" (TBA) market.

Institutions would have greater flexibility to respond in a financial crisis. Financial institutions may prefer to employ government-backed assets for short-term financing, such as repo transactions, and to have the option to sell a government-backed asset readily to raise cash. For example, it may be less costly to deleverage a financial institution that holds guaranteed assets than to deleverage a financial institution that uses guaranteed liabilities to fund illiquid loans. If this is the case, debt overhang problems are less costly in an environment with greater availability of government-backed assets.

While not related directly to runs by guarantee-sensitive investors, another potential advantage of government-backed mortgage instruments is that the scope of bonds that could be purchased by the Federal Reserve would remain similar to what it is now. Currently, the Federal Reserve can purchase Treasury securities and government agency debt and MBS. Creating explicitly guaranteed government MBS would continue to provide the Federal Reserve with more options for dealing with a liquidity crisis. Such options may be valuable in that asset purchases by the Federal Reserve—much like the MBS purchase program that was conducted during January 5, 2009, through March 31, 2010—could potentially reassure guarantee-sensitive investors (for example, insured depositors) more broadly and also provide needed liquidity to the financial system (see Hancock and Passmore 2011).

Is There a Potential Role for Fannie Mae and Freddie Mac to Provide Government-Backed Insurance for Mortgage-Backed Instruments?

An institutional structure for stemming runs analogous to the current setup for the Federal Deposit Insurance Corporation could be deployed to insure catastrophic risks associated with prespecified mortgage-backed instruments (for example, MBS and covered bonds). The FDIC—an independent government agency that provides deposit insurance to U.S. banks—is generally funded by insurance premiums and from earnings on investments in Treasury securities, but it has a statutory line of credit with the U.S. Treasury equal to $100 billion.[39]

39. The Federal Deposit Insurance Corporation is managed by a five-person board of directors, all of whom are appointed by the president and confirmed by the Senate, with no more than three being from the same political party. In the Helping Families Save Their Home Act (enacted on May 20, 2009), the statutory line of credit for the FDIC was increased from $30 billion to $100 billion.

This line of credit is available in the event of an emergency or other unforeseen event that requires an unexpected outflow of cash. Like other insurance providers, the FDIC identifies, monitors, and addresses risks to its fund and charges risk-based premiums. Unlike other insurance providers, the deposit insurance guarantee is backed by the full faith and credit of the U.S. government. No depositor has ever lost a penny of insured deposits.

A government-backed catastrophic insurer for mortgage instruments would likely benefit from the accumulated information on mortgage default, the credit risk–modeling expertise, the securitization know-how, and the infrastructure (for example, workout processes and other real estate–owned management) that are currently embodied in the Fannie Mae and Freddie Mac organizations. Moreover, these entities have substantial experience in actively managing the creation and maintenance of their MBS pools of mortgages that would be useful to a catastrophic insurer of MBS and covered bonds.[40]

As described earlier, to narrow the government's role to that of a catastrophic insurance provider for mortgage-backed instruments, the minimum underwriting criteria for mortgages eligible for purchase by Fannie Mae and Freddie Mac (or a combined restructured entity) could be ratcheted down from mortgage borrowers with a good credit history and loan-to-value ratio of 80 percent or less to mortgage borrowers with a good credit history and a very low loan-to-value ratio (for example, 60 percent or less).[41] Analogously, government insurance for covered bonds issued by prudently managed financial institutions could be provided only for pools of mortgages to borrowers with a good credit history and with a very low loan-to-value.[42] Regardless of the underlying mortgage instrument, the catastrophic risk insurer would guarantee only the performance of MBS or covered bonds backed by mortgages that met or exceeded the strict underwriting criteria, not the performance of the mortgage originator or the covered bond issuer.

40. For a description of the implicit government subsidies provided to Fannie Mae and Freddie Mac and the impacts of such subsidies on mortgage markets, see Passmore (2003, 2005).

41. The recent "white paper" by the Department of the Treasury and the Department of Housing and Urban Development and GAO also suggests this type of approach as one option for reforming the housing finance market. See the Department of Treasury and Department of Housing and Urban Development (2011) and GAO (2009).

42. A primary difference between agency MBS and some other types of asset-backed securities (or covered bonds) is that in the case of agency MBS the collateral of the pool backing the debt is not replaced by the issuer of the pool when the loan defaults. Instead, the guarantor makes the investors in the securities whole by purchasing the defaulted mortgage at par. In contrast, in the case of other types of structures the loan in the pool may be replaced by the issuer of the securities when a loan defaults. In other words, in the case of agency MBS, the pool is static and managed under a trust agreement, but in other cases the pool is actively managed by the security issuer.

Strict underwriting standards on mortgages that are based on a very low loan-to-value ratio test would also ensure that mortgage borrowers, private mortgage insurers, and financial institutions that provide credit enhancements on mortgages would have considerable skin in the game.[43] Like Fannie Mae and Freddie Mac currently do for conforming mortgages, the government-backed catastrophic insurer for mortgage instruments would determine how down payments, private mortgage insurance, and credit enhancements could be used separately or together to create the very low loan-to-value ratio that would be needed to qualify for a guarantee.

The provision of "tail risk" mortgage insurance by the government would also allow it to set standards and determine best practices for mortgage origination, for mortgage data, for mortgage servicing, and for the TBA market. Much like the GSEs have done in the past, the ability to guarantee the performance of mortgages is the key to managing risks and practices in the primary and secondary mortgage markets. Moreover, the provision of catastrophic insurance would afford the government a tool with which to manage its risk associated with a severe downturn in the housing market. Using the information garnered from underwriting insurance, it would be better able to monitor emerging risks in housing and mortgage markets, both idiosyncratic and systemic. For example, it could consider the distribution of debt burdens across U.S. homeowners in different geographic regions to assess the risks of a housing contraction. It could also monitor new types of credit enhancements and other innovations used to facilitate the provision of high-risk mortgages, so as to consider their potential both to inflate home prices and to pose a threat to the financial system.

If the GSEs were restructured into a FDIC-like catastrophic insurer for mortgage-backed instruments, they would strictly be an insurer and would not be permitted to issue debt directly to the public for the purpose of purchasing asset portfolios.[44] That said, the government-backed insurer would be able to invest the (risk-based) insurance premiums it receives in cash, cash equivalents, Treasury bills, and Treasury notes.

The risk-based premiums and size of the fund of the government-backed catastrophic insurer of mortgage instruments would be based on the expectation of losses in market conditions that prevail in all but the most extreme circumstances. This information could potentially be used by both unsecured senior and subordinated debt investors to assess their risks. However, determining how

43. Davidson (2009) has proposed a senior mortgage bond and subordinated mortgage bond structure, with government insurance only on the senior bond.

44. Under the conservatorship and preferred stock agreements, Fannie Mae and Freddie Mac are each required to reduce their portfolio to as little as $250 billion over time.

the government would set risk-based insurance premiums is a much-debated topic, particularly since the government might be prone to misprice systemic risk (see Pennacchi 2000, 2005, 2006). With the explicit pricing of such guarantees, such debates can occur and potentially reduce the misallocation of resources that most certainly results from implicit guarantees that are not priced at all.

One possible pricing rule suggested by our analysis is to set the fee for the government guarantee so that during good economic times the most efficient, profitable, well-capitalized, and well-diversified bank is indifferent between securitizing a qualifying mortgage and holding it. This rule would set a floor on the fee that would be tied to the efficient operation of the banking system and would limit the extent of any arbitrage between the largest banks and the government insurer. Many other financial institutions would still have significant incentives to securitize, thus providing an ongoing and meaningful outlet to mortgage originators and ensuring that the government insurer securitizes a substantial portion of mortgage originations. It is also a pricing rule that would lead to a substantial increase in government backing of the mortgage market during a financial crisis. This pricing rule, of course, is just one possible approach, and its implications need to be explored further.

As is the case with the FDIC, the full faith and credit of the U.S. government would stand behind the proposed catastrophic insurer of mortgage instruments, and the insurer would have access to a line of credit. With the foregoing reforms, the provision of federally backed insurance on prespecified mortgage-backed instruments provided at risk-based premiums could provide a rationale for restructuring the housing-related GSEs to support a public purpose.[45]

---

45. In recent speeches and testimony, Federal Reserve Chairman Ben Bernanke, Secretary of the Treasury Timothy Geithner, and former Secretary of the Treasury Henry Paulson have highlighted the need to reform Fannie Mae and Freddie Mac. See Bernanke (2008a), Geithner (2009, 2010), and Paulson (2009). One potential way to provide government-backed catastrophic insurance is to implement a limited program that would play a significant role in the secondary mortgage markets only during a financial crisis (see chapter 7 of this volume). The idea has many similarities with the approach presented here, but some significant differences. First, we are skeptical that the government can successfully structure a government corporation that needs highly skilled staff that has only minimal participation in the secondary market almost all the time. Second, it not clear how such a program establishes an adequate reserve fund. Third, without significant participation in the secondary mortgage market during a boom, the government insurer will not be able to influence mortgage underwriting standards and, perhaps, mitigate the effects of loose underwriting. Finally, and most important, we are skeptical that guarantee-sensitive investors will be drawn into the secondary mortgage market with such a program unless they perceive that all qualifying mortgages have an implicit government guarantee. When the choice is between guarantees that are implicit or explicit, we would argue that an explicitly priced government guarantee is a better approach.

Conclusion

We have considered the fragility of mortgage securitization and proposed a tailored government remedy that is time consistent. Our analysis of mortgage market equilibriums demonstrates that the additional liquidity provided by mortgage securitization may (or may not) lower primary mortgage rates, but such liquidity comes at the cost of a potential run. More specifically, if guarantee-sensitive investors doubt the credit quality of mortgage-backed securities, significant risk premiums can develop. If a financial crisis ensues, mortgage securitization can disappear from the market entirely, leaving banks that originate just the highest-quality mortgages as the only source of credit. This abrupt increase in lending standards can tighten credit, exacerbate home price declines, and impinge on economic growth. In such circumstances, the government ends up "owning" the "tail risk."

During a credit boom, particularly when home prices are rising, there are many guarantee-sensitive investors who will purchase the debt issued, or mortgage-backed securities guaranteed, by large financial institutions. Since there is a broader range of investors who purchase and sell the debt issued, or securities guaranteed, by large financial institutions, the liquidity of such instruments is greatly enhanced. However, as was seen just prior to when Fannie Mae and Freddie Mac were placed into conservatorships (as well as when some notable investment banks were on the verge of collapse), such liquidity can suddenly dry up when the implicit government guarantee comes into doubt. Indeed, guarantee-sensitive investors are prone to run in a manner similar to what retail depositors did before the establishment of government-provided deposit insurance. Such actions simultaneously drive down security prices and build up liquidity premiums, regardless of the fundamental values of the assets (for example, mortgages and homes) that back the securities. In such circumstances, the issuance of (private-label) mortgage-backed securities can abruptly cease, as occurred in the fall of 2008.

Catastrophic risk insurance provided by the government (and financed using explicit optimal risk-based premiums) would allow for guaranteed mortgage-backed instruments that would likely dominate mortgage-backed instruments that can be offered without such insurance. Moreover, such insurance could be structured to enforce prudent underwriting standards for mortgage-backed instruments and to require parties (for example, homeowners, private insurance providers, and loan originators) to put their own capital on the line in front of taxpayers. Such insurance would also allow for the continuation of a TBA market for mortgage-backed instruments.

We argue that an institutional structure for stemming runs analogous to the current setup for the FDIC could be deployed to insure prespecified mortgage-backed instruments (for example, MBS and covered bonds) using risk-based premiums. Such an insurer would, of course, likely benefit from the accumulated information on mortgage default, the credit risk–modeling expertise, the securitization know-how, and the infrastructure embodied in the Fannie Mae and Freddie Mac organizations. Hence, providing federally backed insurance on prespecified mortgage-backed instruments at risk-based premiums in an effort to stem a potential run by guarantee-sensitive investors could provide a rationale for restructuring the housing-related GSEs to support a public purpose.

Regardless of its institutional structure, a government-backed catastrophic insurer of mortgage-backed instruments would provide greater financial stability and ensure that credit is provided at reasonable cost both in times of prosperity and during downturns. The *explicit* pricing of the government-backed guarantee would mitigate the market distortions that have been created by *implicit* premiums during prosperity in the past. Indeed, *explicit* government provision of catastrophic insurance for mortgage instruments would limit the moral hazard created by *implicit* government guarantees that would likely arise in its absence.

References

Acharya, Viral V., Hyun Song Shin, and Tanju Yorulmazer. 2009. "A Theory of Slow-Moving Capital and Contagion." CEPR Discussion Paper 7147. London: Centre for Economic Policy Research (January).

Adrian, Tobias, and Hyun Song Shin. 2008. "Leverage and Value-at-Risk." Staff Report 338. Federal Reserve Bank of New York (July).

Bernanke, Ben S. 2007. "GSE Portfolios, Systemic Risk, and Affordable Housing." Remarks before the Annual Convention and Techworld. Independent Community of Bankers of America, Honolulu, Hawaii, March 6.

———. 2008a. "The Future of Mortgage Finance in the United States." Presentation at the Symposium "The Mortgage Meltdown, the Economy, and Public Policy." University of California, Berkeley/University of California, Los Angeles, October 31.

———. 2008b. "Liquidity Provision by the Federal Reserve." Presentation at the Risk Transfer Mechanisms and Financial Stability Workshop. Basel, Switzerland, May 29.

Brunnermeier, M. K., and L. H. Pedersen. 2008. "Market Liquidity and Funding Liquidity." *Review of Financial Studies* 22, no. 6: 2201–38.

Caballero, Ricardo. 2009. "The 'Other' Imbalance and the Financial Crisis." Working Paper 09-32. Massachusetts Institution of Technology, Department of Economics (December).

Calem, Paul, Christopher Henderson, and Jonathan Liles. 2010. "'Cream-Skimming' in Subprime Mortgage Securitization: Which Subprime Mortgage Loans Were Sold by Depository Institutions Prior to the Crisis of 2007?" Working Paper. Federal Reserve Bank of Philadelphia (March).

Costello, Glenn, Mary Kelsch, and M. Diane Pendley. 2007. "The Impact of Poor Underwriting Practices and Fraud in Subprime RMBS Performance." U.S. Residential Mortgage Special Report, Structured Finance. New York: Fitch Ratings (November 28).

Covitz, Daniel, Nellie Liang, and Gustavo A. Suarez. 2009. "The Evolution of a Financial Crisis: Panic in the Asset-Backed Commercial Paper Market." Working Paper 2009-36. Washington: Federal Reserve Board (March).

Cutts, Amy C., Robert A. Van Order, and Peter M. Zorn. 2001. "Adverse Selection, Licensing, and the Role of Securitization in Financial Market Evolution, Structure, and Pricing." Working Paper. McLean, Va.: Freddie Mac (July).

Davidson, Andrew. 2009. "GSE Reform and the Future of Agency MBS." Paper prepared for the Sunset Seminar. American Securitization Forum, December 9.

Department of Treasury and Department of Housing and Urban Development. 2011. "Reforming America's Housing Finance Market." Report to Congress. Washington (February).

Diamond, Douglas W., and Philip H. Dybvig. 1983. "Bank Runs, Deposit Insurance, and Liquidity." *Journal of Political Economy* 91, no. 5: 410–19.

GAO (Government Accountability Office). 2009. "Fannie Mae and Freddie Mac: Analysis of Options for Revising the Housing Enterprises' Long-Term Structures." GAO-09-782. Washington (September).

Geanakoplos, J. 2009. "The Leverage Cycle." Discussion Paper 1715. Yale University, Cowles Foundation for Research in Economics (July).

Geithner, Timothy F. 2009. Opening statement before the U.S. Senate, Committee on Appropriations, Subcommittee on Financial Services and General Government, June 9.

———. 2010. Written testimony to the House Committee on Financial Services, March 23.

Gorton, Gary. 2009. "Slapped in the Face by the Invisible Hand: Banking and the Panic of 2007." Paper prepared for the 2009 Financial Markets Conference "Financial Innovation and Crisis." Federal Bank of Atlanta, May 11–13.

Gorton, Gary, and Andrew Metrick. 2009. "Securitized Banking and the Run on the Repo." NBER Working Paper 15223. Cambridge, Mass.: National Bureau of Economic Research (August).

Greenspan, Alan. 2004. "Government-Sponsored Enterprises." Testimony before the U.S. Senate, Committee on Banking, Housing, and Urban Affairs, February 24.

———. 2005. "Regulatory Reform of the Government-Sponsored Enterprises." Testimony before the U.S. Senate, Committee on Banking, Housing, and Urban Affairs, April 6.

Hancock, Diana, Andreas Lehnert, S. Wayne Passmore, and Shane Sherlund. 2005. "An Analysis of the Potential Competitive Impacts of Basel II Capital Standards on U.S. Mortgage Rates and Mortgage Securitization." Basel II White Paper. Washington: Board of Governors of the Federal Reserve System (April).

Hancock, Diana, and S. Wayne Passmore. 2009. "Three Initiatives Enhancing the Mortgage Market and Promoting Financial Stability." *B. E. Journal of Economic Analysis and Policy* 9, no. 3 (symposium): art. 16.

————. 2010. "An Analysis of Government Guarantees and the Functioning of Asset-Backed Securities Markets." Finance and Economics Discussion Series Working Paper 2010-46. Washington: Board of Governors of the Federal Reserve Board (September).

————. 2011. "Did the Federal Reserve's MBS Purchase Program Lower Mortgage Rates?" Forthcoming in *Journal of Monetary Economics*.

Hanson, Samuel G., Anil K. Kashyap, and Jeremy C. Stein. 2011. "A Macroprudential Approach to Financial Regulation." *Journal of Economic Perspectives* 25, no. 1: 3–28.

He, Zhiguo, and Wei Xiong. 2009. "Dynamic Bank Runs." Working paper presented at the Federal Reserve Board, March 25.

Heuson, Andrea, S. Wayne Passmore, and Roger Sparks. 2001. "Credit Scoring and Mortgage Securitization: Implications for Mortgage Rates and Credit Availability." *Journal of Real Estate Finance and Economics* 23 (November): 337–63.

Huberman, Gur, and Rafael Repullo. 2010. "Moral Hazard and Debt Maturity." Columbia Business School and CEFMI (February).

Jaffee, Dwight. 2008. "Catastrophe Insurance and Regulatory Reform after the Subprime Crisis." Working Paper. University of California, Berkeley (November 27).

Jaffee, Dwight, and Thomas Russell. 1997. "Catastrophe Insurance, Capital Markets, and Uninsurable Risks." *Journal of Risk and Insurance* 64, no. 2: 205–30.

Johnson, K., K. Pence, and D. Vine. 2010. "New Vehicle Sales and Credit Supply Shocks: What Happened in 2008?" Working Paper. Washington: Federal Reserve Board.

Kashyap, Anil, Raghuram Rajan, and Jeremy Stein. 2008. "Rethinking Capital Regulation." Paper presented at the symposium "Maintaining Stability in a Changing Financial System." Federal Reserve Bank of Kansas City, Jackson Hole, August 21–23.

Keys, Benjamin J., Tanmoy Mukherjee, Amit Seru, and Vikrant Vig. 2010. "Did Securitization Lead to Lax Screening? Evidence from Subprime Loans." *Quarterly Journal of Economics* 125, no. 1: 307–62.

Lehnert, Andreas, S. Wayne Passmore, and Shane Sherlund. 2008. "Mortgage Rates and Secondary Market Activities." *Journal of Real Estate Finance and Economics* 36, no. 3: 343–63.

Passmore, S. Wayne. 2003. "The GSE Implicit Subsidy and the Value of Government Ambiguity." Finance and Economic Discussion Series Working Paper 2003-64. Washington: Federal Reserve Board.

————. 2005. "The GSE Implicit Subsidy and the Value of Government Ambiguity." *Real Estate Economics* 33, no. 3: 465–86.

Passmore, S. Wayne, and Roger Sparks. 1996. "Putting the Squeeze on a Market for Lemons: Government-Sponsored Mortgage Securitization." *Journal of Real Estate Finance and Economics* 96, no. 13: 27–43.

Paulson, Henry M. 2008. "Paulson Announces GSE Initiatives." Department of Treasury Statement HP-1079. Washington: U.S. Department of the Treasury (July 13).

————. 2009. "The Role of GSEs in Supporting the Housing Recovery." Presentation at the Economic Club of Washington, January 7.

Pennacchi, George. 2000. "The Effects of Setting Deposit Insurance Premiums to Target Insurance Fund Reserves." *Journal of Financial Services Research* 17, no. 1: 153–80.

———. 2005. "Risk-Based Capital Standards, Deposit Insurance, and Procyclicality." *Journal of Financial Intermediation* 14, no. 4: 432–65.

———. 2006. "Deposit Insurance, Bank Regulation, and Financial System Risks." *Journal of Monetary Economics* 53, no. 1: 1–30.

———. 2009. "Deposit Insurance." Paper prepared for the Conference on Private Markets and Public Insurance Programs. American Enterprise Institute, Washington, January 15.

Pozsar, Zoltan, Tobias Adrian, Adam Ashcraft, and Hayley Boesky. 2010. "Shadow Banking." Staff Report 458. Federal Reserve Bank of New York (July).

Shleifer, Andrei, and Robert W. Vishny. 2009. "Unstable Banking." *Journal of Financial Economics* 97, no. 3: 306–18.

Snowden, K. A. 1995. "Mortgage Securitization in the U.S.: 20th Century Developments in Historical Perspective." In *Anglo-American Financial Systems,* edited by Michael Bordo and Richard Sylla, pp. 261–98. New York: Irwin.

———. 2007. "Mortgage Companies and Mortgage Securitization in the Late Nineteenth Century." University of North Carolina at Greensboro (August).

———. 2010. "The Anatomy of a Residential Mortgage Crisis: A Look Back to the 1930s." NBER Working Paper 16244. Cambridge, Mass.: National Bureau of Economic Research (July).

Steinbach, Gordon H. 1998. "Making Risk-Based Pricing Work." *Mortgage Banking* 58, no. 12: 10–19.

Stiglitz, Joseph E., and Andrew Weiss. 1981. "Credit Rationing in Markets with Imperfect Information." *American Economic Review* 71, no. 3: 393–410.

Van Order, Robert A. 2000. "The U.S. Mortgage Market: A Model of Dueling Charters." *Journal of Housing Research* 11, no. 2: 233–55.

White, Eugene N. 2009. "Lessons from the Great American Real Estate Boom and Bust of the 1920s." NBER Working Paper 15573. Cambridge, Mass.: National Bureau of Economic Research (December).

7

The Economics of Housing Finance Reform

DAVID SCHARFSTEIN AND ADI SUNDERAM

There is widespread agreement across the political spectrum that Fannie Mae and Freddie Mac should be wound down. With the two government-sponsored enterprises (GSEs) now guaranteeing or owning about half of all residential mortgages in the United States, this will require nothing less than a complete redesign of the U.S. housing finance system. Unfortunately, there is little agreement about what the new system of housing finance should be.

There are two leading types of housing finance reform proposals. The first type of proposal—offered by numerous industry groups, think tanks, Federal Reserve economists, and other analysts—seeks to replicate key attributes of the current market for GSE-guaranteed mortgage-backed securities (MBS) with explicit, fairly priced government guarantees of MBS. In the typical proposal, private entities are the primary guarantors of MBS, the government provides reinsurance in the event that the private guarantors are impaired, and MBS investors bear no credit risk. The second type of proposal envisions privatizing mortgage markets by eliminating targeted government guarantees of mortgage credit.

We thank our former colleagues at the U.S. Treasury Department and National Economic Council for sharing with us their many insights on housing finance reform. The views expressed in this paper are our own and should in no way be construed as reflecting their views or those of the Treasury or NEC. We are grateful to Martin Baily, Sam Hanson, and Jeremy Stein for very valuable discussions as we worked on this paper. We thank Toomas Laarits for excellent research assistance and the Harvard Business School for financial support.

This chapter starts with an economic analysis of these two types of proposals. We argue that both have significant drawbacks. The government-guarantee proposals reach too far in the scope of their guarantees, while providing little benefit to households under normal financial market conditions. In contrast, privatization proposals do not reach far enough. They ignore flaws in securitization and the fundamental instability of mortgage credit supplied by the private market.

Our analysis of the two leading proposals suggests that we need to reorient the goals of housing finance policy. We argue that *housing finance policy should seek to reduce excess volatility in the supply of housing credit and protect the financial system from adverse shocks to the housing sector.* Specifically, policy should be aimed at reducing the risk of mortgage credit booms, protecting against a drought in mortgage credit, and ensuring that the financial system can withstand a steep downturn in the housing sector.

With these policy aims in mind, we propose a set of housing finance reforms that draw from elements of the two leading reform proposals. Given our skepticism about the benefits of mortgage guarantees under normal financial conditions, *we support the eventual elimination of Fannie Mae and Freddie Mac and significant privatization of mortgage markets.* However, to prevent the kind of mortgage credit boom that characterized the period from 2001 to 2006, *we also advocate significant and stringent regulation of private mortgage markets.* These regulations would combine prohibitions on certain risky mortgages with enhanced capital requirements for financial firms and a new regulatory regime for securitization markets that strengthens the skin-in-the-game regulations put forth in the Dodd-Frank Act. Our proposed regulations include restrictions on the capital structure of securitization trusts as well as restrictions on the financing of MBS purchases. This is the most challenging part of our proposal given the lack of a well-accepted paradigm for the regulation of securitization markets. But it is an essential element of our proposal given the large role that securitization played in the subprime crisis and the broader financial crisis. And regardless of whether housing finance reform results in a greater role for government guarantees of prime mortgages than we would advocate, there will still be a private securitization market for nonprime mortgages and a need to regulate that part of the market.

The second part of our proposal is to establish a government-owned corporation to guarantee MBS. The primary role of this corporation would be *to ensure the supply of high-quality, well-underwritten mortgages during a period of significant market stress* such as the financial crisis of 2007–09. To ensure that the corporation would be able to provide guarantees in a timely fashion during a systemic crisis, we propose that it operate in normal times but with a hard-wired constraint on its market share of no more than 10 percent and possibly less. This market share could only be lifted with the approval of the Financial Stability Oversight Council in response to a systemic crisis.

We propose that this mortgage guarantor be a self-funded government-owned corporation, not a government agency and not a private corporation. As a government-owned corporation with an independent board, it would be less easily influenced by political considerations. More important, as a government-owned corporation it would not likely seek to increase profits by loosening underwriting standards in the way that a private corporation would, making it more likely to be in a strong financial position entering a downturn. In summary, we argue for a carefully regulated, largely private system of mortgage finance in normal times, coupled with a government guarantor to help provide mortgage credit in a severe housing downturn.

The chapter is organized as follows. We begin by analyzing government guarantee proposals and then consider privatization proposals. We then build on the analysis to put forth a set of goals for housing finance reform and lay out our proposal. A final section concludes.

Analysis of Explicit Government Guarantee Proposals

Many leading proposals for housing finance reform involve some form of explicit government guarantee of MBS, usually in conjunction with private market guarantees in a first-loss position. These proposals have two ostensible goals. The first is to preserve key features of GSE-guaranteed MBS, which provide liquidity and credit protection to their holders. The second is to protect the government from losses by charging an explicit fee in exchange for the guarantee.

Proposals along these lines have been advocated by a variety of parties, including industry groups such as the Mortgage Bankers Association, the National Association of Home Builders, and the National Association of Realtors; the Center for American Progress, a progressive think tank; and economists from the Federal Reserve Bank of New York and the Federal Reserve Board of Governors.[1]

We have four main criticisms of these proposals. First, if the government charges the right price for bearing the credit risk associated with its guarantee, the effect on mortgage rates is likely to be small relative to a world without such guarantees. Second, even if government guarantees could lower mortgage financing costs to some extent, the tax code and certain market frictions already make

---

1. See Mortgage Bankers Association (2009), National Association of Home Builders (2010), National Association of Realtors (2010); Center for American Progress (2011); Dechario and others (2010); Hancock and Passmore (2010).

housing investment easier to finance than other socially valuable forms of investment such as education. It may not be desirable to distort investment further in
favor of housing. Third, government guarantee proposals that involve private
financial firms are likely to suffer from governance problems similar to those
that plagued Fannie and Freddie, exposing the taxpayer to significant uncom-
pensated losses in housing downturns. Given the small benefits of government
guarantees during normal market conditions, these costs are probably not worth
bearing. Fourth, in stressed market conditions, private financial firms that guarantee mortgages will themselves be financially impaired. This will limit their
ability to guarantee new MBS issues even if the government guarantee protects
legacy MBS issues. Thus in a crisis the government may have to inject capital
into private guarantors to ensure the continuing flow of mortgage credit, just as
it has done with Fannie and Freddie.

Effect of Properly Priced Government Guarantees on the Cost of Mortgage Credit

Advocates of government guarantees argue that they lower mortgage costs both
because the government can absorb credit risk more efficiently than the market
and because MBS are more liquid when holders do not have to evaluate credit
risk. Guarantee advocates also argue that guarantees can be used to promote
the issuance of long-term, fixed-rate, prepayable mortgages, which are desirable
from a consumer protection point of view. Here we raise several concerns about
the validity of these arguments.

LOWER MBS YIELDS AND MORTGAGE COSTS

It is generally believed that the guarantee fees charged by the two GSEs
(approximately 22 basis points) were too low, given the risks they were bearing
on their guarantee book. They were able to charge low fees and make money on
their guarantee book because lax regulators did not require them to hold much
capital (approximately 45 basis points) against the risk of losses. Despite this
small capital cushion, the implicit government guarantee meant that investors
viewed GSE mortgage-backed securities as essentially riskless.

Nevertheless, numerous studies have raised doubts about how much homeowners benefited from the implicit guarantee on Fannie and Freddie MBS.
These studies, including CBO (2001), Torregrosa (2001), Ambrose, LaCour-
Little, and Sanders (2004), McKenzie (2002), Passmore, Sherlund, and Burgess (2005), and Sherlund (2008), typically examine the differences in rates
between jumbo mortgages, which are securitized without a GSE guarantee,

Figure 7-1. *Mortgage Rates and Treasury Yields, 1998–2009*

Percent

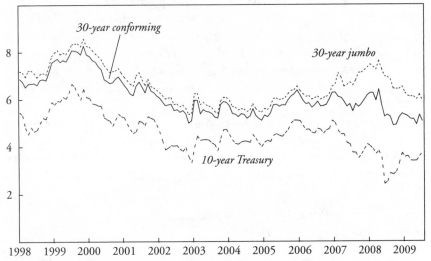

Source: Federal Reserve Statistical Release H.15, Bankrate.

and conforming mortgages, which are securitized with a GSE guarantee.[2] After controlling for borrower characteristics, these studies estimate the benefit of the GSE guarantee on mortgage rates to be anywhere from 7 to 30 basis points, a surprisingly small effect.

To put these estimates in context, figure 7-1 shows the thirty-year conforming mortgage rate, the thirty-year jumbo mortgage rate, and the ten-year Treasury yield. Over most of the period, until the financial crisis hit in mid-2007, the conforming and jumbo mortgage rates were quite similar, and both closely tracked the Treasury yield. Indeed, 90 percent of the variation in both rates over this period was driven by variations in the Treasury yield. The difference between conforming and jumbo rates, which could be attributed to the GSE guarantee, was small in comparison. It was only at the onset of the financial crisis in 2007 that jumbo rates rose relative to conforming rates. Thus the main

2. This spread may underestimate the true value of the government guarantee. In particular, with the GSEs guaranteeing a large share of mortgage credit in the United States, jumbo mortgage lenders may have higher risk-bearing capacity and may be willing to lend at lower rates than they otherwise would if the GSEs were not absorbing so much credit risk. Nevertheless, whatever the effect of lax regulation and the free government guarantee on mortgage rates, it stands to reason that the effect would be even smaller when regulation is tightened and the guarantee is priced.

Figure 7-2. *Originator Concentration and Spreads, 1995–2008*

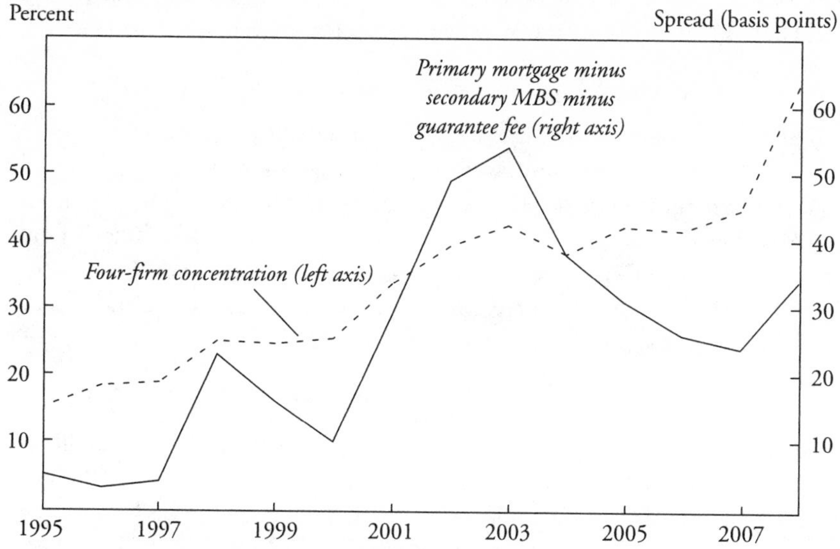

Sources: Freddie Mac Primary Mortgage Market Survey; FHFA (2009).

value of guarantees is that they support the extension of mortgage credit in periods of financial market distress.

As noted by Hermalin and Jaffee (1996), one possible explanation of the small difference between jumbo and conforming mortgage rates is that the beneficiaries of the MBS subsidy are not homeowners, but the GSEs and their shareholders. Another possibility is that the benefits of the subsidy are captured by the banks that originate and then securitize the loan pools into GSE mortgage-backed securities. This would be the case if loan origination itself were imperfectly competitive. Indeed, as shown in figure 7-2, there is some evidence of this. Over the last fifteen years the mortgage origination industry has become significantly more concentrated, according to data from Inside Mortgage Finance. The top four mortgage originators accounted for less than 15 percent of originations in 1995, but more than 60 percent in 2008. At the same time, the spread between the primary mortgage rates available to borrowers (less the guarantee fee) and the yield on Fannie Mae current coupon MBS increased from about 5 basis points to more than 30 basis points.[3] While this evidence is not definitive, it does suggest that the market power of players throughout the mortgage

3. Primary mortgage rates are from Freddie Mac's weekly primary mortgage survey. The current coupon yield on Fannie MBS is from Barclays.

origination chain could be an important consideration when evaluating the benefits of government guarantees. Thus even if government guarantees lower MBS yields, they may not lower the mortgage costs for borrowers very much.

PROPERLY PRICED GOVERNMENT GUARANTEES AND MBS YIELDS

To better understand whether *properly priced* government guarantees lower MBS yields, we start by contrasting pass-through nonguaranteed MBS with ones that are fully guaranteed by the government. Holders of nonguaranteed MBS bear credit risk as well as interest rate and prepayment risks on long-term, fixed-rate, prepayable mortgages. They also bear liquidity risk, which we discuss later. Since holders of guaranteed MBS bear the same interest rate and prepayment risks, our focus is on analyzing differences in the way credit risk is borne across the two types of securities.

Credit risk has two components: expected losses on the securities arising from troubled loans and co-variation of those losses with macroeconomic conditions in which investors suffer other losses. The yields on nonguaranteed MBS must therefore compensate their holders for expected losses and provide a risk premium for the co-variation with other investor losses. In exchange for not bearing credit risk, guaranteed MBS holders pay a guarantee fee to the government analogous to the guarantee fees they pay to the two GSEs.

The guaranteed securities will require a lower yield provided the guarantee fee (*GFee*) is less than the yield required to compensate investors for bearing credit risk. Since the compensation for credit risk is the sum of expected losses on defaults in the loan pool (*EL*) and the risk premium on such losses (*RP*), guaranteed securities will have lower yields than nonguaranteed ones if

$$(5\text{-}1) \qquad\qquad GFee < EL + RP.$$

Ideally, lower yields on guaranteed MBS would be passed along to borrowers in the form of lower mortgage rates, although the evidence above suggests that this may not be the case.

Thus determining the proper *GFee* that the government should charge is critical to analyzing whether a government guarantee of MBS is desirable. The implicit assumption of government-guarantee advocates is that *GFee* should be set equal to the actuarially fair rate that just covers expected losses on the loan pool (*GFee* = *EL*), in which case guaranteed MBS require lower yields than nonguaranteed MBS, as indicated by the inequality above.[4] In this case, the government prices the fee as if it were risk neutral, protecting itself from losses on average, but

---

4. Since 1990, the Federal Credit Reform Act has required the costs of on-budget guarantee programs to be accounted for on an expected-loss basis (that is, without a risk premium).

not charging holders of guaranteed MBS the risk premium, *RP,* for bearing losses at a time when there are losses on other assets. Of course, this risk is ultimately borne by taxpayers. The critical question then is whether the government should include a risk premium in the *GFee* to compensate the government and taxpayers for the systematic risks they are bearing. If it is optimal to charge the full risk premium (*GFee = EL + RP*), then there is no yield advantage to guaranteed MBS.

Arrow and Lind (1970) show that the government, acting in the interest of taxpayers, should not charge a risk premium on government projects as long as a project's costs are independent of taxpayers' income. Because risks are pooled across a large number of taxpayers, the risk associated with the project has only a negligible effect on the welfare of individual taxpayers. As in the capital asset pricing model (CAPM), purely idiosyncratic risk should not receive a risk premium.

However, this assumption of independence does not apply to the mortgage market. The realized costs of guarantees are high when mortgage defaults rise—that is, the costs are high when home prices, and hence taxpayer wealth and income, have fallen. Ultimately, government mortgage guarantees mean that taxpayers will bear greater tax liabilities in states of the world in which their wealth has fallen.[5] As in the CAPM and related models, they should be compensated for bearing this risk. This point applies to a wide range of programs in which the government takes financial risk, as discussed by Lucas and Phaup (2010). *The key point is that risks of mortgage default are always borne by society as a whole. The issue is whether the costs associated with bearing those risks are faced by homeowners through the guarantee fee or by taxpayers through contingent tax liabilities.*

Thus one can argue that the government should embed a risk premium in the *GFee,* although it is an open question whether the risk premium should be the same as would be charged by the private market. One could argue that the government should charge a lower risk premium than the market given that imperfections in capital markets make it more difficult for investors to smooth their consumption than for the government to smooth its expenditures. A large adverse shock to the housing sector that leads to an increase in defaults means that holders of nonguaranteed mortgage-backed pass-through securities would take large losses, requiring them to cut consumption or borrow against future income to maintain consumption. By contrast, when the government takes losses on its guarantees of MBS, it can defer tax increases or expenditure cuts to reduce the contemporaneous burden on taxpayers. However, even if taxpayers do not respond in this way, one has to ask why the government should use its

---

5. This is exactly the situation that taxpayers now face as a result of the costs incurred in supporting the guarantees of the two GSEs. It is not just that the costs are high; it is also that they come at a time when taxpayers have incurred adverse wealth shocks.

risk-bearing and tax-smoothing capacity to support mortgage finance over other forms of finance, such as small business or consumer credit. Moreover, some of the tax-smoothing benefits would be reduced to the extent that taxpayers anticipate greater future tax burdens and therefore choose to cut consumption (Barro 1974).

This discussion assumes that the government is the sole guarantor of MBS. The leading proposals for government guarantees envision private firms, which we refer to as mortgage-guarantee entities (MGEs), that guarantee mortgages and take first losses on mortgage guarantees, while the government acts as a rein-surer against catastrophic losses. In this hybrid system, the MGEs would charge a risk premium for their guarantees because their shareholders would need to be compensated not just for expected losses but also for the co-variation of those losses with the returns on the rest of their portfolio. As discussed above, the government should also charge a risk premium for bearing catastrophic risk. In this case, there would be no difference between the fees the government would charge if it were the sole guarantor and the overall fees charged in the hybrid system. If instead the government does not charge a risk premium for bearing catastrophic risk, overall guarantee fees on MBS would be somewhat lower, but not appreciably different, provided the private firms are well capitalized so that they bear the large majority of the risk.

An implication of this analysis is that in the new housing finance system we should expect to see mortgage rates rise on average regardless of whether the government guarantees mortgages or not. The financial crisis has resulted in a greater understanding of the risks inherent in mortgage lending, and investors will want more compensation for bearing the risks, including a risk premium for bearing systematic risk. The same will be true of all guarantors of mortgage credit, including both MGEs and the government.

What is the likely size of the risk premium—that is, how much compensa-tion will MBS investors require for bearing the systematic risk associated with prime mortgages? The answer will tell us how large the *GFee* would have to be to cover the systematic risk borne by mortgage guarantors. To get a rough estimate of the risk premium on prime MBS, we use the CAPM. According to the CAPM, the risk premium is equal to beta—the co-variation of the asset's return with the overall market return—times the market risk premium, which is usually taken to be about 5 percent. Unfortunately, we do not directly observe beta. However, the losses incurred by Fannie and Freddie during the crisis provide some useful infor-mation that we can use to estimate it. The FHFA's conservative estimate of total GSE credit losses is $337 billion, based on an adverse scenario where home prices decline a total of 45 percent peak-to-trough (put differently, this assumes a 25 per-cent drop from September 2010 to the trough). The FHFA's more moderate baseline estimate is $232 billion. The average of the two estimates is $285 billion.

An estimated 30–40 percent of these losses come from prime loans, which constitute 70–75 percent of the guarantee book of $5.4 trillion.[6] Using the average loss estimate of $285 billion, this implies a loss rate of 1.7 to 3.0 percent. The higher loss estimate of $337 billion implies a loss rate of 2.5 to 3.5 percent.

While losses on prime mortgages were about 3 percent, the stock market was down about 50 percent from peak to trough, implying a beta of 0.06 (3/50 percent). Given a market risk premium of 5 percent, this implies a risk premium of 30 basis points (0.06 × 5 percent) on prime MBS. Under these assumptions mortgage guarantors should embed a risk premium of 30 basis points in their guarantee fees on top of expected losses.[7]

While we have argued that the government should charge a risk premium as a mortgage guarantor, our calculations imply that if the government insures prime mortgages, but does not charge a risk premium (that is, only requires a return equal to the risk-free rate), the *GFee* could be about 30 basis points lower than what private mortgage guarantors would charge. Our conclusion is that, even if the government does not charge a risk premium for its guarantee, the benefit to borrowers in terms of lower mortgage rates would be quite modest. And, of course, even these modestly lower rates would come at the expense of taxpayers who bear this risk for which they have not been compensated.

Government Guarantees and Liquidity

Government guarantees could also lower mortgage rates by increasing the liquidity of MBS. There are two main reasons why government guarantees could increase liquidity and thereby lower the yields required by MBS investors. First, by eliminating credit risk, guarantees reduce asymmetric information problems, which could facilitate trade. Second, to the extent that guarantees are used only for a relatively narrow range of mortgages, they could encourage standardization and thus create a deeper market for securities backed by those mortgages.

6. Fannie Mae (2010a, table 15); Federal Reserve (2010, table L.125).

7. This calculation ignores the nonlinear feature of credit losses. Credit losses do not co-vary strongly with the stock market when the stock market is rising and the housing market is doing well since defaults are likely to be driven by person-specific factors rather than macroeconomic factors such as house values and unemployment. However, credit losses should co-vary more strongly with the stock market when the stock market is falling along with the house values and employment. Thus the beta of credit losses in a time series will tend to be underestimated and result in an underestimate of risk premiums. But, such concerns are alleviated by the fact that our calculations focus on a period when the market is falling and housing credit losses are actually being incurred. Our estimate of the risk premium essentially assumes that credit losses always co-vary as strongly with the stock market as they have in the recent crisis. This overstates the systematic risk of credit losses since they hardly co-vary with the stock market outside of crises. Thus our estimated risk premium and the associated guarantee fee are likely to be overestimates.

Concerns about liquidity loom large in discussions of housing finance reform because GSE mortgage-backed securities are among the most liquid fixed-income securities in the world, with daily trading volumes averaging $300 billion since 2005. In comparison, over the same period, trading in U.S. Treasury securities averaged $520 billion a day, while trading in corporate bonds averaged $16 billion a day.[8] Most trading of GSE mortgage-backed securities occurs in the "to be announced" (TBA) market, a forward market organized by the Securities Industry and Financial Markets Association (SIFMA). The key innovation underlying the TBA market is that a TBA forward contract specifies only a few characteristics of the securities that can be delivered to satisfy the contract. This allows heterogeneous GSE mortgage-backed securities to be traded as though they were homogeneous securities.

Of course, adverse selection could destroy the liquidity of such a market if traders have private information about security payoffs and deliver the worst securities that satisfy a contract. The scope for adverse selection in the TBA market is limited in three ways. First, the guarantee provided by the two GSEs eliminates adverse selection due to credit risk, although adverse selection due to prepayment risk is still present (Downing, Jaffee, and Wallace 2009). Second, the uniform underwriting standards of the two GSEs enforce a degree of homogeneity on the mortgages in each collateral pool. Third, SIFMA maintains additional rules restricting the GSE mortgage-backed securities that are eligible for delivery in the TBA market. TBA-eligible MBS must satisfy certain requirements with regard to geographic diversification and individual loan balances.

While guarantees likely increase liquidity, the size of the effect on yields is probably small, at least most of the time. For example, the yields on newly issued long-term Treasury bonds, which have a deep and active market, are typically about 6 basis points lower than the yields on less liquid long-term bonds that were issued somewhat earlier. However, this spread can increase dramatically during periods of market stress, such as in the fall of 1998, when the spread rose to about 25 basis points (Krishnamurthy 2002). Likewise, Longstaff (2004) estimates that Treasury notes trade at yields 10–15 basis points below government-guaranteed bonds issued by the Resolution Funding Corporation, the government-owned corporation set up to finance assets seized during the savings and loan crisis; he ascribes the spread to the difference in the liquidity of the two instruments. However, some studies on liquidity have found substantially larger effects. For instance, Krishnamurthy and Vissing-Jorgensen (2010) analyze the yields on Treasury bonds and AAA corporate bonds and conclude

---

8. SIFMA compilation of data from the Federal Reserve Bank of New York's primary dealer statistical release (www.sifma.org/uploadedFiles/Research/Statistics/StatisticsFiles/CM-US-Bond-Market-Trading-Volume-SIFMA.xls).

that high liquidity reduces Treasury yields by about 50 basis points. Nevertheless, they find no comparable effect for GSE mortgage-backed securities and suggest that prepayment risk may reduce the liquidity value of MBS.

Perhaps the most relevant study for our analysis is by Vickery and Wright (2010). They estimate the effects of liquidity for GSE mortgage-backed securities by comparing MBS that are eligible for delivery in the TBA market, where the large majority of GSE mortgage-backed securities are traded, with MBS that are not eligible for delivery in the TBA market. The difference in yields between TBA-eligible and -ineligible MBS should largely reflect the value of liquidity for MBS (although TBA-ineligible MBS contain high-balance loans and thus may also have greater prepayment risk than TBA-eligible MBS). They find that TBA-ineligible MBS carry yields approximately 10–15 basis points higher than TBA-eligible MBS in normal times, although the spread was as high as 50 basis points during the height of the financial crisis.

Overall, there is substantial uncertainty over the size of liquidity premiums in asset markets. However, the balance of evidence suggests that, in the context of MBS, 10–20 basis points may be a reasonable estimate in normal times. Moreover, the fact that estimates of liquidity premiums vary substantially across different government securities suggests that all government guarantees do not create equal amounts of liquidity.

In the absence of government guarantees, private markets may be able to generate some liquidity in private-label MBS through financial engineering. In normal times, the cumulative default rate on conforming mortgages is less than 1 percent so that the senior tranches of unguaranteed securitizations should be relatively low risk and informationally insensitive (Standard & Poor's 2010). This means that they could be traded without fear of adverse selection and could be quite liquid. Thus tranching may be able to provide some of the liquidity benefits of government guarantees in normal times. This is the case, for instance, with credit card securitizations where the AAA tranches are quite liquid when markets are functioning properly (Lancaster, Schultz, and Fabozzi 2008).

GOVERNMENT GUARANTEES AND THE PROMOTION OF LONG-TERM, FIXED-RATE MORTGAGES

Beyond their liquidity benefits, many believe that government guarantees help to expand the availability and affordability of thirty-year, fixed-rate, amortizing, prepayable mortgages. These observers have argued that such mortgages are desirable because they protect consumers against interest rate and rollover risks. Concerns that eliminating Fannie and Freddie would reduce the supply of these types of mortgages have at least three sources.

First, long-term, fixed-rate mortgages, while a fixture of the U.S. mortgage market, are rare in other countries. Part of the reason is that the interest rate protection that such mortgages provide borrowers exposes lenders (typically, financial institutions with floating-rate obligations) to considerable interest rate risk. Securitization of mortgages by Fannie and Freddie has enabled investors who are better able to bear interest rate and prepayment risk to hold these mortgages. However, these investors may not be able or willing to evaluate credit risk. In countries where securitization is less developed, mortgages are more likely to be held by financial institutions that are not well positioned to bear interest rate risk because of their floating-rate obligations.

Second, long-term, fixed-rate mortgages have been subsidized through the implicit guarantee of Fannie and Freddie. The subsidy has benefited the suppliers of mortgage credit, which capture some of the subsidy due to imperfect competition, as well as borrowers. Thus the implicit guarantee of Fannie and Freddie has raised the supply of long-term, fixed-rate mortgages. If the subsidy is removed, the long-term, fixed-rate mortgage will have lower supply and rates would be higher.

Third, it has been argued that, without government involvement, the thirty-year, fixed-rate, prepayable, amortizing mortgage would never have gotten off the ground in the first place. Indeed, a Depression-era government program sponsored by the Homeowners Loan Corporation introduced the long-term, fixed-rate, amortizing, mortgage to replace the short-term (about five-year maturity), nonamortizing mortgage (Courtemanche and Snowden 2010). The inability of homeowners to roll over their mortgages because of declining home values was the main reason that the government became involved in mortgage finance. The Homeowners Loan Corporation refinanced many of these underwater borrowers with long-term amortizing mortgages.

These concerns are probably overstated. For one, derivatives markets have developed to the point where financial institutions with floating-rate obligations can hedge interest rate and prepayment risks at relatively low cost. Indeed, at the end of 2009, commercial banks, thrifts, and credit unions owned 21.7 percent of outstanding GSE mortgage-backed securities. These institutions also bear interest rate and prepayment risks in their role as mortgage servicers.[9] Fannie and Freddie themselves own 15.5 percent of the outstanding MBS they guarantee (Inside Mortgage Finance 2010, vol. 2). These institutions already have to hedge their interest rate and prepayment exposures under the current regime and thus are already passing on these exposures to other players in the financial system. It is reasonable to think that they would do the same if they were to hold

---

9. Mortgage servicers bear interest rate risk because they only capture the stream of servicing fees from a mortgage until that mortgage prepays. As of December 2009, the top four mortgage servicers were the four largest banks, and they owned 56.5 percent of mortgage servicing rights (Inside Mortgage Finance 2010, vol. 1).

long-term, fixed-rate mortgages as portfolio loans or to hold securitized, long-term, fixed-rate mortgages.

Moreover, while it may be true that some investors are averse to bearing or evaluating credit risk, if there is a sufficiently large clientele of such investors, securitizations of low-risk mortgages could be tranched to create mortgage products with very little credit risk but with the same interest rate and prepayment exposures as GSE mortgage-backed securities. While securitizers may have misestimated the risk of mortgage products, they are nothing if not clever at designing structured products to meet the risk preferences of investors.

Finally, while it is true that the government introduced and helped to popularize the long-term, fixed-rate mortgage through subsidies, the two GSEs have been purchasing adjustable-rate mortgages since 1981. Thus the GSE subsidy has not uniquely preferenced fixed-rate mortgages over adjustable-rate mortgages for the last thirty years. Yet long-term, fixed-rate mortgages remain popular, suggesting that borrowers now appreciate the value of the long-term, fixed-rate mortgage and that demand for it would likely be robust even in the absence of subsidies.[10] If not, it is possible to preference these loans through other types of government policy.

Efficiency and Effectiveness of Mortgage Credit Subsidies

The government could attempt to subsidize mortgage credit by mispricing its guarantee fee, perhaps by not charging a risk premium. However, lowering the costs of mortgage credit may not be an effective way to achieve broader policy goals for several reasons. First, if government guarantees lower the mortgage interest rates faced by borrowers, some of the benefits get impounded into home prices, benefiting existing owners, not purchasers, of homes. A long literature in economics, including Poterba (1984) and Poterba, Weill, and Shiller (1991), suggests that financing costs are an important determinant of home prices. If the purpose of lowering mortgage rates is to increase affordability, particularly for

10. Vickery (2007) provides some evidence suggesting that demand for long-term fixed-rate mortgages is quite price sensitive. He shows that crossing the conforming loan limit increases the costs of fixed-rate mortgages by 17 basis points relative to adjustable-rate mortgages. This cost increase is associated with a 14 percent decline in the market share of fixed-rate mortgages. Since the two GSEs guarantee both fixed-rate and adjustable-rate mortgages, the cost difference cannot be associated with credit risk and must be driven by the pricing of interest rate risk. However, over the sample period (1992–2005), interest rate hedging technologies evolved substantially, suggesting that guarantees may play a smaller role in maintaining the market share of the fixed-rate mortgage than they once did. Furthermore, the reported price differential between fixed-rate and adjustable-rate mortgages may in part represent the underpricing by the GSEs of interest rate risk in their portfolios, rather than a direct effect of mortgage guarantees.

first-time homebuyers, a mispriced government guarantee may not be particularly effective in achieving this goal.

Second, lowering mortgage financing costs distorts the consumption and investment behavior of households. Because real estate is a tangible asset, it is relatively easy to finance. This can lead to overinvestment in housing relative to other, potentially more valuable, investments such as education. Lowering mortgage financing costs through government programs such as the mortgage interest deduction and government guarantees further exacerbates this distortion.

Finally, one could argue that positive externalities are associated with homeownership (Rossi-Hansberg, Sarte, and Owens 2010), which households do not internalize. In this case, lowering mortgage costs may help to achieve the right level of homeownership. However, lowering mortgage costs does not affect just the decision of whether to own or rent, but also the decision of how much housing to purchase. As noted, it is hard to believe that there is much value in promoting more consumption of housing relative to other investments that are more difficult to finance. More targeted interventions may be better suited to the goal of increasing homeownership.

Government Guarantees and Exposure to Uncompensated Risk

Some of the government guarantee proposals are likely to recreate the governance problems that plagued Fannie and Freddie. For example, both the Mortgage Bankers Association and the Center for American Progress have proposed creating mortgage guarantee entities that would provide guarantees on securitized mortgages. These MGEs would be for-profit entities subject to regulations designed to ensure that they have enough capital to meet their guarantee commitments. In addition, a government agency would be established to "wrap" the MBS—that is, to reinsure the securities themselves in the event the MGEs do not have enough capital to meet their guarantee commitments. The government agency would charge the MGEs a fee in exchange for reinsuring the MBS. Thus the MGEs would hold a first-loss position on any mortgage defaults, and the government would be paid to reinsure the MBS in case an MGE cannot meet its obligation. In essence, these proposals recreate entities like Fannie and Freddie without sizable retained portfolios, government mandates to promote housing affordability, and implicit free government reinsurance of MBS.

In these proposals, the MGEs would be for-profit entities like Fannie and Freddie and continue the tensions that exist when the activities of for-profit firms are guaranteed by the government. These tensions have historically come in two forms. First, for-profit firms are likely to chase market share, engaging in a competitive race to the bottom in underwriting standards during boom periods. That is, when private market participants loosen their underwriting standards,

Figure 7-3. *GSE Share of New Issuance, 2001–09*

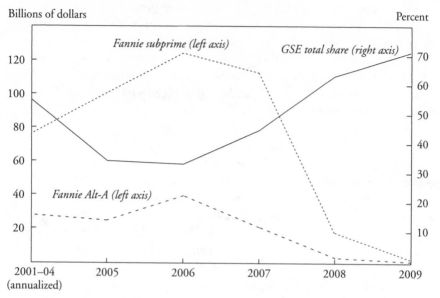

Sources: Fannie Mae (2010b); FHFA (2009); Inside Mortgage Finance (2010).

for-profit MGEs are likely to do the same. Fannie and Freddie are prime examples. Figure 7-3 shows how Fannie Mae expanded into Alt-A and subprime lending in 2006 and 2007 to recapture market share it had lost to the private-label securitization market in the mid-2000s. According to the FHFA conservator's report on the enterprises' financial performance, 40–50 percent of Fannie's and Freddie's credit losses stemmed from their guarantees of Alt-A mortgages (FHFA 2010). Regulators may find it difficult to prevent private MGEs from similarly extending their activities into risky lending. Moreover, the private MGEs will be critical to the extension of new mortgage credit, making it difficult to let them fail in a severe housing downturn. This may weaken market discipline on the MGEs, making them more likely to guarantee high-risk mortgages.

Second, for-profit MGEs will want low government reinsurance fees on MBS and will want their regulator to impose low capital requirements for their mortgage guarantees. Low reinsurance fees and capital requirements increase the chance that taxpayers will bear losses on MBS in a severe housing downturn. There is, of course, ample precedent for regulators setting capital requirements and insurance fees too low in response to lobbying efforts by the for-profit financial firms they regulate. Fannie and Freddie are the most obvious examples, but so too are banks and thrifts. Even after the recent financial crisis, banks have lobbied regulators, with some success, against significant increases in capital requirements as part of the Basel III process. For instance, Bank of America urged the Basel Committee to "balance greater capital and liquidity requirements needed to make the system stronger and safer, on the one hand, against the risk of inappropriately restricting the flow of credit that is critical to economic growth, on the other."[11] Similarly, it is noteworthy that most banks paid no deposit insurance fees between 1996 and 2007 because of provisions in the Deposit Insurance Funds Act of 1996, which were advocated for by the American Bankers Association.[12]

Because of such concerns, some advocates for government guarantees of MBS have proposed alternative governance structures for MGEs that attempt to reduce or eliminate the profit motive. Economists at the New York Fed have proposed establishing a single MGE that would be owned cooperatively by the financial institutions that issue MBS (Dechario and others 2010). This governance structure harkens back to the ownership structure of Fannie Mae established by the Charter Act of 1954, in which thrifts that sold their mortgages to Fannie Mae were required to hold the equity of Fannie Mae. It is also similar to the original ownership structure of Freddie Mac and the current ownership structure of the Federal Home Loan Banks.

While the shareholders in this form of MGE may not chase profits quite as aggressively as Fannie and Freddie did, they would likely still push for low capital requirements. Indeed, the main opposition to the Charter Act of 1954 came from thrifts precisely because they did not want to use their own capital to capitalize Fannie Mae (Bartke 1971). Moreover, a lender-owned cooperative may prove destabilizing for the financial system in a time of crisis. Relying on financial institutions to recapitalize the cooperative MGE when it experiences large losses also decapitalizes the banking sector at a time when it is most likely to need capital.

The proposals of the National Association of Home Builders and the National Association of Realtors attempt to avoid these conflicts by making the MGE a government fund that is capitalized with guarantee fees on MBS. Unlike the other proposals, here the government takes all losses on mortgage defaults; there is no private company in a first-loss position. This structure is closer to the Federal Housing Administration and the Veterans Administration model of guarantees, although it is unclear whether their proposals would have the fund be a government agency or an independent government corporation.

---

11. Bank of America comments on Basel Committee on Banking Supervision (2009) are available at www.bis.org/publ/bcbs165/boac.pdf.

12. American Bankers Association position on FDIC premiums (www.aba.com/Industry+Issues/ FDIC_RBP.htm).

Figure 7-4. *FHA and Subprime Share of New Issuance, 2001–09*

Percent

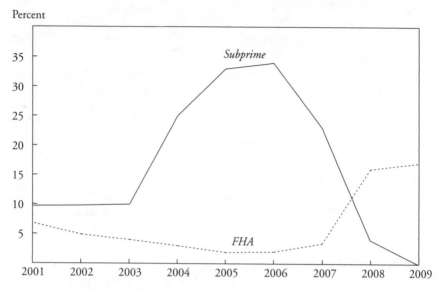

Source: Inside Mortgage Finance (2010).

This structure could work better from a governance perspective. Fannie and Freddie tried to regain market share by guaranteeing riskier loans in 2005 and 2006 in response to the market share gains of subprime lenders earlier in the decade. By contrast, the FHA also lost considerable market share to subprime lenders, but did not chase market share by lowering its mortgage insurance premiums even as subprime lenders were willing to extend credit at much lower rates. As figure 7-4 shows, as subprime mortgages increased from 10 percent to nearly 35 percent of the market, the FHA's share of new origination dwindled to 1.9 percent, from 6.8 percent. Arguably, the FHA did not respond to the competitive pressure from subprime lenders because it was not trying to maximize profit. As a result, the modest size of the FHA's guarantee book meant that its losses were also modest, particularly given the high ratios of loan to value (LTV) on the mortgages it guaranteed.

While the FHA did not chase market share in the subprime boom, it also did not turn away market share in the subprime bust. Instead, it kept mortgage insurance premiums at precrisis levels and quickly regained and then exceeded the market share it had lost during the subprime boom. In 2010 FHA mortgages accounted for 29.4 percent of new mortgages and 14.4 percent of refinanced mortgages. In no small measure, the FHA is now performing the role for which it was originally designed in the 1930s—as a guarantor of mortgage credit during a period in which private sector lenders were unwilling to take mortgage credit risk.[13]

Thus one could argue that a benefit of having a government agency as the mortgage guarantor is that the agency can be directed more easily to play a countercyclical role. Of course, playing such a countercyclical role is no small task: a government agency can make mistakes in determining when intervention is necessary, and it can be influenced by politicians to intervene when it is not necessary or in a way that ends up being costly to the government. We have more to say about these issues when we discuss our policy proposal.

While we have raised moral hazard concerns with respect to government reinsurance of MBS guaranteed by private for-profit entities, this would not be the only type of government guarantee in the financial system. In particular, one may ask whether we also object to deposit insurance, which may create even greater moral hazard problems given the relatively opaque and illiquid nature of a bank's balance sheet.

The core of our response is that, while significant moral hazard costs may be associated with deposit insurance, the *benefits* of providing deposit guarantees are likely to be significantly larger than the benefits of providing MBS guarantees. We make this claim for at least two reasons.

First, a key function of deposit insurance is to prevent bank runs, which force banks to reduce lending, curtail other banking activities, and sell assets to meet deposit redemptions. This creates real inefficiencies. By contrast, a securitization trust is a static collection of assets. If those assets decline in value because of higher-than-expected defaults, investors suffer losses, but there are no direct implications for efficiency.

Second, home purchases have more tangible collateral value (a house) and thus are relatively easy to finance. Banks make risky loans that are subject to asymmetric information and agency problems, often with hard-to-value or limited collateral. Such frictions mean that it is more likely that the private market will underinvest in such loans. Thus there is greater benefit in subsidizing such bank loans through underpriced deposit insurance (and the liquidity premium that deposit insurance creates) than in subsidizing mortgages.

More broadly, one may wonder whether a more efficient way for the government to meet liquidity needs would be to have a financial system with insured

13. The initial increase in market share during the crisis was less a conscious policy decision than a reflection of the insensitivity of FHA loan pricing to market forces. Later, during the Obama administration, there was concern about the risks to the FHA of a considerable expansion of its market share and a conscious decision to try to protect the FHA from future losses while maintaining a large market share. See Streitfeld and Story (2009).

deposits for "narrow banks" that fund only mortgages[14] and long-term unguaranteed debt funding of less transparent credit assets like corporate loans and construction loans. The main benefit of such a system would be that the government would incur less risk because it may be easier to monitor bank risk taking in relatively transparent mortgages than in less transparent credit assets. The main cost would be that the liquidity benefits of guarantees would no longer be channeled toward overcoming underinvestment in asset classes where financial frictions are most severe. While this counterfactual is interesting, such a sweeping reorganization of the financial system is impractical from a policy perspective.

The Functioning of Private Mortgage Guarantee Entities in a Crisis

In hybrid guarantee proposals, where the government reinsures MBS that are guaranteed by private MGEs, government reinsurance protects the holders of existing MBS from taking losses. In these hybrid systems, many or all MGEs are likely to experience financial difficulty in a systemic crisis. Thus the ability of the system to guarantee *new* mortgages will be significantly impaired, impeding the extension of new mortgage credit, even if the government protects *existing* MBS holders. For new MBS to be guaranteed, existing MGEs would have to raise capital, but their ability to do so would be very limited given their financial distress. Moreover, as an MGE's financial condition worsens, it is likely to scale back on guaranteeing mortgages in an attempt to conserve capital. Thus in any hybrid system of mortgage guarantees, the government would likely step in during a crisis to guarantee mortgages directly or to inject capital into existing MGEs.

The recent financial crisis provides ample evidence that MGEs would find it difficult to guarantee new mortgages. Fannie and Freddie are the most obvious examples. The government is not just protecting existing MBS holders; it is helping the two GSEs to guarantee new MBS. Recent experience with private mortgage insurers also provides evidence that MGEs would have problems in a crisis. The leading mortgage insurers, Mortgage Guarantee Insurance Corporation, PMI Group, Genworth Financial, and Radian Group, all had significant financial difficulties during the financial crisis. Their debt was downgraded, and their credit default swap spreads reached very high levels. They also had difficulty meeting regulatory capital requirements. At the peak of the crisis, their condition was so dire that they applied for capital injections from the Troubled Asset Relief Program, but were denied. The government was able to deny this

---

14. See Gorton and Metrick (2010a) for a proposal in which "narrow funding banks" can only hold asset-backed securities. Given that a large share of asset-backed securities consists of mortgage-backed securities, this would amount to a narrow bank with a large exposure to real estate.

support because it was already supporting the mortgage market through Fannie, Freddie, and the FHA. But if MGEs were the only guarantors, it is likely that the government would be forced to provide capital, just as it has done with Fannie and Freddie.

To summarize, we make five key points about government guarantee proposals.

—Government guarantees provide little benefit to borrowers during normal times if guarantee fees are set properly; these fees should incorporate a risk premium that closely approximates the market risk premium on guarantees with systematic risk.

—The liquidity benefits of guarantees in normal times are probably relatively small. In the absence of government guarantees, private-label MBS would likely be tranched to create near-riskless securities that could be quite liquid.

—Guarantees are not necessary to ensure the supply of long-term, fixed-rate mortgages. Borrowers have strong preferences for such mortgages, and the private financial institutions have evolved sophisticated hedging strategies to supply them.

—Proposals that mix private guarantees with public guarantees risk the same sort of governance conflicts that ultimately led to the downfall of Fannie and Freddie.

—Private mortgage guarantee entities may find it difficult to guarantee new mortgages during periods of significant financial stress and may need government infusions of capital to guarantee new mortgages.

None of this is to say that government guarantees are never valuable. Indeed, we argue that government guarantees are valuable during periods of significant market stress. This does not mean that government-guaranteed mortgages should constitute a large share of the market during normal times. Instead, we argue later in this chapter that government guarantees should be offered when they are needed most, namely during periods of financial crisis. By implication, private markets should provide the lion's share of mortgage finance in normal times. The next section considers some of the challenges of increased use of private markets in mortgage finance.

Analysis of Privatization Proposals

Privatization proposals in some form have been part of the public debate about the GSEs almost since Fannie Mae's creation in 1938. Over the last twenty years, the government has repeatedly considered privatization, beginning with the President's Commission on Privatization in 1987. The report noted that Fannie and Freddie provided little value to the mortgage market while exposing the government to considerable risk. However, Congress did not act on the commission's recommendation to privatize the two entities.

A series of reports by the U.S. Government Accountability Office in the early 1990s documented that Fannie and Freddie continued to expose the government to large risks, that they held insufficient capital against these risks, and that they were inadequately supervised by the Department of Housing and Urban Development (HUD). In response, the Federal Housing Enterprises Financial Safety and Soundness Act of 1992 established the Office of Federal Housing Enterprise Oversight (OFHEO) as an independent regulator within HUD and empowered it to set capital standards and ensure the safety and soundness of Fannie and Freddie. It also mandated that HUD, the Treasury, the Congressional Budget Office, and the Government Accountability Office study whether Fannie and Freddie should be privatized. HUD opposed privatization, writing in conclusion, "There remains a substantial public-purpose rationale for the current GSE system. Given the recently improved housing goals and safety and soundness oversight by OFHEO, the Department recommends that it be continued." The other reports noted that the shareholders of Fannie and Freddie were the main beneficiaries of the implicit government guarantee and reinforced the idea that the two companies exposed the government to considerable risk. Nevertheless, none of the reports came out in support of privatization, and no legislative action was taken.

Over the years, however, numerous policy analysts and economists, including Vern McKinley, Peter Wallison, and Charles Calomiris, have argued forcefully for privatization. Their criticisms echo many of the same concerns in the government reports, but they argue further that the two GSEs serve no useful public purpose (see McKinley 1997; Wallison and Ely 2000; Calomiris 2001; Wallison, Stanton, and Ely 2004). More recently, Dwight Jaffee, an early critic of the GSEs, Edward Pinto, a former Fannie Mae executive, and Alex Pollock, a long-time president of the Federal Home Loan Bank of Chicago, itself a GSE, have argued for full privatization of Fannie Mae and Freddie Mac (see Jaffee 2010; Pinto 2010; Pollock 2010). Given the immense cost to taxpayers from supporting Fannie and Freddie through the recent crisis, the case for privatization appears to be a strong one.

However, the advocates for privatization, while generally on target in their criticism of the GSEs, have not provided much detail on the kind of housing finance system that would emerge in place of the current one or how it would be regulated. This is a significant shortcoming of their proposals, given that a good deal of responsibility for the subprime crisis resides with private market participants. While Fannie and Freddie were exposed to a very large share of Alt-A loans, they had a relatively small share of subprime mortgages. At the peak of the mortgage credit boom in 2006, Fannie and Freddie accounted for approximately 30 percent of new Alt-A and subprime mortgage lending.[15] While this is a large

15. Calculations based on Inside Mortgage Finance (2010); Fannie Mae (2010b); FHFA (2009, 2010).

exposure, many other market participants had to be involved to fuel the growth of low-quality credit. Thus there is a case to be made for more stringent regulation of private mortgage markets.

However, most of the focus of privatization advocates has been on how to transition from a system in which the government guarantees 54 percent of all outstanding mortgages and the vast majority of all newly issued mortgages. Essentially, they support a continued winding down of the GSEs' retained portfolio, as prescribed in the Housing and Economic Recovery Act of 2008, guaranteeing legacy obligations of the GSEs, but then gradually scaling back guarantees on newly issued MBS. Without a clear idea of the end point of the transition, it is difficult to evaluate the costs and benefits of privatization.

This section discusses the implications of privatization. As noted, privatization is unlikely to have a material effect on mortgage interest rates during normal financial market conditions, although it could have a large effect when financial markets become significantly stressed. Privatization also has implications that require an enhanced regulatory regime. For one, "privatization" will not eliminate the government's exposure to housing finance given the large scope of implicit and explicit government insurance of the financial system. Moreover, privatization will increase the credit risk borne by financial institutions and may increase the transmission of shocks from the housing sector to other sectors. Finally, privatization will increase the use of private securitization, which the recent crisis has shown to have serious flaws both in the quality of underwriting and in the incentives for renegotiation.

The Effect of Privatization on the Costs of Mortgages Provided by Banks

As noted, private securitization is unlikely to lead to appreciably more expensive mortgages than a regime with properly priced government guarantees of MBS. However, one possible implication of winding down Fannie and Freddie is that a much larger share of residential mortgage credit would be held directly by banks on their balance sheets, an increase from the current level of 28 percent. Indeed, some of the growth in GSE mortgage-backed securities over the years, and corresponding decline in the share of mortgage credit risk held by banks, can be attributed to the fact that under Basel I the financial system as a whole had to hold about 75 basis points less capital against mortgage losses if the mortgages were securitized by the GSEs.[16]

---

16. Specifically, portfolio loans on bank balance sheets get a 50 percent risk weight, which means that they have to hold 200 basis points of tier 1 capital (given a capital requirement of 400 basis points). By contrast, GSE mortgage-backed securities get a 20 percent risk weight, which corresponds to 80 basis points of capital. In combination with the 45 basis points that the GSEs hold, the total financial system capital held against loans in GSE mortgage-backed securities is only 125 basis points.

Thus a benefit of moving mortgage credit back to the banks in the form of portfolio loans is that the financial system will have a greater buffer against mortgage risk. This buffer will be even bigger as the more stringent Basel III capital regime gets phased in over the next decade. This may encourage more prudent lending, although the long history of imprudent bank lending should give pause to those who think that higher capital requirements are an effective deterrent to making bad loans.

In theory, the increase in bank capital could lead to higher mortgage rates because bank capital is a more expensive source of finance than debt. However, market participants probably overstate the size of this effect.[17] Academic studies argue that bank capital is only modestly more expensive than debt because equity becomes less risky as a bank's capital is increased. For example, Kashyap, Stein, and Hanson (2010) place an upper bound of 45 basis points on the increase in funding costs from a 10 percentage point increase in bank capital.[18] Thus if banks have to hold 1 or 2 percentage points more capital than the nonbank financial system, the effect on mortgage rates would likely be very modest.

The Effect of Privatization on the Government's Exposure to Mortgage Risk

While winding down the GSEs will eliminate one form of government guarantee, it will also increase the use of other explicit and implicit government guarantees. As of the third quarter of 2010, 40.5 percent of the commercial banking sector was financed by government-insured deposits.[19] Although banks pay deposit insurance premiums to the Federal Deposit Insurance Corporation (FDIC), these premiums have arguably been underpriced (Pennacchi 2009). Thus GSE privatization could put the FDIC's deposit insurance fund at greater risk. This would be particularly true if community and regional banks expand their portfolio of residential real estate loans, both because their portfolios would be less geographically diversified and because deposits are a larger source of

---

17. See, for example, the comment letters of market participants in response to Basel Committee on Banking Supervision (2009). Comments can be found at www.bis.org/publ/bcbs165/cacomments.htm.

18. Bank debt is less expensive than equity for two reasons in the framework of Kashyap, Stein, and Hanson (2010). First, interest payments are tax deductible, while dividends are not. Second, to the extent that banks can raise deposit financing or access other liquid short-term funding sources they benefit from the liquidity premium that depositors and short-term lenders are willing to pay, enabling banks to borrow more cheaply. However, the tax benefit is a transfer to the banking sector and is not really a social benefit of debt financing (Admati and others 2010). Moreover, if one thinks that banks are excessively reliant on short-term funding and do not incorporate its systemic risk when making their funding decisions (as suggested by the proposed Basel III liquidity requirements), then the liquidity premium understates the true cost of debt.

19. Authors' calculations from FDIC (2010, table III-B, p. 18).

funding for them than for large banks. Whereas banks with less than $10 billion in assets funded 64 percent of their assets with insured deposits, the top four banks funded only 26.4 percent of their assets with insured deposits. One has only to look at the losses that community and regional banks have incurred on their commercial and residential real estate loans in the recent crisis to get a sense of the risk that real estate poses to the FDIC. The savings and loan crisis of the 1980s, which was also related to excessive real estate lending, resulted in even larger losses to deposit insurers as a share of GDP than the current crisis (1.7 and 0.5 percent, respectively; Curry and Shibut 2000; CBO 2010a, 2010b).

The government's exposure to losses in the banking sector is not restricted to deposit insurance. The four largest financial institutions—JP Morgan Chase, Wells Fargo, Bank of America, and Citigroup, with combined assets of $5.4 trillion—originated 58.2 percent of all new residential mortgages in 2009.[20] While they now securitize a large share of these loans through Fannie and Freddie (62.7 percent in 2009),[21] privatization may lead them to hold a larger share of their loans on their balance sheets. Although the Dodd-Frank Act took some steps to facilitate the resolution of large, systemic financial institutions, it is difficult to know whether the legislation will succeed in ending "too-big-to-fail." If not, then there is an implicit guarantee on the loans made by the largest financial institutions even if only 26.4 percent of their liabilities are insured deposits. Thus it is misleading to suggest that eliminating the GSEs would eliminate government guarantees from the housing finance system.

The Effect of Privatization on the Banking Sector's Exposure to Mortgage Risk

Eliminating government guarantees on MBS increases the banking sector's exposure to mortgage credit risk both from portfolio loans and from their holdings of MBS. This increases the likelihood that shocks to the housing sector will get transmitted to other sectors by impairing banks' capital and reducing their willingness to lend. A large literature documents spillovers of this type (Peek and Rosengren 1997; Gan 2007; Khwaja and Mian 2008). If there is any silver lining in the failure of Fannie and Freddie, it is that they limited the exposure of banks to residential real estate losses. Had banks suffered the $229 billion of losses that Fannie Mae and Freddie Mac have suffered to date, they would have been in worse shape than they are today, further impairing their willingness to lend to other sectors of the economy. With losses to date of $229 billion, tier 1 capital in the banking sector would be 7.0 percent rather than 8.7 percent. Moreover, given that large banks rely heavily on uninsured short-term funding,

---

20. Authors' calculations from Inside Mortgage Finance (2010, vol. 1, p. 41).
21. Authors' calculations from Inside Mortgage Finance (2010, vol. 1, p. 41; vol. 2, p. 161).

it is possible that greater exposure to residential mortgages would have exacerbated the withdrawal of funding from large banks in the fall of 2008. This is not to say that it is necessarily undesirable for banks to bear more credit risk in residential real estate, perhaps to reduce moral hazard in underwriting, but it does suggest that absorbing such risk is not without cost.

The Effect of Privatization on Securitization Markets

Eliminating Fannie and Freddie would drive more activity into private-label MBS. It is important to analyze the effects of such a shift given that subprime mortgage lending funded largely by private-label securitizations, and securitization in general, played such a prominent role in the recent financial crisis. Indeed, the crisis exposed several flaws in the securitization process. Some of these flaws emerged because regulation was lacking, others because regulations encouraged regulatory arbitrage. Privatization advocates have not addressed these flaws in securitization. We discuss them in detail to provide context for our proposal for the regulation of securitization.

MORAL HAZARD IN ORIGINATION, UNDERWRITING, AND CREDIT RATINGS

Numerous observers have suggested that because underwriters of MBS held very little, if any, of the securities they underwrote, they had little incentive to assess the quality of the mortgages that went into the mortgage pools. Keys and others (2010) present evidence to this effect, showing that mortgages with FICO (credit) scores above 620 performed worse than mortgages with FICO scores just below 620. Securitizers profited instead from the underwriting fees they received and proceeds from the sale of the securitization tranches in excess of the cost of mortgages in the pool. Originators, in turn, profited from the fees they earned by supplying mortgages to securitizers. These poor incentives resulted in the extension of mortgages to uncreditworthy borrowers. For instance, Mian and Sufi (2010) show that securitization is associated with increased availability of mortgage credit in subprime areas from 2002 to 2005 and elevated mortgage defaults in 2007.

There were also incentive problems with credit rating agencies, which were paid by underwriters to provide ratings of the various tranches. The conflicts inherent in the ratings process have been widely noted, resulting in AAA ratings for senior securitization tranches that were far from immune to a nationwide decline in home prices. For instance, Griffin and Tang (2010) show that the rating agencies frequently adjusted the output from their statistical models to increase the size of the AAA tranches in some securitizations. In addition, Ashcraft, Goldsmith-Pinkham, and Vickery (2010) show that ratings do not incorporate readily available information on the riskiness of the loans in subprime and

Alt-A MBS. These AAA tranches were, in turn, highly valued for their ostensible safety and the ability to include them in "safe" investment portfolios while earning spreads over Treasuries or agency MBS.

The Dodd-Frank Act attempts to deal with these problems in four ways. First, it requires "skin in the game"; securitizers and originators must collectively hold 5 percent of the risk of mortgages that are not "qualified residential mortgages." Precisely how this requirement will be implemented is not yet known. Second, to reduce the conflicts of interest between securitizers and credit rating agencies, Dodd-Frank requires the Securities and Exchange Commission to study the feasibility of a system where credit rating agencies are randomly assigned to rate-structured products. Third, Dodd-Frank reduces the use of credit ratings by government entities in an attempt to reduce the perception that the government endorses credit ratings. Fourth, Dodd-Frank abolishes the exemption of the credit rating agencies from full disclosure, eliminating their government-granted special status as information providers. The critical question here is whether these new regulations will be enough to solve the problems in origination, securitization, and credit ratings.

While a good first step, the answer may be no. First, the 5 percent risk retention requirement may be too low to incentivize good underwriting practices. As suggested by Shleifer and Vishny (2010), the incentives created by risk retention must be compared to the fee income generated by mortgage origination. If the fee income is large, only a large retention requirement will encourage good underwriting. Second, risk retention addresses only problems in underwriting that arise due to moral hazard on the part of mortgage originators. There may be other causes for a deterioration in underwriting standards, including competition among securitizers and investor sentiment, which are better addressed through more direct regulation. Third, regulation of the credit rating agencies may improve their performance but is unlikely to change fundamentally the way that issuers and securitizers interact with the agencies. Investors are likely to continue relying on the rating agencies for credit analysis as long as doing so is more cost effective than generating their own analysis. Securitizers still have incentives to push for larger AAA tranches in order to maximize the profits from structuring MBS.

Complexity in Loan Modifications and Excess Foreclosures

The foreclosure crisis has also revealed the difficulty of modifying mortgages in private-label securitizations. Piskorski, Seru, and Vig (2010) show that foreclosure rates on delinquent borrowers are higher when mortgages are securitized than when they are held as whole loans in a bank's portfolio. In addition,

Agarwal and others (2011) show that portfolio loans are 26 to 36 percent more likely to be renegotiated than securitized loans and that these renegotiations have lower post-modification default rates.[22]

It is difficult to modify loans in securitizations for many reasons. Pooling and servicing agreements (PSAs), which govern the management of mortgage loan pools in securitization trusts, often prohibit servicers from modifying loans or constrain the number of modifications they can make (Gelpern and Levitin 2009). While servicers are compensated for the costs of foreclosure, they are not compensated for the costs of modification. Although successful modification enables servicers to continue to earn servicing fees, foreclosure may still have higher present value to the servicer (Piskorski, Seru, and Vig 2010).

In normal times, when foreclosure rates are low, foreclosing on delinquent borrowers may maximize the expected payoffs to MBS investors. Thus the PSA that encourages foreclosure may be optimal from an ex ante perspective. However, in the current environment, when foreclosure rates are high, foreclosure may no longer maximize the value of payments to investors. But changing a PSA to encourage mortgage modifications is extremely difficult, as it requires the consent of a large number of investors in the securities. Moreover, investors in the senior tranches do not bear the costs of foreclosure and have little incentive to agree to a change in the PSA. They could be encouraged to go along with such a modification to the PSA by changing the terms of their securities, but the Trust Indenture Act of 1939 would require unanimous consent, making such a change nearly impossible (Gelpern and Levitin 2009).

The key point here is that, while the privately negotiated contracts that govern securitization *may* be optimal during normal times, it is far from clear that they are optimal during a crisis. One cannot expect private parties to internalize the foreclosure externalities that such contracts create. Therefore, it may be necessary to regulate securitization agreements in such a way as to discourage excessive foreclosure.

Fragility of Securitization More Broadly

The financial crisis also revealed that securitization can be a fragile form of financing. One of the supposed benefits of securitization is that it allows tranching of claims into senior and junior securities. This allows relatively uninformed investors (or those with mandates to invest only in "safe" securities) to provide financing by enabling them to buy the senior tranches, leaving the more junior

---

22. Adelino, Gerardi, and Willen (2010) dispute this view. They present evidence that there is no difference between the modification rates on securitized and portfolio loans.

tranches to better-informed investors (Gorton and Pennacchi 1990; Duffie and DeMarzo 1999; DeMarzo 2005). As a result, more credit is supplied. Adelino (2010) shows that the pricing of MBS supports this hypothesis. The prices at which the junior tranches of MBS were sold at issue contain information about the quality of the underlying loans beyond the information in the ratings of those tranches; the prices of the AAA tranches contain no such information.

While such tranching works well during normal times, it is prone to break down during periods of crisis. Dang, Gorton, and Holmstrom (2009) suggest that secondary market trading of senior tranches will be disrupted when there is large uncertainty about the value of the collateral because the uninformed investors who hold them fear adverse selection. Hanson and Sunderam (2010) argue that instability is an intrinsic feature of securitization: securitizers will structure the trusts with too large a senior tranche so as to attract uninformed investors who require low returns on their investments precisely because they do not invest in information acquisition. Thus securitizers fail to take into account the financing difficulties that are created when there is uncertainty about collateral values and there are too few informed investors in the market. Gennaioli, Shleifer, and Vishny (2011) suggest that securitization is inherently unstable because securitizers and investors are prone to neglect low-probability downside risk. Securitization structures that work well during normal times collapse when low-probability events materialize. Securitization collapsed during the recent crisis, but also during prior episodes, such as the 1994 breakdown in the market for collateralized mortgage obligations. Such arguments could provide a rationale for regulating the capital structure of securitizations.

USE OF ASSET-BACKED SECURITIES AS COLLATERAL IN SHORT-TERM FUNDING AND FINANCING VEHICLES

Asset-backed securities (ABS) are used as collateral in repo funding by financial firms and as collateral in off-balance-sheet entities such as structured investment vehicles (SIVs). These entities are themselves funded with commercial paper. Concerns about the quality of ABS collateral, particularly private-label MBS, led repo lenders to financial firms and commercial paper holders in SIVs to withdraw funding. Covitz, Liang, and Suarez (2009) show that the withdrawal of SIV funding was initially indiscriminate, unrelated to the quality of the assets being financed. This modern-day (non-deposit) run on financial firms led to a sequence of interventions by the Federal Reserve and Treasury to stabilize the financial system, including the Term Auction Facility, the Commercial Paper Funding Facility, and guarantees of money market mutual funds. Given that mortgages make up a large fraction of the financial sector's long-term assets, how they are funded is of critical importance for financial stability; their regulation cannot be ignored.

In summary, any proposal advocating privatization must address concerns that privatization will create a larger role for private-label securitization, which proved deeply flawed in the recent crisis. As we discuss later in this chapter, we believe that careful regulation of private-label securitization must be a key component of any privatization plan.

Are Covered Bonds the Solution?

Former Treasury secretary Henry Paulson and privatization advocates have tried to promote covered bonds as an alternative to agency MBS. Indeed, since July 2008, several bills have been introduced in Congress to promote and regulate covered bond usage, although none has passed.[23]

Covered bonds are an important form of securitization in Europe, where they have been used since the 1700s (Treasury Department 2008). They are issued by financial institutions, backed by a pool of assets (the "cover pool"), and protected from the insolvency of the issuer. They are similar in this regard to MBS, but they differ in at least two important respects. Unlike MBS, the asset pool that backs covered bonds is dynamic in the sense that loans in default or loans that have been prepaid have to be replaced with other loans. Even more important, covered bondholders have recourse to the issuer. Thus if the covered bond defaults, covered bondholders have an unsecured claim on the assets of the issuer to the extent that the face value of the bond exceeds the value of the cover pool. Because the issuing bank ultimately bears the credit risk of the mortgages, the covered bond stays on the bank's balance sheet as a liability.

Covered bond advocates have made much of the benefits of recourse to the issuer, arguing that covered bonds reduce moral hazard and adverse selection problems relative to MBS (Quinn 2008; Packer, Stever, and Upper 2007). Because the issuer bears the cost of mortgage defaults, it has more incentives to engage in due diligence on mortgage quality and less incentive to sneak low-quality mortgages into the cover pool. In this view, one gets the liquidity benefits of MBS, without the adverse selection and moral hazard problems that have been associated with them.

However, the good performance of covered bonds is likely to derive less from the benefits of recourse to the issuer and more from government regulations requiring either that only high-quality mortgages can be included in the cover pool or that issuers must add cash or other liquid assets to the cover pool if they include lower-quality mortgages in it (see table 7-1). For example, in Denmark—which has been held up by many as a model for covered bond usage—only mortgages with an LTV at or below 80 percent can be included in the cover

23. Most recently the U.S. Covered Bond Act of 2010, sponsored by Representatives Garrett, Kanjorski, and Bachus, was not voted on by the House of Representatives.

Table 7-1. *Covered Bond Legislation in Europe*
Percent

Country and bond	Special covered bond legislation?	Ratio of 2009 outstanding covered bond to GDP	Required over-collateralization	Loan-to-value limit	
				Residential	Commercial
Austria	Yes, since 1905	1.9	2	60	60
Denmark	Yes	143.3	8[a]	80	70
Finland	Yes, since 2000	4.5		60	
France, obligations foncières, CRH	Yes, since 1999	9.1	0	80	
Germany, Pfandbriefe	Yes, since 1927	9.4	2	60	60
Greece	Yes, since 2007	2.7		80	60
Hungary	Yes	7.6		70	60
Ireland, asset covered securities	Yes, since 2001	18.2	3	75	60
Italy, OBG	Yes, since 2007	0.9	10	80	60
Luxembourg, lettres de gage	Yes, since 1997	0.0	2	80	60
Netherlands	Yes, since 2008	5.0		80 or 125	
Poland	Yes	0.2			
Portugal	Yes, since 1990	12.4	5	80	60
Slovakia	Yes	5.7		70	
Spain	Yes, since 1999	31.8	11	80	
Sweden	Yes	46.5		75	70
United Kingdom, regulated covered bonds	Yes, since 2003	12.9	10	80	

Sources: European Covered Bond Council (2010); European Mortgage Federation (2009).
a. Percent of risk-weighted assets.

pool; Germany requires extra collateral for lower-quality mortgages (European Covered Bond Council 2010). If such restrictions were placed on the mortgages included in private-label MBS or agency MBS, these securities would also perform well. Thus it is not recourse to the issuer per se that promotes mortgage quality, but rather government regulation.[24] As further evidence that recourse

24. In the United States, only Washington Mutual and Bank of America have issued a few covered bonds. The mortgages backing these bonds were generally of very high quality, even though there was no government restriction against including lower-quality mortgages (Bergstresser, Greenwood, and Quinn 2009). Given the small number of such issues, it is difficult to conclude that all covered bond issues would be backed by high-quality mortgages without regulation.

alone does not solve the problem, one has only to look at the current crisis. Many banks failed in the United States precisely because of recourse: they issued very risky mortgages and kept them in their portfolios. And Acharya, Schnabl, and Suarez (2010) show that banks provided recourse to many investors who purchased securitized products. Thus a covered bond system without strict controls on what types of mortgages can be included in the cover pool runs the risk of transmitting housing shocks to bank balance sheets in a way that destabilizes the financial system. This risk could be mitigated by restricting the quality of mortgages in the cover pool, but off-balance-sheet securitization would likely work just as well. One could also mitigate transmission to the financial sector by making the covered bond issuers separate mortgage finance companies. The success of such an approach relies on those financial institutions being very well capitalized, again through strict regulation.

To summarize, we make three main points about privatization proposals, all of which suggest that privatization must be accompanied by a strong regulatory regime for housing finance:

—Privatization does not eliminate the taxpayer's exposure to mortgage risk because of the presence of deposit insurance and other implicit or explicit government safety nets.

—Privatization would increase the banking sector's exposure to mortgage risk and thus increase the probability that distress in the housing market is transmitted to other sectors.

—Privatization would increase the use of private-label securitization, which has significant structural flaws.

The Goals of Housing Finance Reform

Proponents of explicit government guarantees for MBS believe that a properly designed system of guarantees can significantly lower mortgage costs at minimal risk to the government. Advocates of privatization believe that such guarantees would do little to lower mortgage costs and would expose the government to considerable risk. The debate therefore centers on how costly guarantees would be and how much they would lower average mortgage financing costs.

We do not think that this should be the central issue in the debate on housing finance reform for the following reasons:

—If guarantee fees are properly determined it is hard to argue that mortgage financing costs would be materially lower during normal market conditions.

—Guarantee programs that lower required yields on MBS do not necessarily benefit borrowers.

—Lowering mortgage financing costs may not be an effective way to achieve policy goals related to housing or investment more broadly.

This is not to say that there is no role for the government in housing finance. Indeed, we argue that the government's main goals in designing housing finance policy should be to *reduce excessive volatility in the supply of housing credit and protect the financial system from adverse shocks to the housing market.*

These goals have three distinct components. The first is to support mortgage markets when support is needed most—during crises like the Great Depression and the one we are now experiencing. During such periods, private markets are likely to function poorly, and the government can have a significant impact by ensuring the proper supply of housing finance. The second component is to reduce the likelihood that a housing-related crisis starts in the first place. This can be done through regulatory measures that prevent the kind of excess supply of housing credit that characterized the period from 2001 to 2006 in the United States. The third component involves ensuring that the financial system does not collapse if there is a housing-related crisis.

Because real estate values are so dependent on credit terms, reducing excess volatility in housing finance can help to mitigate booms and busts in this sector. Doing so is important because such booms and busts have significant consequences for the real economy. Since housing assets are the principal asset for most families in the United States, the bursting of a housing bubble is particularly damaging to the U.S. economy. For instance, Case, Quigley, and Shiller (2005) find that the marginal propensity to consume out of housing wealth is two to three times larger than the marginal propensity to consume out of other financial wealth. Furthermore, when a housing bubble bursts, it can lead to an increase in foreclosures, which imposes negative externalities on neighbors. For instance, Campbell, Giglio, and Pathak (2009) show that a single foreclosure reduces the value of each home within 0.05 mile of that foreclosure by 1 percent. Moreover, Mian, Sufi, and Trebbi (2011) show that foreclosures lead not only to a decline in home prices, but also to a sharp decline in durable consumption. And, as noted by Guiso, Sapienza, and Zingales (2011), mortgage defaults may make strategic default more socially acceptable, leading to more defaults. Such costs are not borne by the defaulting borrower or the lender who forecloses on the borrower. Housing finance policy must play a role in mitigating these spillovers.

Housing finance policy should also ensure that, when there are large adverse shocks to real estate, the financial system has adequate levels of capital and liquidity so that its ability to lend is not too adversely affected. As we have seen in the recent crisis and in numerous other crises both in the United States and abroad, when a housing bubble bursts it impairs the ability of financial firms—particularly leveraged financial firms—to extend credit because their capital and liquidity are eroded. Since housing credit is the single-largest type of credit in the economy—there is $10.6 trillion of housing credit outstanding—a crisis in housing has a particularly severe effect on the ability of banks and other leveraged financial institutions to lend. Indeed, $9 trillion of wealth was lost when the Internet bubble burst. That led to a recession, but not a financial crisis, as leveraged financial institutions did not have a large exposure to this sector. Reinhardt and Rogoff (2009) document that real estate crashes are a big part of most financial crises, and these crises have large long-term negative effects on economic growth.

These policy goals are consistent with the government's regulatory approach to the banking sector. Capital requirements exist in part to ensure that banks do not lend too much during good times and have a buffer during bad times so that they do not cut lending excessively. Indeed, the macroprudential approach to bank regulation attempts to reduce excess volatility in the supply of credit by raising capital requirements in good times and cutting them in bad times. Moreover, deposit insurance is designed to prevent bank runs, which can lead to drastic reductions in lending. And, as the lender of last resort, the Federal Reserve can supply liquidity to the banking sector so that banks are not forced to cut lending and sell assets at fire-sale prices to generate liquidity. Collectively these policies are consistent with the three policy goals for housing finance: they lean against excessive volatility in credit supply, they protect the financial system from adverse shocks, and, in so doing, they help to soften the blow of an adverse shock on the economy.

If all housing credit were supplied by banks, one could conceivably rely on macroprudential bank regulation to limit excess volatility in the supply of housing credit. However, given the importance of securitization in housing finance, bank regulation alone will not be enough. Moreover, tight regulation of mortgage credit in the banking sector would just move more credit into private securitization. Unfortunately, we do not have a complete regulatory regime for securitization.

The Proposal

This section outlines a policy proposal to achieve the goals of housing finance reform articulated above. We first discuss approaches to regulating mortgage financing that would help to reduce excess volatility in the supply of housing credit. We then turn to policies for stabilizing housing finance in periods of market stress. Finally, we discuss issues surrounding the transition to a new system of mortgage finance.

Regulation of Private Forms of Housing Finance

The most direct way to achieve the basic goals of housing finance policy—limiting excess volatility in the supply of housing credit and insulating financial firms from adverse shocks to real estate values—is through strict regulation of mortgage underwriting. For example, one might allow only mortgages with loan-to-value ratios below 80 percent and borrower FICO scores above 700. However, such restrictions, while helping regulators to satisfy core goals of housing finance policy, may be at odds with broader goals of housing policy. Indeed, if a primary goal of housing policy is to promote homeownership, then one might want looser underwriting standards. There is a clear trade-off, then, between housing *finance* policy, which targets financial stability, and housing policy, which targets sustainable homeownership.

Of course, the goal of promoting homeownership is itself somewhat controversial. Many blame the financial crisis on the affordability and homeownership goals established for Fannie and Freddie by Title XIII of the Housing and Community Development Act of 1992 as well as the tightening of the Community Reinvestment Act in 1995; see, for example, Wallison (2011). Furthermore, it is unclear that policies designed to increase the availability of financing have a large effect on the long-run rate of homeownership. At the same time, few policymakers would support extremely strict underwriting standards to ensure the absolute safety of housing finance—say, LTVs below 60 and FICO scores above 740. So implicitly policymakers are trading off homeownership goals and housing finance goals. How these competing goals are traded off is not for us to decide. Instead, we describe the approaches one could adopt to deal with the risks inherent in relaxing underwriting standards to promote homeownership.

One such approach is to use monetary policy to dampen mortgage credit cycles. However, as suggested by Bernanke (2010) and Bernanke and Gertler (2000), monetary policy may be a blunt tool for countering a mortgage credit bubble because monetary tightening in the face of a bubble may have significant costs for the rest of the economy. By contrast, regulation can target more precisely the source of the credit bubble, with less adverse spillover to the rest of the economy. Next, we consider three regulatory levers that policymakers can use to deal with the risks inherent in relaxing underwriting standards to promote homeownership: regulation of mortgage products, setting of bank capital requirements, and regulation of securitization.

REGULATION OF MORTGAGE PRODUCTS

Subprime lending became a subprime crisis because subprime borrowers—those with low FICO scores and little or no documentation of income—did not just get mortgages, they got mortgages with very risky mortgage terms, such as loans with high LTV ratios, seller-financed down payment assistance, adjustable rates, and negative amortization. This toxic combination was a recipe for default. For example, Agarwal and others (2010) show that, controlling for LTV and FICO, delinquent borrowers with adjustable-rate mortgages are 5 percentage points more likely to end up in foreclosure. The FHA also reports that mortgages with seller-financed down payment assistance are three times more likely to become delinquent than those without such assistance (HUD 2010).

One could argue that offering toxic mortgages was a one-time mistake that lenders will not make again; however, financial history is full of examples in which imprudent lending practices are repeated. For instance, the junk bond boom of the late 1980s was followed by a similar boom in the mid-2000s, both resulting in high default rates. Greenwood and Hanson (2010) show that the corporate credit markets routinely experience episodes of lax credit followed by poor performance on corporate bonds. The boom, and subsequent bust, in commercial and residential real estate values in New England and California in the late 1980s was, in part, the result of banks' lax underwriting practices (FDIC 1997). These practices included qualifying buyers for mortgages they could only afford at low teaser rates. One could argue that this episode was caused by a one-time innovation in securitization that market participants, including rating agencies, poorly understood. While true, it is also the case that many imprudent loans were made by banks and retained in their portfolios. This is one of the reasons why bank failure rates were so high.

Furthermore, even if lenders become better at protecting themselves from losses when they extend risky mortgages to borrowers, we may want to regulate those products for consumer protection reasons. A wide range of research, including Lusardi (2008), Lusardi and Mitchell (2008), and Barr, Mullainathan, and Shafir (2009), has shown that the typical consumer does not understand many features of the financial products they use. When negotiating with more sophisticated lenders, these consumers may end up unknowingly bearing excessive risks.

Thus there is a case to be made for prohibiting mortgages with very risky characteristics. For example, one could allow high LTV loans for borrowers with less-than-perfect FICO scores, but require that they be fixed-rate, full-documentation, amortizing mortgages with no seller-financed down payment assistance. More generally, there could be a matrix of allowable mortgage products determined by LTV, FICO score, debt-to-income ratio, fixed or floating rate, and amortizing or not. Some combinations would be allowable; others would not. This approach has recently been introduced by Fannie, Freddie, and the FHA. In choosing which types of mortgages to allow, policymakers would have to trade off broad housing policy goals against housing finance policy goals.

One caveat in the design of such regulations is that the relationships between measurable characteristics and true mortgage default risk can change over time. For instance, Rajan, Seru, and Vig (2010) argue that the default risk models used by the credit rating agencies failed because they were calibrated on a sample of well-underwritten loans in which FICO and LTV were the key risk factors. As a result, lenders began to ignore other measures of borrower quality. This changed the set of loans being made, resulting in default behavior that was not predicted by the models. Regulators must be watchful for innovations in the mortgage market that change the risk profiles of mortgages.

Despite these concerns, LTV is a measure of mortgage riskiness that deserves special scrutiny for several reasons. First, high LTV mortgages are at risk of strategic default because even small declines in home prices result in borrowers who are underwater on their loans. Studies in 2009 by Amherst Securities and the credit scoring agencies Equifax and Experian suggest that strategic defaults among underwater borrowers make up a meaningful fraction of mortgage defaults. Second, as suggested by Geanakoplos (2009), asset prices are strongly affected by the LTV that lenders are willing to accept from borrowers who want to purchase the assets. In the context of housing, this means that variations in the LTVs accepted by mortgage lenders have a strong impact on the potential for bubbles in home prices. Third, borrowers can alter the LTVs they face by taking out second mortgages or home equity lines of credit without the knowledge of the first mortgage lender. Private mortgage insurance (PMI) can similarly drive a wedge between the LTVs faced by the borrower and by the lender. Both second mortgages and PMI increase the riskiness of loans by introducing frictions into the workout process for distressed loans, increasing the probability that those loans will be foreclosed upon. These considerations suggest the need for strict regulatory scrutiny of high LTV loans.

SETTING OF BANK CAPITAL REQUIREMENTS

Another way to protect financial stability while allowing somewhat riskier mortgages is to make bank capital requirements sensitive to mortgage risk. Currently, all one-to-four-family residential mortgages get a 50 percent risk weight in capital regulations "presum[ing] that such loans will meet . . . prudent underwriting standards."[25] In practice, banks are given fairly wide latitude in determining what constitutes prudent underwriting standards. A better policy would be to make risk weights dependent on mortgage characteristics. This is done with multifamily mortgages where only fixed-rate mortgages with LTVs below 80 percent or floating-rate mortgages with LTVs below 75 percent get a 50 percent risk weight. Increasing capital requirements for riskier loans creates a larger buffer against loss. It also raises the cost of making riskier loans to a modest degree, and it puts more bank capital at risk, which may mitigate moral hazard problems.

A critical lesson from the crisis is that bank exposure to housing has to be measured on a *consolidated* basis, including contributions from whole loans, mortgage-backed securities, repo collateral, loan warehousing, underwriting

---

25. Code of Federal Regulations, Title 12, ch. 1, pt. 3, app. A.

income, and servicing income. Leading up to the crisis, neither regulators nor financial firms themselves understood the full extent of this consolidated exposure. Capital requirements should be based on this consolidated exposure.

In determining the correct capital requirement, a macroprudential approach is needed along the lines suggested by the Basel Committee on Banking Supervision as well as the Dodd-Frank Act.[26] Specifically, capital requirements should be set based not just on the risk to the specific financial institution making the loan, but also on the risk to the system if that loan, and loans like it, become distressed.

The financing that banks use for their mortgage holdings should also be regulated. Mortgages are long-duration financial assets. While there may be some benefits to financing these assets with short-term funding in terms of maturity transformation or liquidity creation, doing so significantly increases the risks of runs and fire sales. Intermediaries are unlikely to internalize all of these costs when making their financing decisions. This logic applies to bank holdings of both whole loans and mortgage-backed securities. Financing security holdings with repo or asset-backed commercial paper opens the door for runs, as does financing whole loans with uninsured deposits.[27]

REGULATION OF SECURITIZATION

Higher and more risk-sensitive capital requirements could be used to make the banking sector safe, but they threaten to move all risky mortgages outside of banks and into the securitization market to avoid such capital requirements. Such an outcome would not meet our proposed goals for housing finance policy. The supply of mortgage credit would still be subject to booms and busts with potentially severe consequences for the real economy. Furthermore, the core banking system would still have significant indirect exposures to unregulated risky mortgage lending through its effects on prices and foreclosures. Thus if capital requirements are to be enhanced, as part of both the Basel III capital reforms and housing finance policy reforms, regulation of securitization must also be enhanced. Unfortunately, there is no well-accepted paradigm for such regulation. Here we discuss a few possibilities.

One possible approach is simply to prohibit risky mortgages from being securitized. There is some merit in this approach, given the difficulty of regulating securitization and the fact that renegotiation of distressed mortgages is made more difficult by agency problems between servicers and MBS investors (Agarwal and others 2011; Piskorski, Seru, and Vig 2010). However, such

---

26. Dodd-Frank Act, sec. 171.7; Basel III: A Global Regulatory Framework for More Resilient Banks and Banking Systems, Part IV.

27. For example, see Gorton and Metrick (2010b) for documentation of the withdrawal of repo funding from large financial firms.

a prohibition means that considerable mortgage risk would be on the balance sheets of leveraged financial institutions, the very ones we want to insulate from such risk because of the important role they play in intermediating credit to other sectors of the economy. Ideally, and as originally conceived, securitization would improve financial stability by transferring exposure to housing away from large, highly leveraged financial institutions and into long-term, "real money" investors like pension funds and mutual funds.

An intermediate solution would be to require a single investor in the securitization of a risky mortgage to hold a "vertical strip" in all of the tranches equal to some percentage—say, 20 percent—of the economic interest in the loan. This investor would have to be a qualified financial institution with the capability to deal with a distressed borrower and would have all the decision rights with respect to its dealings with the borrower. This would provide some of the benefits of securitization, while ensuring that some party has the proper economic incentives to deal with distressed borrowers and to evaluate credit risk. This would provide greater incentives than the 5 percent skin-in-the-game requirement in the Dodd-Frank legislation.

Another approach would be to allow securitization of risky mortgages, but to regulate the capital structure of securitization trusts in much the same way that we regulate the capital structure of financial institutions. For example, there could be a prohibition against having more than two tranches—a debt tranche and an equity tranche—along with the requirement of a minimum equity percentage (or maximum debt-tranche percentage). Those parameters could then vary with the risk of the underlying loan pools.

Ideally, the rating agencies would properly assess the risk of senior and junior tranches, but they failed to do so in the current crisis, and it is not clear that they will do so in the future. If the size of the senior tranche is limited so that it is nearly safe, relatively uninformed fixed-income investors are unlikely to overpay for these securities, which they did during the subprime boom. If they do not overpay, this reduces the likelihood that the underlying mortgages in the loan pool will be overpriced and that borrowers will be able to borrow on excessively attractive terms. This helps to prevent a credit-induced housing boom.

Furthermore, as the recent crisis has demonstrated, many investors now rely heavily on the credit rating agencies for managing risk and analyzing credit quality (Adelino 2010). Thus the functioning of the financial system relies critically on the credibility of the credit rating agencies and, in particular, the credibility of AAA ratings. While the agencies value the credibility of their ratings, they are unlikely to internalize their full importance within the financial sector. Although Dodd-Frank takes steps to reduce regulatory reliance on ratings, this effort is unlikely to result in significantly less reliance on them among private investors. Limiting the size of senior tranches would decrease the likelihood of a wave of downgrades in a housing downturn, helping to preserve the credibility of the rating agencies and improve financial stability.

It is possible that, even if the debt tranche is safe and properly valued, the equity tranche of the securitization could be overvalued. It is difficult to know how to deal with this possibility, but it is no different than when a bank overvalues a mortgage in its portfolio. However, one could adopt additional regulations to reduce the likelihood of such overvaluation. First, one could prohibit resecuritization of junior tranches (or so-called CDO squared). Coval, Jurek, and Stafford (2009) show that the value of a resecuritization is highly sensitive to the assumed correlation in the default rates of mortgages in the underlying loan pools. Second, one could regulate the leverage used to finance the purchase of a junior tranche. If the market is willing to finance such purchase on very favorable terms, this could lead to overvaluation of these tranches and thus to overvaluation of the underlying mortgage pools.

Bank capital requirements and regulation of securitization structures are likely to improve the ability of the housing finance system to absorb and work through a housing downturn. However, by the logic of the Modigliani-Miller theorem, total financing costs do not depend strongly on the mix of financing used. Thus these interventions would probably have only small effects on the costs of risky mortgages and may be only modestly effective at preventing bubbles from developing in the housing market.

Government Backstop

The regulations proposed here are an important part of ensuring the stability of housing finance. However, other shocks to the financial system may significantly impair the extension of mortgage credit. For instance, adverse shocks to bank capital originating outside the housing sector may constrain mortgage lending. Alternatively, as argued by Hanson and Sunderam (2010), investors may grow wary of securitized products, which happened during the recent financial crisis and on several previous occasions, leading to a drought in securitized mortgage financing.[28] Furthermore, despite their best efforts, regulators may fail to oversee private forms of housing finance properly, resulting in a credit boom and a subsequent collapse in mortgage credit. Such regulatory failures are far from uncommon, both in the United States and abroad. Finally, as suggested by Gennaioli, Shleifer, and Vishny (2011), securitizers and investors may simply neglect

---

28. The recent financial crisis is not the first time that investors have become wary of mortgage-backed securities. In 1994 collateralized-mortgages obligations, which resecuritize agency MBS into various tranches for separate claims on principal and interest, collapsed when interest rates rose dramatically (Carroll and Lappen 1994). In addition, commercial mortgage-backed securities were popular in the 1920s and then disappeared for many years out of concern about the quality of the underlying mortgages (Bartke 1971).

the risk of low-probability events and choose forms of mortgage finance that perform very poorly when those risks emerge.

Thus even if there is a carefully regulated, largely private system of mortgage finance, it is still possible to have a collapse in the availability of private mortgage financing. Given the importance of credit for the housing market, such an episode could result in a severe housing downturn, with serious consequences for the macroeconomy.[29] As a result, if the goal of housing finance policy is to achieve some measure of financial stability, the government should be prepared to step in and support mortgage markets during periods of significant market stress.

To this end, we propose establishing a "guarantor of last resort" for the housing market. This entity would be a government-owned corporation responsible for guaranteeing and securitizing *new* high-quality, well-underwritten mortgages when private securitization and bank balance sheets are significantly constrained. As shown in figure 7-1, guarantees are most valuable in a crisis. In the current crisis, they significantly reduced the costs of conforming mortgages relative to jumbo mortgages and have probably increased mortgage availability. The proposed corporation would function like Ginnie Mae in that it would issue MBS, while guaranteeing full and timely payments to MBS holders. Unlike many of the government guarantee proposals, no private party would be in a first-loss position. It would also not insure existing mortgages; the goal is not to protect banks and investors from losses on legacy mortgage assets that they purchased in normal or boom times.[30] Instead, it is to ensure the continued availability of relatively low-risk, high-quality mortgages as losses from those legacy assets are absorbed by private sector entities. Having a small footprint most of the time helps to insulate taxpayers from losses that inevitably occur in the aftermath of a credit boom.

At present, Fannie Mae and Freddie Mac (with government backing) and the FHA are effectively playing this guarantor-of-last-resort role. With private capital still on the sidelines, the GSEs and the FHA are together responsible for almost all new mortgage originations today. The backstop we are proposing would formalize this guarantor-of-last-resort role in a separate government-owned corporation, rather than having existing organizations fill the role on an ad hoc basis.

The backstop's market share during normal market conditions would be small, in the range of 5–10 percent. The reason it should have even a small

29. One way that loose monetary policy can stimulate the economy during a financial crisis is to encourage refinancing of fixed-rate mortgages as interest rates fall. If such refinancing is hampered by a decline in the supply of mortgage credit, then monetary policy may be less effective.

30. Of course, guaranteeing legacy assets may help to maintain financial stability. However, it may be unnecessary to commit to bailing out all legacy security holders ex ante, as proposals involving government reinsurance would do. If particular holders of legacy securities are particularly important for financial stability, they can be selectively supported in a crisis.

market share is to maintain the risk management infrastructure, personnel, and private market contacts necessary for it to act effectively and expeditiously in a severe downturn. In a typical year this would mean that the government-owned corporation would guarantee MBS of between $100 billion and $300 billion. This is about roughly the same market share that the FHA had prior to its loss of market share during the housing boom leading up to the financial crisis. To ensure that the market share stays small in normal times, the guarantor could have a preset limit on its market share that could only be waived with a determination of systemic risk from the Financial Stability Oversight Council, established as part of the Dodd-Frank Act.

The small share of the backstop in normal times could be achieved by manipulating either the prices or the quantities of the guarantees. The backstop could set guarantee fees high enough that its market share would be low. However, to the extent that the market demand for guarantees is relatively elastic, as it would be in the absence of frictions, it may be difficult to control market share through price alone; the guarantor's share would be 100 percent if the market found the price of guarantees attractive and 0 percent if it did not. Alternatively, the backstop could directly control the quantity of guarantees offered, selling a fixed supply on a daily or weekly basis. If guarantees were sold through an auction, clearing prices would reflect market conditions. However, reserve prices in these auctions would have to be set appropriately to protect the government at times when the private market underprices credit risk. Like any mortgage guarantor, the backstop is at risk of adverse selection; mortgage originators could try to put the lowest-quality mortgages into pools guaranteed by the backstop. The guarantor could control the scope for such adverse selection by offering guarantees on mortgages with a relatively specific set of observable characteristics. Giving the guarantor the ability to levy significant penalties on originators who pass on low-quality mortgages would also help to mitigate adverse selection problems.

In a significant housing downturn, the backstop, with the approval of the Financial Stability Oversight Council, would increase the quantity of guarantees it makes available to ensure continuity in the availability of mortgage credit. This would likely increase the backstop's market share substantially. Presumably the price of the guarantee would also increase given the withdrawal of private mortgage credit, although the extent of the increase would depend on how much the backstop increases its supply of guarantees. Like any lender of last resort, the backstop would face significant risk management challenges. It would have to decide whether a drought in the supply of mortgage credit reflects a malfunctioning of the private market or the appropriate reluctance on the part of private market participants to lend to borrowers that are not creditworthy. This issue confronts any government entity extending credit or liquidity in the midst of a crisis.

A key feature of this proposal is that the backstop entity should be in the form of a government-owned corporation. Given that a severe nationwide downturn is likely to impair the balance sheets of most or all private sector financial firms, the government is likely to be the most effective—possibly the only effective—guarantor of last resort. Indeed, virtually all proposals that retain some government involvement in the mortgage market involve government reinsurance of privately guaranteed mortgage-backed securities for exactly this reason. Moreover, as the recent experiences of Fannie and Freddie (as well as the monoline insurers) demonstrate, private firms seeking to maximize shareholder value have strong incentives to chase market share during normal or boom times. This means they are likely to be highly exposed to housing credit entering a bust and thus too impaired to play a countercyclical role (just as Fannie and Freddie would have been without government support). A government-owned corporation would have much weaker incentives to seek market share in normal times and would have the "dry powder" necessary to guarantee new loans at the onset of a crisis.

In this respect, the backstop would resemble the FHA. As the subprime market took off in 2001 and peaked in 2005, the FHA's market share dwindled from 7 percent down to 2 percent. In part because it is a government agency, the FHA had little incentive to chase market share and was able to increase the size of its guarantee program to play a countercyclical role over the past three years. It did take losses on high LTV loans guaranteed during the boom, but this can be ascribed to its mission of providing credit to underserved borrowers. Moreover, the losses were not so large as to prevent it from increasing its guarantee program.

The backstop may also be subject to political pressure. In particular, it could face strong pressure to intervene at the first hint of a downturn. It could also face pressures to reduce guarantee fees and loosen eligibility standards during a longer crisis. These changes would then likely be difficult to reverse after the crisis. Making the backstop an independent government-owned corporation, rather than a government agency, would help to alleviate these concerns.

Political economy concerns also argue against embedding the guarantor-of-last-resort function within an existing housing agency such as the FHA, which has separate policy objectives in normal times. As the track records of Fannie and Freddie show, giving housing organizations multiple objectives opens the door for mission creep and weakens the institutional focus on risk management. Setting up the mortgage guarantor as a separate entity from the Federal Reserve would have similar benefits, maintaining the distinction between fiscal and monetary policy.

Transitioning to the New System

Since we are in the midst of a housing crisis, transitioning to the new system could take many years. One element of this transition is already taking place through minimum 10 percent annual reductions in the two GSEs' portfolios of mortgages and MBS, which were mandated by the Housing and Economic Recovery Act of 2008. These reductions will occur mainly by natural runoff as mortgages either mature or are prepaid. In the end, the GSEs' portfolios, which once reached a combined total of $1.9 trillion, will have been eliminated.[31]

The more difficult question is how and when to phase out the GSEs' guarantee function. The GSEs, with support of the government, are currently playing the role of the backstop entity that we envision as part of the new housing finance system. They should continue to play this role as long as it is necessary, but there should be a gradual reduction in the fraction of new mortgages that the GSEs guarantee. This can be achieved, as Jaffee (2010) suggests, by gradually increasing guarantee fees, which would stimulate private market lending, including securitizations. This gradual transition would give market participants who have traditionally purchased GSE mortgage-backed securities the time to develop the expertise necessary to evaluate and manage credit risk. It would also allow for the slow reallocation of capital from investors who are constrained to purchasing guaranteed MBS (by regulation or investment charter) to investors with broader investment mandates. At some point, the GSEs' guarantee capabilities, including information systems and personnel, should be transferred to the new backstop entity, which would take over the GSEs' guarantee function. The GSEs' legacy obligations would remain with the GSEs, which would be transferred from a conservatorship to a receivership and wound down.

Availability and Affordability of Housing for Low- and Moderate-Income Households

Our focus here has been on enhancing the safety of the housing finance system. As noted, the easiest way to achieve this goal is by enforcing strict regulation on underwriting standards. To the extent that underwriting standards are relaxed, it is presumably to meet the policy objective of promoting the availability and affordability of mortgage credit to low- and moderate-income households. The benefits of meeting this policy objective have to be traded off against the benefits of financial stability. This trade-off is probably better implemented by regulating underwriting standards rather than by targeting quantities of lending to low- and moderate-income households, which was done in the Community Reinvestment Act and Title VIII of the Housing and Community Development Act. To the extent that the private market fails to provide mortgage credit to low- and moderate-income households on reasonable terms, the FHA would be able to do so.

---

31. In the new system, the government backstop entity would have only a de minimus portfolio simply because it would have to purchase loans that default to satisfy its guarantees of those loans. These loans would ultimately be sold.

Figure 7-5. *Share of Multifamily Mortgages, 1990–2010*

Percent

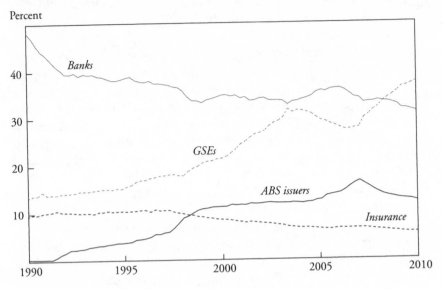

Source: Federal Reserve Board (2010).

Multifamily rental housing, while only providing housing for 13 percent of all households, is an important source of housing for low- and moderate-income households. Most multifamily housing units have rents that are considered afford-able for households at the median level of income in a metropolitan area. As of the third quarter of 2010, almost 38 percent of multifamily housing debt was owned or guaranteed by GSEs.[32] Their total exposure is more than $315 billion. Most of the GSEs' involvement has been with multifamily housing properties of greater than fifty units. While most are considered affordable, there are notable exceptions, such as the GSEs' disastrous funding of the private-equity investment in Stuyvesant Town, an 80-acre luxury apartment complex in New York City.

Figure 7-5 plots the market share of the GSEs in multifamily mortgages since 1990 as well as the market shares of banks, insurance companies, and ABS issuers. Over the years, the GSEs have increased their shares substantially, from 13.4 percent in 1990 to the current peak of 37.5 percent. During the mid-2000s, the GSEs lost market share to ABS issuers, but that market collapsed in 2007, and their share has grown. Indeed, all of the growth in net multifamily residential credit from the start of the financial crisis through the third quarter of 2010 has come from the GSEs. Thus they appear to be playing a countercyclical

32. Authors' calculations based on Federal Reserve Board (2010).

role (with government backing) in the current crisis, but there is no evidence that they played a countercyclical role when markets were more modestly disrupted at other times.

It is natural to ask whether our proposal should be applied to multifamily housing—that is, whether multifamily housing deserves the same level of regulatory scrutiny as single-family housing and whether the government should be backstopping this market as well. The answer is arguably no. The main issue in a severe housing downturn is whether the owner of a multifamily property can roll over the debt. If the owner cannot, then the property either is sold to a real estate investor who can put in equity or is foreclosed by the lender and then sold to a real estate investor. Unlike owner-occupied housing, no one is evicted and financial losses are borne by real estate investors and lenders. Although this can have adverse effects on the capital of leveraged financial firms, disruptions in multifamily housing have less important wealth effects and foreclosure externalities for individual households. Thus the multifamily housing sector would seem to warrant the same level of regulatory oversight as other forms of commercial real estate, but probably not more. The backstop function is also probably less important in the multifamily market, given that individual wealth effects and foreclosures are not significant issues.

Some observers, however, believe that multifamily housing is undersupplied by the private market relative to single-family housing. If true, it may be better to address this concern through some type of direct subsidy. This subsidy could be funded by taxes on single-family mortgage credit or a rollback of the mortgage interest deduction for single-family homes.

Conclusion

Housing finance was at the center of the recent financial crisis, just as it has been in other financial crises in the United States and abroad. This is not surprising given that residential mortgage debt is the single largest type of credit in the U.S. economy. And it suggests that reform of the housing finance system should have financial stability as its main policy objective.

Unfortunately, the two leading proposals have largely ignored financial stability. Instead, advocates of broad-based, explicit, properly priced government guarantee programs have had as their objective the reduction of mortgage interest rates. We think that this approach is problematic: *properly priced guarantees will do little, if anything, to lower mortgage interest rates.* The only way that such guarantees can lower rates is if the government takes on risk for which it is not compensated. Ultimately, that risk is borne by taxpayers. Given the moral hazard associated with government guarantee programs, the likely costs of such a large program outweigh the benefits.

Privatization advocates have made much of these moral hazard costs and have argued that the government should not guarantee mortgages. We note, however, that government guarantees elsewhere in the financial system mean that "privatization" does not eliminate the government's exposure to mortgage risks. Indeed, the private housing finance system, not just the two GSEs, performed poorly during the past decade, leading the government to intervene extensively in financial markets. Privatization advocates have provided little guidance about how to reform housing finance to avoid the need for such interventions in the future.

Drawing on this analysis, we craft our own reform proposal, which has three components. First, we argue that private markets can provide attractively priced mortgage credit without government guarantees in normal times and that the private market should be the main supplier of mortgage credit. Second, we argue that privatization must be combined with careful regulation because private markets are prone to destabilizing boom and bust cycles. Third, we propose the creation of a government-owned corporation that would play the role of "guarantor of last resort" during periods of crisis, when government guarantees of MBS are most valuable.

This chapter proposes some fundamental reforms of the housing finance system. None will be easy. But such reform is necessary for promoting the overall stability of the financial system and, ultimately, the real economy.

References

Acharya, Viral, Philipp Schnabl, and Gustavo Suarez. 2010. "Securitization without Risk Transfer." Working Paper. New York University; Federal Reserve Board.

Adelino, Manuel. 2010. "Do Investors Rely Only on Ratings? The Case of Mortgage-Backed Securities." Working Paper. Dartmouth College, Tuck School of Business.

Adelino, Manuel, Kristopher Gerardi, and Paul Willen. 2010. "Why Don't Lenders Renegotiate More Home Mortgages? Redefaults, Self-Cures, and Securitization." Working Paper 10-2. Federal Reserve Bank of Boston.

Admati, Anat, Peter DeMarzo, Martin Hellwig, and Paul Pfleiderer. 2010. "Fallacies, Irrelevant Facts, and Myths in the Discussion of Capital Regulation: Why Bank Equity Is Not Expensive." Working Paper 86. Stanford University, Rock Center for Corporate Governance.

Agarwal, Sumit, Gene Amromin, Itzhak Ben-David, Souphala Chomsisengphet, and Douglas Evanoff. 2010. "Market-Based Loss Mitigation Practices for Troubled Mortgages Following the Financial Crisis." Working Paper 2010-03-019. Fisher College of Business.

———. 2011. "The Role of Securitization in Mortgage Renegotiation." Working Paper 2011-03-002. Fisher College of Business.

Ambrose, Brent, Michael LaCour-Little, and Anthony Sanders. 2004. "The Effect of Conforming Loan Status on Mortgage Yield Spreads: A Loan-Level Analysis." *Real Estate Economics* 32, no. 4: 541–69.

Arrow, Kenneth, and Robert Lind. 1970. "Uncertainty and the Evaluation of Public Investments." *American Economic Review* 60, no. 3: 364–78.

Ashcraft, Adam, Paul Goldsmith-Pinkham, and James Vickery. 2010. "MBS Ratings and the Mortgage Credit Boom." Staff Report 449. Federal Reserve Bank of New York.

Barr, Michael, Sendhil Mullainathan, and Eldar Shafir. 2009. "The Case for Behaviorally Informed Regulation." In *New Perspectives on Regulation,* edited by David Moss and John Cisternino. Cambridge, Mass.: Tobin Project.

Barro, Robert. 1974. "Are Government Bonds Net Wealth?" *Journal of Political Economy* 82, no. 6: 1095–117.

Bartke, Richard. 1971. "Fannie Mae and the Secondary Mortgage Market." *Northwestern University Law Review* 66, no. 1: 1–78.

Basel Committee on Banking Supervision. 2009. "Strengthening the Resilience of the Banking Sector." Consultative Document. Basel (December).

Becker, Bo and Todd Milbourne. 2010. "How Did Increased Competition Affect Credit Ratings?" HBS Working Paper. Harvard Business School (September).

Bergstresser, Daniel, Robin Greenwood, and James Quinn. 2009. "Washington Mutual's Covered Bonds." Case 209-093. Harvard Business School.

Bernanke, Ben. 2010. "Monetary Policy and the Housing Bubble." Speech given at the annual meeting of the American Economic Association (www.federalreserve.gov/newsevents/speech/bernanke20100103a.htm).

Bernanke, Ben, and Mark Gertler. 2000. "Monetary Policy and Asset Price Volatility." NBER Working Paper 7559. Cambridge, Mass.: National Bureau of Economic Research (February).

Calomiris, Charles. 2001. "An Economist's Case for GSE Reform." In *Serving Two Masters, Yet Out of Control: Fannie Mae and Freddie Mac,* edited by Peter J. Wallison. Washington: AEI Press.

Campbell, John, Stefano Giglio, and Parag Pathak. 2009. "Forced Sales and House Prices." NBER Working Paper 14866. Cambridge, Mass.: National Bureau of Economic Research.

Carroll, Michael, and Alyssa Lappen. 1994. "Mortgage-Backed Mayhem." *Institutional Investor* 7 (July): 81–96.

Case, Karl, John Quigley, and Robert Shiller. 2005. "Comparing Wealth Effects: The Stock Market Versus the Housing Market." *Advances in Macroeconomics* 5, no. 1: 1–34.

Center for American Progress. 2011. "A Responsible Market for Housing Finance: A Progressive Plan to Reform the U.S. Secondary Market for Residential Mortgages." Washington.

CBO (Congressional Budget Office). 2001. "Federal Subsidies and the Housing GSEs." Washington: Government Printing Office.

———. 2010a. "The Budgetary Impact of Fannie Mae and Freddie Mac." Washington (November 16).

———. 2010b. "Report on the Troubled Asset Relief Program—November 2010." Washington (November).

Courtemanche, Charles, and Kenneth A. Snowden. 2010. "Repairing a Mortgage Crisis:

HOLC Lending and Its Impact on Local Housing Markets." NBER Working Paper 16245. Cambridge, Mass.: National Bureau of Economic Research.

Coval, Joshua, Jakub Jurek, and Erik Stafford. 2009. "The Economics of Structured Finance." *Journal of Economic Perspectives* 23, no. 1: 3–25.

Covitz, Daniel, Nellie Liang, and Gustavo Suarez. 2009. "The Evolution of a Financial Crisis: Panic in the Asset-Backed Commercial Paper Market." Working Paper. Washington: Federal Reserve Board (March).

Curry, Timothy, and Lynn Shibut. 2000. "The Cost of the Savings and Loan Crisis: Truth and Consequence." *FDIC Banking Review* 13, no. 2: 26–35.

Dang, Tri Vi, Gary Gorton, and Bengt Holmstrom. 2009. "Opacity and the Optimality of Debt for Liquidity Provision." Working Paper. Yale University; National Bureau of Economic Research; Massachusetts Institute of Technology (November 30).

Dechario, Toni, Patricia Mosser, Joseph Tracy, James Vickery, and Joshua Wright. 2010. "A Private Lender Cooperative Model for Residential Mortgage Finance." Staff Report 466. Federal Reserve Bank of New York.

DeMarzo, Peter. 2005. "The Pooling and Tranching of Securities: A Model of Informed Intermediation." *Review of Financial Studies* 18, no. 1: 1–35.

Downing, Chris, Dwight Jaffee, and Nancy Wallace. 2009. "Is the Market for Mortgage-Backed Securities a Market for Lemons?" *Review of Financial Studies* 22, no. 7: 2457–94.

Duffie, Darrell, and Peter DeMarzo. 1999. "A Liquidity-Based Model of Security Design." *Econometrica* 67, no. 1: 65–99.

European Covered Bond Council. 2010. *Fact Book*. Brussels.

European Mortgage Federation. 2009. *Hypostat 2009—A Review of Europe's Mortgage and Housing Markets*. Brussels (www.hypo.org/Objects/6/Files/Hypostat%202008%20-%20light%20version.pdf).

Fannie Mae. 2010a. "Fannie Mae 2010Q3 10-Q Filing." Washington (November 5).

———. 2010b. "Fannie Mae 2010 Third-Quarter Credit Supplement." Washington (November 5).

FDIC (Federal Deposit Insurance Corporation). 1997. "History of the Eighties." Washington (www.fdic.gov/databank/hist80).

———. 2010. *FDIC Quarterly* (third quarter). Washington.

Federal Reserve Board. 2010. *Flow of Funds Accounts of the United States: 2010 Quarter 3*. Washington: Board of Governors of the Federal Reserve System.

FHFA (Federal Housing Finance Agency). 2009. *Report to Congress*. Washington.

———. 2010. *Conservator's Report on the Enterprises' Financial Performance, Third Quarter 2010*. Washington.

Gan, Jie. 2007. "The Real Effects of Asset Market Bubbles: Loan- and Firm-Level Evidence of a Lending Channel." *Review of Financial Studies* 20, no. 6: 1941–73.

Geanakoplos, John. 2009. "The Leverage Cycle." In *NBER Macroeconomic Annual 2009*, vol. 24, pp. 1–65. University of Chicago Press.

Gelpern, Anna, and Adam Levitin. 2009. "Rewriting Frankenstein Contracts: The Workout Prohibition in Residential Mortgage-Backed Securities." Working Paper. American University Washington School of Law; Georgetown University Law Center.

Gennaioli, Nicola, Andrei Shleifer, and Robert W. Vishny. 2011, "A Model of Shadow Banking." NBER Working Paper 17115. Cambridge, Mass: National Bureau of Economic Research.

Gorton, Gary, and Andrew Metrick. 2010a. "Regulating the Shadow Banking Sector." Working Paper. Yale University; National Bureau of Economic Research (October).

————. 2010b. "Securitized Banking and the Run on Repo." ICF Working Paper 09-14. Yale University (November).

Gorton, Gary, and George Pennacchi. 1990. "Financial Intermediaries and Liquidity Creation." *Journal of Finance* 45, no. 1: 49–71.

Greenwood, Robin, and Samuel Hanson. 2010. "Issuer Quality and Corporate Bond Returns." Working Paper 1734528. Harvard Business School.

Griffin, John, and Dragon Tang. 2010. "Did Subjectivity Play a Role in CDO Credit Ratings?" Working Paper. University of Texas at Austin, Department of Finance; University of Hong Kong, Department of Economics and Finance (September 30).

Guiso, Luigi, Paola Sapienza, and Luigi Zingales. 2011. "The Determinants of Attitudes towards Strategic Default on Mortgages." ECO Working Paper 2010/31. Florence: European University Institute, Department of Economics.

Hancock, Diana, and Wayne Passmore. 2010. "An Analysis of Government Guarantees and the Functioning of Asset-Backed Securities Markets." Finance and Economics Discussion Series Paper 46. Washington: Federal Reserve Board.

Hanson, Samuel, and Adi Sunderam. 2010. "Are There Too Many Safe Securities? Securitization and the Incentives for Information Production." Working Paper. Harvard University (December 29).

Hermalin, Benjamin, and Dwight Jaffee. 1996. "The Privatization of Fannie Mae and Freddie Mac: Implications for Mortgage Industry Structure." In *Studies on Privatizing Fannie Mae and Freddie Mac,* pp. 225–302. Washington: U.S. Department of Housing and Urban Development, Office of Policy Development and Research.

HUD (Department of Housing and Urban Development). 2010. *Annual Report to Congress Regarding the Financial Status of the FHA Mutual Mortgage Insurance Fund Fiscal Year 2010.* Washington (November 15).

Inside Mortgage Finance. 2010. *The 2010 Mortgage Market Statistical Annual.* 2 vols. Bethesda, Md.

Jaffee, Dwight. 2010. "How to Privatize the Mortgage Market." *Wall Street Journal,* October, 25.

Kashyap, Anil, Jeremy Stein, and Samuel Hanson. 2010. "An Analysis of the Impact of 'Substantially Heightened' Capital Requirements on Large Financial Institutions." Working Paper. University of Chicago Booth School of Business; Harvard University.

Keys, Benjamin, Tanmoy Mukherjee, Amit Seru, and Vikrant Vig. 2010. "Did Securitization Lead to Lax Screening? Evidence from Subprime Loans." *Quarterly Journal of Economics* 125, no. 1: 307–62.

Khwaja, Asim, and Atif Mian. 2008. "Tracing the Impact of Bank Liquidity Shocks." *American Economic Review* 98, no. 4: 1413–42.

Krishnamurthy, Arvind. 2002. "The Bond/Old-Bond Spread." *Journal of Financial Economics* 66, no. 2: 463–506.

Krishnamurthy, Arvind, and Annette Vissing-Jorgensen. 2010. "The Aggregate Demand for Treasury Debt." Cambridge, Mass.: National Bureau of Economic Research (May 12).

Lancaster, Brian, Glenn Schultz, and Frank Fabozzi. 2008. *Structured Products and Related Credit Derivatives: A Comprehensive Guide for Investors.* Hoboken, N.J.: John Wiley and Sons.

Longstaff, Francis. 2004. "The Flight-to-Liquidity Premium in U.S. Treasury Bond Prices." *Journal of Business* 77, no. 3: 511–26.

Lucas, Deborah, and Marvin Phaup. 2010. "The Cost of Risk to the Government and Its Implications for Federal Budgeting." In *Measuring and Managing Federal Financial Risk,* edited by Deborah Lucas, pp. 29–54. University of Chicago Press.

Lusardi, Anna Maria. 2008. "Financial Literacy: An Essential Tool for Informed Consumer Choice?" Working Paper UCC08-11. Harvard University, Joint Center for Housing Studies (February).

Lusardi, Anna Maria, and Olivia Mitchell. 2008. "How Much Do People Know about Economics and Finance? Financial Illiteracy and the Importance of Financial Education." Policy Brief. Ann Arbor: Michigan Retirement Research Center.

McKenzie, Joseph. 2002. "A Reconsideration of the Jumbo/Non-Jumbo Mortgage Rate Differential." *Journal of Real Estate Finance and Economics* 25, no. 2-3: 197–213.

McKinley, Vern. 1997. "The Mounting Case for Privatizing Fannie Mae and Freddie Mac." Cato Policy Analysis 293. Washington: Cato Institute.

Mian, Atif, and Amir Sufi. 2010. "House Prices, Home Equity–Based Borrowing, and the U.S. Household Leverage Crisis." NBER Working Paper 15283. Cambridge, Mass.: National Bureau of Economic Research .

Mian, Atif, Amir Sufi, and Francesco Trebbi. 2011. "Foreclosures, House Prices, and the Real Economy." NBER Working Paper 16685. Cambridge, Mass.: National Bureau of Economic Research.

Mortgage Bankers Association. 2009. "MBA's Recommendation for the Future Government Role in the Core Secondary Mortgage Market." Washington.

National Association of Home Builders. 2010. "Future of Fannie Mae and Freddie Mac and the Housing Finance System." NAHB Resolution 3. Washington.

National Association of Realtors. 2010. "Recommendations for Restructuring the GSEs." Washington.

Packer, Frank, Ryan Stever, and Christian Upper. 2007. "The Covered Bond Market." *BIS Quarterly Review* (September): 43–55.

Passmore, Wayne, Shane M. Sherlund, and Gillian Burgess. 2005. "The Effect of Housing Government-Sponsored Enterprises on Mortgage Rates." *Real Estate Economics* 33, no. 3: 427–63.

Peek, Joseph, and Eric Rosengren. 1997. "The International Transmission of Financial Shocks: The Case of Japan." *American Economic Review* 87, no. 4: 495–505.

Pennacchi, George. 2009. "Deposit Insurance." Paper prepared for the Conference on Private Markets and Public Insurance Programs. American Enterprise Institute, January 15.

Pinto, Edward J. 2010. "The Future of Housing Finance." *Wall Street Journal,* August 17.

Piskorski, Tomasz, Amit Seru, and Vikrant Vig. 2010. "Securitization and Distressed Loan Renegotiation: Evidence from the Subprime Mortgage Crisis." *Journal of Financial Economics* 97, no. 3: 369–97.

Pollock, Alex. 2010. "To Overhaul the GSEs, Divide Them into Three Parts." *American Banker,* August 26.

Poterba, James. 1984. "Tax Subsidies to Owner-Occupied Housing: An Asset-Market Approach." *Quarterly Journal of Economics* 99, no. 4: 729–52.

Poterba, James, David Weill, and Robert Shiller. 1991. "House Price Dynamics: The Role of Tax Policy and Demography." *Brookings Papers on Economic Activity* 2: 143–83.

Quinn, Brian. 2008. "Failure of Private Ordering and the Financial Crisis of 2008." *New York University Journal of Law and Business* 5, no. 2: 549–615.

Rajan, Uday, Amit Seru, and Vikrant Vig. 2010. "Statistical Default Models and Incentives." *American Economic Review Papers and Proceedings* 100 (May): 506–10.

Reinhardt, Carmen, and Kenneth Rogoff. 2008. "This Time Is Different: A Panoramic View of Eight Centuries of Financial Crises." NBER Working Paper 13882. Cambridge, Mass.: National Bureau of Economic Research.

———. 2009. *This Time Is Different: Eight Centuries of Financial Folly.* Princeton University Press.

Rossi-Hansberg, Esteban, Pierre-Daniel Sarte, and Raymond Owens III. 2010. "Housing Externalities." *Journal of Political Economy* 118, no. 3: 409–32.

Sherlund, Shane. 2008. "The Jumbo-Conforming Spread: A Semiparametric Approach." Finance and Economics Discussion Series 2008-01. Washington: Federal Reserve Board.

Shleifer, Andrei, and Robert Vishny. 2010. "Unstable Banking." *Journal of Financial Economics* 97, no. 3: 306–18.

Standard & Poor's. 2010. "U.S. Residential Mortgage Default Index: Defaults Are Waning But Cumulative Default Rates Remain Extremely High for Recent Vintages." New York (May 24).

Streitfeld, David, and Louise Story. 2009. "F.H.A. Problems Raising Concern of Policy Makers." *New York Times*, October 9.

Torregrosa, David. 2001. "Interest Rate Differentials between Jumbo and Conforming Mortgages, 1995–2000." Washington: Congressional Budget Office.

Treasury Department. 2008. *Best Practices for Residential Covered Bonds.* Washington.

Vickery, James. 2007. "Interest Rates and Consumer Choice in the Residential Mortgage Market." Working Paper. Federal Reserve Bank of New York.

Vickery, James, and Joshua Wright. 2010. "TBA Trading and Liquidity in the Agency MBS Market." Staff Report 468. Federal Reserve Bank of New York.

Wallison, Peter. 2011. "Financial Crisis Inquiry Commission, Dissenting Statement." Washington: Financial Crisis Inquiry Commission (January).

Wallison, Peter, and Bert Ely. 2000. *Nationalizing Mortgage Risk: The Growth of Fannie Mae and Freddie Mac.* Washington: AEI Press.

Wallison, Peter, Thomas Stanton, and Bert Ely. 2004. *Privatizing Fannie Mae, Freddie Mac, and the Federal Home Loan Banks: Why and How.* Washington: AEI Press.

Contributors

MARTIN BAILY
Economic Studies
The Brookings Institution

KAREN DYNAN
Economic Studies
The Brookings Institution

DOUGLAS ELLIOTT
Economic Studies
The Brookings Institution

TED GAYER
Economic Studies
The Brookings Institution

ALAN GREENSPAN
Greenspan Associates, LLC

DIANA HANCOCK
Board of Governors of the Federal
    Reserve System

WAYNE PASSMORE
Board of Governors of the Federal
    Reserve System

ROBERT C. POZEN
Harvard Business School

DAVID SCHARFSTEIN
Harvard Business School

ADI SUNDERAM
Harvard Business School

PETER J. WALLISON
American Enterprise Institute

Index

ABS (asset-backed securities). *See* Securities and securitization

Access *2000*, 35

Accounting: banks and, 105; failures at GSEs, 6, 57; FHA and, 95, 106; SPEs and, 43–44

Acharya, Viral, 177

Adelino, Manuel, 174

Agarwal, Sumit, 173, 180

Agriculture, U.S. Department of (USDA), 26, 34, 36, 37, 39. *See also* Rural Housing Service

Ambrose, Brent W., 83, 149

American Bankers Association, 162

Amherst Securities, 182

Arizona, 29

Arrow, Kenneth, 153

Ashcraft, Adam, 171

Asset-backed securities (ABS). *See* Securities and securitization

Australia, 32, 33, 34, 51, 59

Bank of America, 51, 162, 170

Banks and banking: bank runs, 15, 81, 164, 179, 183; capital hoarding by, 122, 169; capital requirements of, 5, 45–46, 161–62, 179, 182–83; covered bonds and, 51–53, 175; current total amount of U.S. bank loans, 42; debt and losses of, 169n18, 170–71; decision and funding issues of, 118–21, 125, 128; deposit insurance and, 164, 169; deposits in, 169–70; effects of guarantee-sensitive investor participation on funding costs, 121–25; effects of privatization on the costs of mortgages provided by banks, 168–69, 177; exposure to housing of, 182–83; failures and insolvency of, 52, 177, 181; GSEs and, 170; housing crises and, 178–79; loans and lending of, 102–03, 117, 164, 169–70, 173; portfolios of, 118; privatization and, 170–71; recommendations for, 45–46; reserves for, 105; risks and, 45, 117, 165, 168–69; securitization and, 42–43, 53, 61; special-purpose entities and, 43–45, 55; strategies of, 117–18, 130–32. *See also* Housing finance system; Mortgages; Regulation; Securities and securitization

Barclays Capital, 95

Barr, Michael, 181

Basel I, III process, 161–62, 168, 169, 183